Beyond Boundaries?

SUNY series in Global Politics
James N. Rosenau, editor

A complete listing of books in the series can be found at the end of this volume.

BEYOND BOUNDARIES?

Disciplines, Paradigms, and Theoretical Integration in International Studies

EDITED BY
Rudra Sil
and
Eileen M. Doherty

STATE UNIVERSITY OF NEW YORK PRESS

Published by
State University of New York Press, Albany

For information, address State University of New York Press,
State University Plaza, Albany, NY, 12246

Production by Cathleen Collins
Marketing by Anne M. Valentine

Library of Congress Cataloging in Publication Data

Beyond boundaries? : disciplines, paradigms, and theoretical integration in international
studies / edited by Rudra Sil and Eileen M. Doherty.
    p.   cm. — (SUNY series in global politics)
  Includes bibliographical references and index.
  ISBN 0-7914-4597-6 (alk. paper) — ISBN 0-7914-4598-4 (pbk. : alk. paper)
    1. International relations. 2. International cooperation. 3. Boundaries. I. Sil, Rudra.
II. Doherty, Eileen M. III. Series.
JZ1305 .B49 2000
327'.01—dc21
                                           99-050267

10 9 8 7 6 5 4 3 2 1

To Our Teachers at Berkeley

CONTENTS

Part Two
Reorienting the Foundations?

FIGURES

ACKNOWLEDGMENTS

We are grateful to our colleagues and students at the University of California at Berkeley, the University of Pennsylvania, Case Western Reserve University, and elsewhere who read and commented on various portions of the manuscript. We are especially appreciative of the support and encouragement we received from Emanuel Adler, Thomas Callaghy, Beverly Crawford, Yale Ferguson, William Hazleton, Sai Felicia Krishna Hensel, and Steven Weber. We are also grateful to the W. P. Jones Fund at the College of Arts and Sciences at Case Western Reserve University and the School of Arts and Sciences at the University of Pennsylvania for providing support at various stages of this project. We would also like to thank our series editor, James Rosenau, and two anonymous reviewers at State University of New York Press. Finally, we are grateful to Zina Lawrence, Cathleen Collins, and Carol Inskip for their assistance in preparing this volume.

Rudra Sil
Eileen M. Doherty

1

THE QUESTIONABLE STATUS OF BOUNDARIES

The Need for Integration

RUDRA SIL

Extreme differentiation without unification mistakes the trees
for the forest.
—Ernst B. Haas[1]

This book is concerned with the role and limits of boundaries separating scholarly endeavors in the study of international life. It is specifically concerned with two different kinds of boundaries: (1) the enduring and seemingly entrenched boundaries defining and separating disciplines and subfields in the social sciences (e.g., the boundaries between political science, psychology and economics, or the boundaries between "political economy" and "historical sociology"); and (2) the boundaries that divide distinct theoretical schools or research traditions regularly vying for supremacy as "paradigms" in the analysis of international life (e.g., the boundaries between neorealism, pluralism, and constructivism).

For the better part of the past century, both sets of boundaries have been thought of as playing an important and necessary role in the advancement of "knowledge" in the social sciences, albeit for quite different reasons. The first set of boundaries—those defining distinct disciplines and subfields—is often thought to reflect a necessary and valuable division of labor in the quest for knowledge. This division supposedly enables investigators to gain a more detailed knowledge of a particular set of phenomena and to share their research products with a community of scholars who can more efficiently grasp the significance of these findings since they share a certain preexisting set of skills, vocabularies, research tools, and common stocks of knowledge bearing on the phenomena around which a discipline originally emerged.

The second set of boundaries—those defining research traditions, theoretical schools, or "paradigms"—has enabled individual investigators to systematically and confidently carry out their research projects on the basis of shared fundamental assumptions concerning the nature of social life, the goals of social science, the appropriate objects of empirical analysis, and standard methods for conducting and evaluating scientific inquiry. The emergence of a research tradition in a particular field is thought to provide a necessary foundation for defining and carrying out specific research projects deemed meaningful by others working in that tradition, while the competition among research traditions espousing different epistemological and methodological assumptions is often regarded as a precursor for the emergence of a new Kuhnian "paradigm"[2] or, at least, progressively more sophisticated conceptual frameworks.

It is an open question, however, as to whether these two sets of boundaries are presently serving the purposes invoked to justify their existence. Is the division of labor between disciplines, subfields, or programs serving the purpose of more efficiently and thoroughly acquiring empirical knowledge concerning different actors, structures, and processes in international life? Are the present debates among adherents of competing theoretical schools or research traditions indeed contributing to the progressive cumulation of theoretically significant knowledge about international life by spurring revolutionary breakthroughs or by producing incremental advances in concepts and research methods? This book is motivated by the strong suspicion that the separate stocks of "knowledge" being produced by social scientists are not being sufficiently integrated across different disciplines, subfields, and competing research traditions so that we can see the forest *and* the trees.

The essays in this volume are by scholars who are formally trained in the discipline of political science, but who, in pursuing their varied substantive interests in the study of international life, have found it necessary and valuable to cross the existing boundaries that, on the one hand, define and separate the various social science disciplines, subfields, or multidisciplinary programs, and on the other hand, define and separate competing research traditions or "paradigms." The authors do not share a single epistemology or a single research agenda; nor are they interested in offering an alternative unifying foundation for social science research. What they share is a common concern for concrete problems of cooperation and collective action in international life, along with a conviction that "normal" research in the social sciences has not paid sufficient attention to the *integration* of potentially related stocks of knowledge produced in different disciplines, subfields, or research traditions. The remainder of the chapter (1) discusses the origins of boundaries separating disciplines, subfields and specialized multidisciplinary research programs; (2) examines the impact of the contentious debates among distinct research traditions on "progress" in the field of international relations; and (3) emphasizes the value of question-driven integrative theoretical frameworks while providing an overview of the chapters to follow.

Disciplinary Structures and Specialization in the Social Sciences

Boundaries clearly serve an important and valuable function in the organization of social life. Indeed, a complex division of labor has been viewed as an integral feature of the "modern" era ever since the nineteenth century when the predecessors of contemporary social science—Spencer, Durkheim and Weber, for example—all pointed to the emergence of clearly defined roles and spheres of competence within increasingly rational bureaucratic structures. Through most of the twentieth century, the growing complexity of this division of labor became widely regarded as an intrinsic characteristic of "progress" in social and international life.[3]

Until recently, it was not unreasonable to assume that, as with the increasingly complex division of labor in society, an increasingly complex division of labor in the social sciences would contribute to the efficient expansion of the total reservoir of knowledge in society. Scholars focusing on different processes and objects of analysis could specialize in their tasks, developing further the skills necessary to investigate and analyze these particular processes and objects. Even before the nineteenth century, the natural sciences had already come to be separated from the study of law and philosophy; the former was defined as an experimental, empirically based scientific endeavor, and the latter was increasingly regarded as a nonscientific, and hence less privileged, realm of discourse. By the late nineteenth century, the Comtean ideal of a unified science of the natural and social worlds had not only been fractured but had given rise to distinct social science disciplines, with history first separated from the nomothetic social sciences, and the latter then developing into the distinct disciplines of economics, political science, and sociology. Anthropology and geography also emerged as distinct disciplines, but were confined to the margins of the social sciences, while psychology became a component of the natural sciences.[4] Finally, toward the end of World War I, international relations (IR) emerged as a field in its own right—either as a discipline or subfield—separated from the faculties of law and history within which international phenomena were previously studied.

This increasingly complex and "rational" division of labor in the social sciences was deemed to be intellectually productive because it was believed that "systematic research required skilled concentration on the multiple separate arenas of reality, which was partitioned rationally into distinct groupings of knowledge."[5] More significantly, once emergent, these disciplinary boundaries became so deeply entrenched that their significance and necessity became taken for granted. The fundamentally discipline-focused character of social sciences became a defining feature of the organization of research and education, shaping the roles and identities of every component and every actor within academia. In effect, disciplinary structures acquired "the force of necessity, implying that the academic institution could hardly be structured otherwise and emplotting knowledge in a narrative of increasingly specialized material."[6]

In the postwar period, the emergence of distinct subfields and distinct clusters of research based on particular areas in the world or particular actors (belonging to a particular gender, race, or ethnicity) came to occupy an important place in the division of labor in the social sciences. These new programs of research, often spanning at least two disciplines, posed new challenges for the existing disciplinary structure of the social sciences, but ultimately came to be incorporated as permanent fixtures within a more specialized division of labor. There was, for example, the emergence of subfields in each of the disciplines defined in relation to contributions from other disciplines (e.g., the emergence of "historical sociology" and "economic sociology" and the reappearance of "political economy").[7] While this enabled a few scholars belonging to two particular disciplines to work on similar phenomena or similar problematics, it remained unclear why politics was not relevant for economic sociologists or sociology was not relevant for political economists.[8] More generally, the fact that the new subfields were defined in terms of preexisting disciplines meant that the social sciences remained grounded in assumptions concerning the separability of social phenomena and the desirability of studying these separate phenomena within distinct realms of specialized research. Similarly, the disciplinary structures within the social sciences were challenged by, but ultimately managed to coopt, the multidisciplinary research programs that emerged for the study of particular areas of the world or particular sets of actors.[9] Such fields as the various area-studies, ethnic studies, or women's studies certainly did more to integrate the insights from various disciplines than the new subfields discussed above. Yet, it is important to recognize that these interdisciplinary research programs also became permanent institutional fixtures that took for granted the importance of the bounded knowledge gained by focusing in detail on particular sets of actors employing particular combinations of concepts, methods, and metatheoretical assumptions.

Although "boundary-crossing" has slowly become an integral aspect of the social sciences in practice,[10] the principles undergirding the division of labor in the social science research have remained firmly entrenched. Thus, most members of multidisciplinary research programs continue to regard their departmental affiliations as primary while the few scholars primarily affiliated with multidisciplinary research programs (ethnic or gender studies, for example) are still regarded within the social sciences as performing marginal roles at best. Graduate training remains linked to the dominant social science departments as does the administration of research grants and training fellowships. While the emergence of dual-discipline subfields and multidisciplinary research programs demonstrate the questionable status of the disciplinary boundaries that developed prior to World War II, neither of these developments has resulted in any fundamental reassessment of disciplinary structures. Efforts to create interdisciplinary research structures around particular areas or actors, rather than prompting a serious reexamination of the purpose, limits, and structure of social science research, simply came to coexist with disciplinary structures as part of an even more complex division of labor in the social sciences. Thus, as one social scientist has recently pointed out, "[t]he intellectual eco-system has with time been carved up into 'separate' institutional and professional niches through the continuing processes of boundary-work designed to achieve an apparent differentiation of goals, methods, capabilities and substantive expertise."[11]

In order to more seriously reassess the merits of increasing differentiation and the role of disciplinary structures in the social sciences, a brief comparison of the role of boundaries within the social sciences and natural sciences might serve as a valuable point of departure. To the extent that disciplinary boundaries may be defended in the natural sciences (and the status of these boundaries, too, is certainly open to question), it is at least conceivable that the boundaries serve an essential function in specifying distinct domains of scientific analysis and providing a set of distinct concepts, assumptions, and research tools for efficiently acquiring and organizing stocks of knowledge pertaining to those domains. It is possible, for example, that while chemical, biological, and physical processes may affect one another, a large set of phenomena can be reasonably defined as purely chemical, biological, or physical outcomes that merit a distinct mode of observation and analysis. In the social sciences, however, while economic, psychological, political, or cultural processes and structures may be analyzed within separate realms of inquiry, this is primarily driven by which aspect of a complex social reality *is of interest to the investigator*. It is far from clear that most of the questions addressed within each of the disciplines correspond to *objectively separable, empirically distinct outcomes* that must necessarily be analyzed on the basis of distinct analytic frameworks and research methods. The gravitational attraction between two celestial bodies is a phenomenon that can be analyzed and understood entirely by astrophysicists without any assistance from biologists or chemists. Explanations of why wars occur or how democracy emerges, however, require us to simultaneously consider several phenomena normally studied independently within the domains of economics, sociology, psychology, or political science. It is highly unlikely that the specialists within any one of these disciplines will be able to offer a convincing model or interpretation of international conflict or democratic transitions without transgressing at least partially into the proclaimed intellectual domains of the other disciplines.[12]

This point may have been *implicitly* recognized within the context of the area studies programs that emerged in the 1950s. It is also implicitly acknowledged in the work of some scholars who have come to partially appreciate the interconnectedness of the "political," "economic," "psychological," or "sociological" dimensions of such major events and processes as the two world wars, the rise and fall of Nazism and Leninism, East Asian development, North-South cooperation, and more recently, "globalization." What has yet to be *explicitly* considered, however, are the possibility that knowledge about social and international phenomena is *essentially* interdisciplinary in character, and the implications of this possibility for the organization of social science research. The boundaries that separate disciplines and subfields in the study of social and international phenomena, while they clearly serve an analytic purpose, cannot be taken for granted. And, in the absence of complementary mechanisms designed to integrate research in the social sciences, inflexible disciplinary structures may very well come to constitute a hindrance to whatever "progress" is possible in our collective efforts to understand aspects of international life.

Expert knowledge is certainly an essential component of all inquiry, but "[o]nce expertise is thought of in terms of tools and instruments as opposed to the privilege it may assume in theoretical terms, then its status is open to changes all the time."[13] In other words, the formation and proliferation of permanent specialized structures supposedly organized around intellectually and empirically distinct objects of research, needs to be accompanied by efforts to study a particular set of actors, processes, or events in a manner that *brings to bear on particular questions the full range of relevant concepts, theoretical frameworks, hypotheses, interpretations, insights, and methods, regardless of their disciplinary origins,* and simultaneously recognizes that *this cluster of concepts and tools are not necessarily applicable to a different set of questions, even where the same actors, processes, or events may be involved.*[14] This does not require that we dismantle or reject all existing disciplinary structures; it simply requires that we make more room in the division of labor for those scholars who consciously and deliberately approach their questions and objects of analysis in an *essentially* interdisciplinary manner, integrating the relevant concepts, facts, ideas, and insights from different disciplines, subfields or narrowly focused multidisciplinary programs.

Interparadigm Debates and "Progress" in the Study of International Life

This volume is also motivated by a desire to explore the intellectual returns to be gained from transcending—or ignoring—a second set of boundaries: the sharp, sometimes bitter, divisions separating adherents of competing research traditions in social science disciplines. I argue below that ever since Thomas Kuhn published his analysis of scientific "paradigms" in 1962, the stakes have been raised in the competition among theoretical schools and research traditions in the social sciences (arguably much more so than in the natural sciences, the primary subject of Kuhn's analysis). The intensity of the resulting "interparadigm debates"[15] has paradoxically undermined the efforts of those committed to developing a unifying paradigm, and, more importantly, has tended to marginalize the significance of more eclectic scholarly research transcending the divisions among competing research traditions. As a result, "progress" in the field of international relations has primarily taken the form of *intraparadigm* advances in theoretical sophistication and empirical knowledge; but these advances have been at the expense of incremental, *trans-paradigm* advances in our collective ability to understand the complexity of international life. The latter type of progress, I contend, is more significant and will require more room in the social sciences for deliberately eclectic and integrative conceptual frameworks designed to illuminate concretely defined problems.

In Kuhn's treatment of scientific knowledge, "progress" was marked not by the steady cumulation of objective knowledge through the standardized application of universally valid methods, but by the emergence of new "paradigms," each breaking with past strands of research and offering a new foundation for research consisting of a fundamentally different *system* of concepts, assumptions, questions, methods, and evaluative standards. A paradigm would first emerge when such a revolutionary foundation enabled a group of scientists to pioneer unprecedented achievements, and when these new achievements attracted scholars previously committed to other research programs and inspired them to pursue a new set of research questions framed within a common conceptual, epistemological, and methodological foundation. The initial appearance of a paradigm marked the achievement of "maturity" for a discipline, ending a period of initial competition among a variety of theoretical schools and research traditions. Subsequently, each new paradigm represented a fundamental departure from past research, setting new boundaries for research under conditions of "normal science." When these boundaries started to become blurred and the consensus undergirding key concepts and assumptions began to fade, conditions were ripe for a "scientific revolution" that would involve a new era of competition among a variety of research programs until one would emerge as the new dominant paradigm.[16]

Kuhn's treatment of scientific knowledge was predictably met with a flurry of criticism almost immediately. Most positivists, in both the natural and social sciences, challenged the notion that the development of knowledge is not cumulative but rather marked by a series of "new beginnings" that "occur in a random and unpredictable way."[17] They were also critical of the idea that most knowledge claims resulted from paradigm-bound practices rather than from the application of uniform scientific methods capable of revealing universally valid, objective laws of nature.[18] Others challenged the sharpness of the distinction Kuhn drew between "normal science" and "scientific revolutions," and faulted him for failing to recognize the value of "trans-paradigm" components of knowledge or the gradual evolution of new "conceptual variants" paradigm shifts.[19] In fact, in his subsequent writings, including the second edition to the book, Kuhn himself chose to downplay the relativistic implications of his work, dropped the language of "paradigms," and had to back away from some of his earlier claims about the sharp difference between "normal" and "revolutionary" aspects of scientific research.[20]

Nevertheless, ever since *The Structure of Scientific Revolutions* was first published in 1962, the very idea of a unifying "paradigm" for research has come to exert a powerful hold on students of international and social life. The concept has since been used widely by scholars across social science disciplines in referring to clusters of related research agendas organized around particular collections of concepts, assumptions, questions, and methodologies. Intellectual histories of disciplines and subfields have been rewritten using the language of "paradigms" and "paradigm-shifts."[21] A variety of research traditions, methodological approaches, and epistemologies have repeatedly attempted to claim the mantle of new "dominant" paradigms under a variety of labels often encompassing overlapping assumptions. As a result, most scholarly analyses of international life (and indeed, the analysts themselves) have come to be identified with one research tradition or another, with most new research being framed as a contribution toward turning one of these research traditions into a unifying "paradigm" (neorealism, neoliberalism or constructivism, for example).

This fixation on "paradigms" over the last three decades, if anything, has actually had an adverse effect on whatever "progress" may be possible in the social sciences by raising the stakes of the competition between research traditions, by subsequently raising the status of those contributing to the advancement of one research tradition in the estimation of others also working in that tradition, and by marginalizing (even penalizing) eclectic research agendas not founded on the system of concepts, assumptions, methods, or evaluative standards provided by one of the established research traditions. As a result, as Hirschman has noted, the "search for paradigms" has constituted more of a "hindrance to understanding," prematurely closing off possibilities for pursuing many socially important problems and slowing down whatever "progress" may be possible in the study of the social world.[22]

This view is informed by three related observations on the applicability of the "paradigm" concept to the social sciences and on the prospects for "progress" in international relations. These have to do with the prevalence and endurance of supposedly dominant research traditions, the degree to which the core concepts and assumptions of the competing traditions are fundamentally novel and mutually exclusive, and the extent to which research designed to promote a prospective paradigm has contributed to some sort of "progress" in the field at large.

First, while there have been periods when certain theoretical schools or approaches have been prevalent in the social sciences, nowhere in the history of IR or any other social science discipline do we find research traditions comparable to Kuhnian scientific paradigms in terms of their predominance in the field and their "staying power." In every discipline or subfield in the social sciences, except for brief periods of time, several contending schools have typically been in existence simultaneously, competing with each other for dominance, and intensifying intellectual debates over ontological, epistemological, methodological, and/or normative issues, rather than paving the way for the emergence of a unifying paradigm. To the extent that the status of "paradigm" is achieved by a research tradition's ability to attract away adherents of competing traditions, it is significant that in every decade since the establishment of the first IR department in 1919, there have been at least two clear alternatives schools or approaches, each with sufficient adherents to challenge the claims of others to dominance in the field.[23] Certainly, in the postwar period, behavioralism and structural realism (or "neorealism") have been strong contenders for the status of "paradigm" at different points in time; but even at the height of their popularity within IR, neither achieved the kind of dominance represented by the Newtonian paradigm in physics, and neither survived more than a decade before being subjected to severe criticisms and spurring the growth of competing research traditions.[24] Even the more recent attempt to erect a unified "rationalist" tradition[25] combining several of the concepts and assumptions of neorealism and neoliberalism has not had the effect of drawing away adherents from "reflectivist" alternatives as evident in the attention received by many poststructuralists, critical theorists, and a new generation of constructivists and cultural theorists in IR.[26]

Second, it is important to note that many of the ontological, epistemological, methodological, and/or normative orientations of different research traditions overlap substantially, and that many of the points of contention among these traditions involve recurrent debates over familiar issues. The problem of mutual exclusivity is nowhere more evident perhaps than in the aforementioned attempt of neorealists and neoliberalists/pluralists—the two most popular contestants in the 1970s "interparadigm debate"—to combine forces by offering a unified "rationalist" approach to IR, to be distinguished from older behavioralist approaches and newer "reflectivist" alternatives. Such a synthesis would not have been possible had the neorealist and pluralist research traditions consisted of mutually exclusive systems of concepts, assumptions, and research methods as would be the case with Kuhnian paradigms. Moreover, the recurrence of certain familiar ontological, epistemological, and methodological debates since the beginning of the century makes it difficult to define "progress" in IR or any other social science field in terms of either a succession of paradigm shifts or the transition from a "preparadigmatic" stage to an age of "maturity." It is important to note, for example, that many of the epistemological differences between contemporary rationalists and reflectivists are essentially similar to the epistemological differences between the adherents of the "behavioral" and "classical" approaches in the 1950s–1960s, not to mention the differences evident in the nineteenth-century debate between British empiricists and German idealists.[27] Similarly, it is worth noting that the debate over culture and identity in the 1990s is not new in either international relations or in any other discipline or subfield; for over a century now, social scientists have been at odds with regard to the possibility of operationalizing nonobservable factors such as values, beliefs, and attitudes in a truly "scientific" analysis of social and international life.[28] Moreover, many of the core assumptions and concepts of self-proclaimed paradigms survive or reemerge within the disciplines or subfields within which they were originally conceived,[29] while the alternative research programs developed on the basis of the critique of these paradigms end up announcing the "return" of some concept or another, or "bringing back in" some actor or another.[30] It is therefore difficult to classify research traditions in the social sciences as Kuhnian paradigms that are supposed to be based on *fundamentally different, and mutually exclusive* systems of concepts, assumptions, and methods based on revolutionary departures from past strands of research.[31]

Third, while the most recent "interparadigm debates" in IR involve different combinations of ontological, epistemological, methodological, and normative stances than may have been the case in the 1950s or 1970s,[32] these shifting debates do not represent a substitute for Kuhnian paradigm-shifts or an alternative path to the cumulation of knowledge, especially when one considers the absence of consensus on what constitutes "progress" in the study of international life. Many of the supposed "break-throughs" and "syntheses" have reflected little more than the efforts of a particular community of scholars to come to grips with new, unexpected, empirical phenomena on the basis of new vocabularies and different per-mutations of ontological, epistemological, methodological, and normative assumptions. At the same time, critiques of particular research traditions have ended up pointing the way not to a single, unifying alternative para-digm, but to several different kinds of alternative theoretical projects each with its own standards of "progress." Thus, just as one distinguished scholar sets out to ponder the "growing relevance of pluralism," another equally distinguished scholar simultaneously insists on the "timeless wis-dom of neorealism."[33] Moreover, as Haggard has noted, where "progress" in IR theory can be said to have occurred, it is not as a result of the emer-gence of a dominant paradigm, but because research traditions claiming this mantle have *lost* their hegemonic positions, allowing for more flexible approaches that raise new questions and introduce new factors. Structural realism, for example, has contributed to "progress" in IR theory, but not as a paradigm breaking with past research and providing a new system of concepts, assumptions, methods, and questions; the progress has come from the *unintended* consequences seen in theories and research into non-systemic factors designed to *challenge* the claims of structuralists![34] Under these conditions, "interparadigm" debates may indeed contribute to increasing theoretical sophistication and new empirical research *within* a given research tradition, each offering scholars the ability to investigate empirical phenomena in far greater detail than previously possible.[35] But, if we are interested at all in some sort of theoretical "progress" that can be shared by a wider community of scholars subscribing to different episte-mological, ontological, and methodological assumptions, then a different approach must be taken to appreciating the roles and limitations of differ-ent research traditions.

It is possible—and much more reasonable in our view—to opt for an altogether different notion of "progress" than the one assumed by social sci-entists invoking the language of "paradigms" or "scientific revolutions." One such reasonable approach may be found in Stephen Toulmin's evolu-tionary view of a part-rational, part-instrumental selection of useful concep-tual variants from an expanding population of concepts. Toulmin focuses on concepts as "micro-institutions" rather than full-blown logical systems that constitute Kuhnian paradigms. He examines the gradual expansion of "conceptual populations" as new variants emerge over time. Certain variants then come to be "selected" for their staying power, partly because of their utility in solving certain conceptual problems, partly because of their value in connection with various disciplinary and professional considerations, and partly because of their unanticipated payoffs for certain interests crucial to the maintenance or reproduction of the academe as a whole. The result is not a purely "rational" process of progress through purely objective procedures and evaluative processes, but it is progress nonetheless with the "selected" concepts at least contributing to the collective ability of scientists to define and solve the crucial problems of their time.[36]

The question remains, however, as to how this kind of progress can emerge and how the utility of new conceptual variants may be recognized if social scientists remain focused exclusively on the advancement of a single research tradition or theoretical school vying for supremacy as paradigms. For example, while the recent efforts to "bridge" neorealism and certain strands of pluralism or neoliberal institutionalism may have yielded some new concepts for those seeking a structured understanding of regularities in international behavior, this bridge is designed to advance a single unifying paradigm while marginalizing several other research traditions and dismissing the core concepts and assumptions of the latter. At the same time, the renewed interest in culture, identity, and norms, albeit helping to illuminate much of the complexity in international life in the eyes of many "reflectivist" theorists, by and large ignores the concepts and assumptions embedded in the "rationalist" formulation offered by neorealists or neoliberal institutionalists. In the end, most scholars remain inclined to take for granted the importance of defending particular research traditions, and as a result, we are left with incommensurable theories, each designed to advance a research tradition—and a particular system of concepts—without regard for whether or not this advancement is appreciated by a community of scholars larger than the adherents of one of the traditions. If research into problems of international life is ever going to bear any resemblance to even the modest view of evolutionary progress offered by Toulmin, it will only be as a result of people hitting on particular concepts for their utility in defining and addressing certain problems regardless of which research tradition these concepts or problems originated within.

Beyond Boundaries?

These observations concerning disciplinary structures and "interparadigm" debates are not meant to suggest that the ideal of cumulative knowledge must be sacrificed to an ever-increasing "proliferation of incommensurable theories."[37] Nor can we ignore the fact that specialized research has produced significant—indeed, critical—contributions to our understanding of international phenomena. This volume simply offers a modest plea for a more extensive and more flexible realm of interdisciplinary social analysis, and for a shift away from contentious (and probably unresolvable) "interparadigm" debates toward a focus on substantive problems and issues. Such a shift would be oriented neither toward the permanent establishment of new programs or fields of inquiry, nor toward the construction of dominant paradigms, but toward a more integrative approach to concrete empirical objects, structures, and processes that brings to bear a wider range of relevant concepts, theories, evidence, and interpretations regardless of which discipline or research tradition these originated within.

It is also essential to recognize that it is historically emergent *questions* and concretely defined categories of phenomena that represent the driving force for social research rather than *a priori* commitments to disciplinary traditions or methodological perspectives. If *questions* are what drive social scientists, then the debates in the social sciences ought to be focused on questions, and not on whether a particular study is appropriate for a particular discipline or whether a given approach is consistent with the epistemological and methodological assumptions of an identifiable research tradition. As James Rosenau has recently noted: "Instead of focusing prime attention upon the substance of world politics and/or criticising each other for their conceptions of how the system functions and changes, all too many analysts drift into a preoccupation with what constitutes the proper route to understanding and/or faulting each other for their methodological premises."[38]

Moreover, different questions can be posed at different levels of analysis and different levels of abstraction, and in order to shed light on these different questions, it will be necessary to invoke different theoretical frameworks and different combinations of methods. But the choices made by different scholars interested in a given problem cannot then be turned into monolithic theoretical foundations designed to inform each and every analysis of each and every social phenomenon. Once we abandon *a priori* commitments to disciplinary traditions or particular analytic perspectives, it becomes possible to determine the relationships between the concepts and assumptions driving the various frameworks. It also becomes possible to discern how apparently contradictory assertions about social phenomena stemming from competing research traditions may, in fact, simultaneously represent partial "truths" about broader, more complex international phenomena that defy elegant, mono-causal explanations.

Constructing Integrative Frameworks

The chapters in this volume can be separated into two groups, each addressing the problem of boundaries in the social sciences at different levels of abstraction. The four essays in Part I of the volume—by Eileen Doherty, Anne Clunan, Norrin Ripsman and Jean-Marc Blanchard, and Tadashi Anno—all tackle the problem of boundaries concretely by consciously incorporating important concepts and analytic theories from various disciplines, subfields, and research traditions in order to construct innovative, integrative theoretical approaches for analyzing substantive problems in the study of international life. These authors, albeit interested in different substantive questions, share a common interest in aspects of cooperation and collective action in international life as well as a common intellectual orientation toward a question-driven social science. Each of the essays serves to highlight the *essentially* interdisciplinary nature of certain core concepts and problems in international life, and each of the approaches builds on a variety of methodological approaches linked to integrative theoretical "toolboxes," designed to shed light on different aspects of cooperation and collective action in international life—ranging from the dynamics of international bargaining to the study of collective identity and the relationship between interdependence and conflict.

The chapter by Eileen Doherty, "Negotiating Across Disciplines: The Implications of Judgment and Decision Making Research for International Bargaining Theory," explores the ways in which two research traditions in the discipline of psychology—prospect theory and social judgment theory—can be incorporated into a more comprehensive and useful theoretical approach to the study of international bargaining. Doherty begins with a discussion of traditional rational choice models of human behavior and briefly examines well-known variations on these models (bounded rationality, satisficing behavior and incremental decision making). She then turns the possibility of integrating into the study of international relations two distinct bodies of research in the field of judgment and decision making (JDM) in psychology, both of which question the validity of rational choice models. Prospect theory emerged from within (and as a reaction to) the tradition of rational choice, while social judgment theory (SJT) developed as a parallel tradition based on a different set of assumptions, methodological techniques, and assessment criteria for evaluating human decision making. Each of these research traditions offers a separate set of hypotheses about the factors that shape human cognition, but taken together, these hypotheses promise to offer novel and valuable insights in the study of certain problems traditionally thought to be strictly within the domain of international relations specialists. Doherty proceeds to develop some of her own preliminary hypotheses based on the implications of these two research traditions for the analysis of international bargaining. She notes, for example, that negotiations often break down even when actors' preferences begin to converge. A complete understanding of the dynamics of international bargaining, she concludes, requires taking seriously the cognitive obstacles to successful negotiation, and this, in turn, requires integrating the contributions of theoretical traditions in the field of judgment and decision making with existing rationalist approaches in IR to the study of cooperation.

In their chapter, "Contextual Information and the Study of Trade and Conflict: The Advantage of a Cross-Disciplinary Approach," Norrin Ripsman and Jean-Marc Blanchard argue that to reach definitive judgments about the relationship between international trade, economic interdependence, and international conflict, researchers must reach beyond the boundaries of political science and economics to employ the relevant concepts and tools of geographers and historians. Their question driven analysis leads them to define and measure economic interdependence not merely with reference to the quantity of international or bilateral trade, but also with reference to more contextual concepts introduced by political geographers and geopoliticians, such as the material composition of trade and its importance to each state as a function of its geographical location and access to strategic resources. Furthermore, they employ the historian's method of primary-source, decision-making analysis to assess whether national leaders are actually aware of the constraints of economic interdependence and how such awareness conditions national security decision-making. Employing this interdisciplinary approach in concrete historical contexts, Ripsman and Blanchard demonstrate that interdependence prior to World War I, while not uniformly high as previous studies indicated, was not insignificant in 1930s Europe. They also ascertain that decision makers in Germany, France, and Great Britain were aware of the constraints of interdependence, yet did not consider their dependence relevant to national security decisions in times of crisis, when they were motivated primarily by strategic considerations and domestic political imperatives. Thus, Ripsman and Blanchard cast doubts on both the commercial liberal argument and the conventional neorealist assumptions concerning the origins of national security decisions while developing a more integrative, cross-disciplinary approach to the study of trade and conflict.

In her chapter, "Constructing Concepts of Identity: Prospects and Pitfalls of a Sociological Approach to World Politics," Anne Clunan emphasizes that the interests of actors are best understood by analyzing how their identities shape those interests. She notes that international politics, however defined, is shaped not only by interests, but to a large extent, by how actors construct sets of ideas, norms, and identities, in order to cope with their interactions with other human beings. Clunan shares with Doherty a common desire to challenge the universality of rationalist assumptions, but her focus on the problem of shared norms and identities leads her to engage the efforts of a new generation of "constructivists" who are seeking to integrate the insights of sociology and political science in their search for approaches that more fully illuminate the growing complexity of international life. While some continue to claim that the fuzzy causal logic and fuzzy variables of constructivism are a hindrance to the pursuit of knowledge, Clunan's chapter demonstrates that sociological approaches can complement, and even partially reconcile, competing mainstream approaches as long as careful attention is paid to the articulation and framing of the core analytic concepts. Clunan recognizes important differences among scholars labeled "constructivist," but points out that these theorists generally agree that the reality we see is socially constructed, and that therefore the analysis of social forces (particularly, identity, cultures, and norms) must accompany studies of individual rationality or material forces in the study of international processes. She also notes that constructivists are in a unique position to develop a new, more integrated research program for examining the roles of learning and emergent shared interests in the development of international society. As an example of the utility of a sociological approach, Clunan demonstrates how a constructivist analysis of identity formation allows us to "unpack" some of the most problematic assumptions smuggled into mainstream theories and paves the way for more integrated explanations of specific aspects of state behavior. Finally, Clunan considers the potential returns of integrating the constructivist agenda into the study of socially constructed international life: the investigation of new substantive issues, the cumulation of knowledge already produced by many constructivists, and the progressive refinement of such knowledge through comparison and critique with works in the rationalist tradition; and she concludes that these intellectual gains are worth the sacrifice of universal models of choice and behavior.

In the final chapter of Part I, titled "Collective Identity as an 'Emotional Investment Portfolio': An Economic Analogy to a Psychological Process," Tadashi Anno notes that "identity" has become a "buzzword" not only in international relations, but in various other disciplines in the social sciences and humanities as well. Like Clunan, he notes that discussions of "collective identity" in the field of international relations are characterized by a fuzziness that makes many mainstream social scientists uncomfortable, and he suggests that a more in-depth understanding of identity *formation* and the relationship between interests and identity can help us get beyond the apparently fruitless and endless debate between rational-choice theorists and students of identity. However, unlike Clunan who focuses on the contributions of sociology to a constructivist research agenda, Anno focuses on the problem of individual motivation and on the partial convergence between psychological and economic understandings of the sources of that motivation. His chapter begins by attempting to clarify the relationship between the concept of "collective identity" and the broader theoretical models for the study of choice and action, focusing especially on the possible linkages between identity-based and interest-based explanations of group behavior. Anno's own approach to the problem of collective identity-formation is based on the notion of an "emotional investment portfolio," a concept derived from the strong analogy between, on the one hand, the processes and politics of identity formation, and on the other hand, the investment decisions of investors and their impact on the "fund managers." While fully aware of the limits of analogies for the purposes of theory building, Anno nonetheless makes a compelling and original case for simultaneously appreciating the importance of both, interest-driven explanations of group behavior and the emotional aspects of individual commitment to a group identity. In order to demonstrate more concretely the utility of the "emotional investment portfolio" approach, Anno examines the process of national identity-formation in Japan, with comparative references to Russian national identity.

Reorienting the Foundations?

The essays in Part II of the volume—by Rudra Sil, Wade Huntley, and Timothy Luke—address the problem of boundaries at the level of ontology and epistemology, offering critical reflections on how to understand and reconceptualize the role of boundaries in defining what constitutes "truth," "knowledge," and "method" in international studies. The authors reject simplistic notions of a unified, discipline-bound, positive science applicable to each and every human endeavor, but at the same time, they seek to constructively identify alternative foundations for a social science characterized by a greater tolerance for different modes of inquiry carried out in a variety of settings by a larger and more diverse community of scholars. The authors share a common view that whatever cumulation may be possible in the study of international life can only take place when genuinely interdisciplinary analysis is accompanied by conscious efforts at a more philosophical level to reorient our thinking about the intellectual and practical significance of the various disciplinary, methodological, and epistemological boundaries in social science research. Each of the essays then offers a distinctive perspective on the what role boundaries might play in furthering or hindering the quest for a more pragmatic or inclusive social science.

In the first essay in Part II, "Against Epistemological Absolutism: Toward a 'Pragmatic' Center," Rudra Sil notes how the contemporary debates between positivists and postmodern relativists—over issues that are at least a century old—has resulted in the fragmentation of communities of scholars who share a common interest in a general phenomenon or a particular historical instance thereof. Only the most agnostic of scholars are able to take full advantage of the insights garnered from the range of hypotheses, descriptive inferences, interpretations, or narratives that pertain to the phenomenon or episode in question. Seeking to improve the possibilities for communication among a wider community of scholars embracing a variety of epistemological positions, Sil rejects epistemological "absolutism" and proceeds to identify a wide range of more nuanced, intermediate positions undergirding many of the great works of social science on such foundational issues as the objective/subjective nature of social reality, the inductive/deductive character of theory building, the purpose of social analysis, the significance of the fact/value distinction, and the question of how interpretations and theories might be evaluated in the absence of uniform methods of verification/falsification. In between the positivist and relativist extremes, Sil identifies a "spectrum" of epistemological perspectives on these issues, and he attempts to locate a "pragmatic" center in which the social construction of reality is acknowledged, but historical and empirical observations remain the primary basis for persuading audiences that theories, descriptive inferences, or context-sensitive interpretations are plausible and deserving of further exploration. Such a center is offered not as a superior or definitive alternative to positivist social science or postmodern relativism, but as a more flexible and practical approach to facilitate greater communication among scholars adhering to competing research traditions in the absence of a clear consensus on foundational issues.

In his contribution, "Thresholds and the Evolution of Scientific Knowledge: A Cautionary Note on Boundaries," Wade Huntley takes another approach to the problem of boundaries, or "thresholds" as he refers to them. A "threshold," as Huntley conceptualizes it, is meant to be crossed even as it marks a separation between fields or styles of inquiry. Thus, while Sil seeks to identify a pragmatic epistemological "middle ground" as a first step to overcoming deeply entrenched boundaries, Huntley argues that before we can even begin to consider strategies for transcending boundaries, it is essential to gain a more nuanced understanding of why thresholds emerged in the first place. He employs analogies from the natural sciences in conjunction with a Kantian epistemology to suggest that there may be sound reasons why distinctions between disciplines and paradigms have emerged and why further thresholds are likely to emerge in the future. As the "universe of knowledge" expanded, boundaries became essential to the management and further expansion of that knowledge. The emergence of international relations as a discipline in its own right, a discipline whose concerns were separated from those of students of law and philosophy, was also a part of this process. Even the appearance of cross-disciplinary research, he notes, is essentially a component of this trend, reflecting rather than rejecting the process of increasing specialization. Finally, Huntley turns to one of the problems that distinguishes the social sciences from the natural sciences, the problem of the relationship of knowledge to action, or specifically, social knowledge to political action. It is this threshold—and not the boundaries between disciplines or paradigms—that Huntley considers to be the most fundamental challenge if the foundations of social science are to be made more meaningful. Considering the "constructivist" turn in international relations as well as "postmodern" and "critical" perspectives, he concludes by suggesting that while Kant may provide some answers for coping with fundamental epistemological problems in the social sciences, it is Marx who may provide some help in the search of logics to justify crossing the threshold between the "good citizen" and the "good scholar."

Finally, Timothy Luke, in a chapter titled "The Discipline as Disciplinary Normalization: Networks of Research," offers a critical—and provocative—analysis of the "normalizing effects of disciplinary practices and values in contemporary American political science." Drawing in part on his own experiences and in part on his observations, he applies the "strong program" of the sociology-of-science perspective to "read" the discipline of political science. He does so by analyzing in Foucaultian fashion how the construction and application of professional "standards," along with the system of departmental rankings, reputational concerns, doctoral training, and pressures on thousands of individual careers in different university settings, combine to produce "an implicit system of rules, which exerts, in turn, a normalizing effect upon both thought and action." Luke's chapter concentrates on three specific aspects of discipline in the discipline of political science. First, most generally, he examines the problem of how the discipline serves to provide an "ontological stability" for the larger social order by bringing to bear its own dominant constructions of power and knowledge to reproduce existing systems of social control. Second, he considers the requirements of "success" in the discipline, and links these requirements to the expectations of "professional correctness" that serve to normalize and provide symbolic order to professional-technical life. Finally, Luke investigates the question of reputation as institutionalized in "nomenclatures" that define the visibility of individual scholars and their departments, and carry with them imputations of prominence or insignificance without reference to the teaching or research practices of the thousands of scholars who make up the discipline.

The concluding chapter by Eileen Doherty provides a tentative appraisal of the intellectual returns to be had from the various chapters in Parts I and II of this volume. Doherty aims to show how the integrative frameworks contained in these may serve to improve the lines of communication between different disciplines, subfields and research traditions in order to bring together related stocks of knowledge. She also compares the payoffs of the different essays in light of the others, and considers the different ways in which each of the authors may be able to further extend his or her analytic frameworks and theoretical perspective by incorporating or accounting for insights and concepts from the work of the other authors in this volume.

Conclusion

If the sources of change in social and international life are complex, so must be the division of labor within the social sciences. However, as mechanisms of integration are essential to the preservation of order in society, so must we make room within this complex division of labor for scholars who, rather than deriving their projects within existing disciplinary structures or research traditions, consciously and deliberately pursue interdisciplinary, eclectic and integrative approaches organized around empirically grounded problematics. Original, question-driven integrative frameworks that transcend boundaries between disciplines or subfields and eschew *a priori* methodological commitments may very well interfere with attempts to construct a new universal system of concepts or a new analytic paradigm leading the social sciences to an age of scientific "maturity." But, rather than social proceeding blindly along the path of further specialization into progressively narrower "turfs," it may be worthwhile to seek a better understanding of how different concepts and units of analysis from across disciplines, subfields, and methodological traditions relate to each other in the study of particular aspects of international life. In order to do this, however, we need to place less emphasis on the definition of disciplinary boundaries or the formulation of new "paradigms," and we need to place a much greater premium on methodological pluralism and theoretical integration developed in the context of discrete, empirically-grounded questions. That is, we need a shift in focus away from the competition among research traditions and toward the expansion of "interdiscursive communities" in which there is a division of labor between those who seek to work within the framework of an established research tradition and those who seek to pursue eclectic, "paradigm-less" approaches that might produce more useful, more integrated conceptual schemes accompanied by different methodological tools for analyzing different kinds of substantive problems at different levels of abstraction.[39] Such approaches may not result in unifying grand theories, objective laws, or the achievement of scientific "maturity" for a discipline, but as the chapters in this volume aim to demonstrate, they may at least pave the way for some modest steps forward in our collective ability to generate deeper understandings and partial, middle-range explanations of concretely defined problems in international life.

Notes

1. Ernst B. Haas, "Reason and Change in International Life: Justifying a Hypothesis," *Journal of International Affairs* (Spring/Summer 1990), p. 213.
2. Thomas Kuhn, *The Structure of Scientific Revolutions* (Chicago: University of Chicago Press, 1962).
3. On this point, see Andrew Janos, *Politics and Paradigms* (Stanford: Stanford University Press, 1986), chapters 1–2, passim.
4. For a concise and insightful discussion of the emergence of disciplinary structures in the social sciences, see Immanuel Wallerstein et al., *Open the Social Sciences: Report of the Gulbenkian Commission on the Restructuring of the Social Sciences* (Stanford: Stanford University Press, 1996), pp. 1–32.
5. Wallerstein, et al., p. 7. Wallerstein et al. further note (pp. 9–10) that in the early stages, the disciplines were neatly correlated with distinct epistemological positions. On the one end, there stood mathematics as the model of logical positivism, followed by experimental natural sciences (physics, chemistry, and biology), and on the other end, there was were the humanities and arts, anchored by the normative discourse of philosophers.
6. Julie Thompson Klein, *Crossing Boundaries: Knowledge, Disciplinarities and Interdisciplinarities* (Charlottesville: University Press of Virginia, 1996), p. 6.
7. On the emergence of the dual-discipline subfields, see Wallerstein et al., pp. 44–46.
8. For example, although economists and political scientists both addressed problems of economic development and underdevelopment, the economists engaged each other within the subfield of "development economics" and, for the most part, did not directly engage political scientists studying the "political economy of development." Examples of these two approaches include, respectively, Albert Hirschman, "The Rise and Decline of Development Economics," in Hirschman, *Essays*

in Trespassing: From Economics to Politics and Beyond (New York: Cambridge University Press, 1981); and Stephan Haggard and Robert Kaufman, eds. *The Politics of Economic Adjustment* (Princeton: Princeton University Press, 1992).

9. For a discussion of the emergence of area studies, see Wallerstein et al., pp. 36–38.

10. Klein, p. 2.

11. Thomas Gieryn, "Boundary-Work and the Demarcation of Science from Non-Science: Strains and Interests in Professional Ideologies of Scientists," *American Sociological Review*, 48 (1983): 783; also quoted in Ellen Messer-Davidow, David Shumway and David Sylvan, "Disciplinary Ways of Knowing," in Messer-Davidow, Shumway and Sylvan, eds. *Knowledges: Historical and Critical Studies in Disciplinarity* (Charlottesville: University Press of Virginia, 1993), p. 4.

12. Some theorists of international relations have certainly incorporated insights from one or another discipline, most notably, from psychology or economics. However, as Doherty notes, these interdisciplinary explorations have only given way to new debates over the relative merits of "economic" and "psychological" approaches as evident in recent annual meetings of the International Studies Association and the American Political Science Association. See Doherty's chapter in this volume, "Negotiating Across Disciplines: The Implications of Judgment and Decision Making Reserach for International Bargaining Theory."

13. Raphael Sassower, *Knowledge Without Expertise: On the Status of Scientists* (Albany: State University of New York Press, 1993), p. 130.

14. In this sense, this volume is in keeping with the spirit of the proposals recently advanced by Wallerstein and the Gulbenkian Commission on the Restructuring of the Social Sciences. The commission distinguishes between two understandings of "interdisciplinary" research: (a) the standard interdisciplinary programs established on a permanent basis which only add to the number of entrenched, bounded units in the disciplinary structure of the university; and (b) integrated research programs cutting across all traditional disciplinary structures that are funded on a temporary basis for the purpose of addressing particular questions or urgent themes. See Wallerstein et al., pp. 104–105.

15. I am using the term "interparadigm debate" here to capture any debate between competing research traditions in any social science field or discipline. It should be noted, however, that the term was originally coined by Michael Banks and subsequently employed by British scholars in response to the growing interest in the language of "paradigms" to describe the debates between neorealists, pluralists and Marxists in 1970s international relations theory. On this point, see Ole Waever,

"Figures of International Thought: Introducing Persons Instead of Paradigms," in Iver Neumann and Waever, eds. *The Future of International Relations: Masters in the Making* (London: Routledge, 1997), p. 12; and Michael Banks, "The Evolution of International Relations Theory," in Banks, ed. *Conflict in World Society: A New Perspective on International Relations* (London: Harvester, 1984), pp. 1–21.

16. Kuhn, pp. 10–13, 77–90.

17. Andrew Janos, "Paradigms Revisited: Productionism, Globality and Postmodernism in Comparative Politics," *World Politics*, 50, 1 (October 1997), p. 121.

18. While the "paradigm" concept could be—and was—interpreted as pointing to a strictly relativistic epistemology, it should be noted that nowhere did Kuhn ever suggest that new paradigms did not, in fact, represent means to acquire new stocks of knowledge previously beyond the grasp of those whose research was limited by earlier paradigms or by the confusion of a preparadigmatic stage of research. It is true that only a sharp break with the fundamental assumptions of Newtonian physics was necessary in order for Einstein to introduce his theory of relativity, and the contributions of the latter could not be evaluated within the theoretical framework of the Newtonian paradigm. Nevertheless, the absence of a single uniform set of evaluative criteria did not mean that these were merely two different sets of subjective interpretations given the absence of a single uniform set of evaluative criteria.

19. See the discussion of Kuhn and his critics in Stephen Toulmin, *Human Understanding* (Princeton: Princeton University Press, 1972), pp. 98–117. The last of the criticisms constitutes the basis for Toulmin's own evolutionary theory of progress in scientific knowledge based on the steadily increasing variation in "populations" of concepts and "selection" of certain concepts on the basis of both their intellectual utility and their instrumental value in maintaining disciplinary or professional interests.

20. Toulmin, pp. 113–115; Janos, *Politics and Paradigms,* p. 157, fn. 2; and Janos, "Paradigms Revisited," p. 120. See also Kuhn, *The Structure of Scientific Revolutions,* 2nd ed. (Chicago: University of Chicago Press, 1970), and his "Second Thoughts on Paradigms," in Frederick Suppe, ed. *The Structure of Scientific Theories* (Urbana: University of Illinois Press, 1974).

21. On the use of the "paradigm" concept in international relations, see, for example, Banks; Michael Smith, Richard Little, and Michael Shackleton, eds. *Perspectives on World Politics* (London: Croom Helm, 1981); Steve Smith, "Paradigm Dominance in International

Relations: The Development of International Relations as a Social Science," in Hugh C. Dyer and Leon Mangasarian, eds. *The Study of International Relations: The State of the Art* (New York: St. Martin's Press, in association with Millennium: Journal of International Studies, 1989); Stephen Haggard, "Structuralism and Its Critics: Recent Progress in International Relations Theory," in Emmanuel Adler and Beverly Crawford, ed. *Progress in Postwar International Relations* (New York: Columbia University Press, 1991); Paul Viotti and Mark Kauppi, *International Relations Theory: Realism, Pluralism, Globalism* (New York: Macmillan, 1993); and Ole Waever, "The Rise and Fall of the Inter-Paradigm Debate," in Steve Smith, Ken Booth and Marysia Zalewski, eds. *International Theory: Positivism and Beyond* (Cambridge, UK: Cambridge University Press, 1996). On paradigms in other social science fields or subfields, see previously cited works by Janos as well as Sheldon Wolin, "Paradigms and Political Theories," and Douglas Eckberg and Lester Hill, "The Paradigm Concept and Sociology: A Critical Review," both in Gary Cutting, ed. *Paradigms and Revolutions* (South Bend: Notre Dame University Press, 1980).

22. Albert Hirschman, "The Search for Paradigms as a Hindrance to Understanding," *World Politics,* 22 (April 1970); see also Janos, "Paradigms Revisited," p. 118.

23. The 1930s-1940s witnessed the first debate in IR between interwar idealists and their realist critics. Subsequent decades saw debates between those advocating a unifying paradigm under "scientific behavioralism" and adherents of a "classical" approach, followed by the "third inter-paradigm debate" between those attempting to defend a realist paradigm and the adherents of pluralism and Marxism in the 1970s (which turned into the neorealist-neoliberalist debate in the 1980s as Marxist approaches fell out of favor), and more recently, a debate between "rationalists" (working at the intersection of neorealism and neoliberalism) and "reflectivists" (e.g., critical theorists, poststructuralists, or constructivists). See Waever, "The Rise and Fall of the Inter-Paradigm Debate," pp. 155–165.

24. The "behavioral" approach to international relations may be found in Morton Kaplan, *System and Process in International Politics* (NY: Wiley, 1957); for the debate between behavioralists and advocates of a "classical" alternative, see Morton Kaplan, "The Great Debate: Traditionalism vs. Science in International Relations," *World Politics,* 19, 1 (1966), and Hedley Bull, "International Theory: The Case for a Classical Approach," in Klaus Knorr and James Rosenau, eds. *Contending Approaches to International Politics* (Princeton: Princeton University Press, 1969), pp. 20–38. By the late-1970s, "neorealism" or "struc-

tural realism" (inspired primarily by Waltz) had replaced both behavioral and classical approaches to realism, but, like its predecessors, came to be criticized from a variety of perspectives; see Kenneth Waltz, *The Theory of International Politics* (Reading: Addison-Wesley, 1979); and Robert Keohane, ed. *Neorealism and Its Critics* (New York: Columbia University Press, 1984).

25. This unified rationalist tradition is described by Waever as the "neo-neo synthesis," and is rooted in Robert Keohane's observation in the late 1980s that neorealism and neoliberalism could be distinguished from "reflectivist" alternatives on the basis of certain shared assumptions, such as their desire to explain behavioral regularities by examining the nature of the decentralized international system and their desire to transcend the interpretation of texts and provide explanatory understanding of an objective international political reality. See Waever, "Figures of International Thought," pp. 18–19; Robert Keohane, *International Institutions and State Power* (Boulder: Westview, 1989), esp. p. 165; and Stephen Krasner, "The Accomplishments of International Political Economy," in Smith et al., pp. 108–127.

26. On the growing interest in a "reflectivist" alternative to the rationalist approach, see the extensive discussion of constructivism in Anne Clunan, "Constructing Concepts of Identity: Prospects and Pitfalls of a Sociological Approach to World Politics," chapter 4 in this volume; and Ronald Jepperson, Alexander Wendt and Peter Katzenstein, "Norms, Identity, and Culture in National Security," in Katzenstein, ed. *The Culture of National Security* (New York: Columbia University Press, 1996). On other "reflectivist alternatives," see Hayward Alker and Thomas Biersteker, "The Dialectics of World Order: Notes for a Future Archeologist of International Savoir Faire," *International Studies Quarterly*, 28, 2 (1984): 121–142; Richard Ashley, "The Achievements of Post-Structuralism," in Smith et al., pp. 250–253; and James Der Derian, ed. *International Theory: Critical Investigations* (New York: New York University Press, 1995).

27. On the recurrence of certain core ontological and epistemological problems in the social sciences since the end of the nineteenth century, see Rudra Sil, "Against Absolutism in International Studies: Towards a 'Pragmatic' Epistemological Center," chapter 6 in this volume.

28. Michael Desch notes that the 1990s proliferation of interest in norms, identities, and culture, rather than representing a new challenge to realist IR theories, is in fact the latest in a succession of waves in cultural theorizing since the Second World War. More generally, the recent debate between "culturalists" and "rationalists" in both IR and comparative politics echoes the same points of contention employed since

the end of the nineteenth century in defining what Janos characterizes as the competing "materialist" and "idealist" paradigms in the nomothetic social sciences at large. See Desch, "Culture Clash: Assessing the Importance of Ideas in Security Studies, *International Security* (Summer 1998): 141–170; and Janos, "Paradigms Revisited," p. 121. See also the discussion of the role of culture and rationality in Rudra Sil, "The Foundations of Eclecticism: The Epistemological Status of Agency, Culture, and Structure in Social Theory," *Journal of Theoretical Politics* 12.3 (2000).

29. For example, as noted above, the pluralist, Marxist, and constructivist critiques of neorealism may have reduced the popularity of the neorealist research tradition, but many of the latter's central assumptions have remained intact and are even embedded in the "rationalist" tradition currently thought to represent the dominant mode of research in IR. Similarly, in comparative politics and sociology, some of the assumptions of universal convergence in the so-called modernization paradigm of the 1950s-1960s, although subject to an intense barrage of criticisms for more than two decades, have reemerged in the 1990s with the decline of Soviet communism, the spread of "globalization," and the renewed interest in transitions to liberal capitalist democracy. For critical appraisals of this phenomenon, see Robert Boyer, "The Convergence Hypothesis Revisited: Globalization but Still the Century of Nations?" in Suzanne Berger and Ronald Dore, ed. *National Diversity and Global Capitalism* (Ithaca: Cornell University Press, 1995); and Rudra Sil, *Historical Legacies, Late-Industrialization and Institution-Building* (Ph.D. Dissertation, University of California, Berkeley, 1996), pp. 99–133.

30. See, for example, Yosef Lapid and Friedrich Kratochwil, eds. *The Return of Culture and Identity in IR Theory* (Boulder: Lynne Rienner, 1996); Peter Evans, Dietrich Rueschmeyer and Theda Skocpol, eds. *Bringing the State Back In* (New York: Cambridge University Press, 1984); and Roger Friedland and Roger Alford, "Bringing Society Back In: Symbols, Practices and Institutional Contradictions," in Walter Powell and Paul DiMaggio, eds. *The New Institutionalism in Organizational Analysis* (Chicago: University of Chicago Press, 1991).

31. Steve Smith, among others, does view "realism" as a dominant IR "paradigm" that held sway for several decades. However, Smith views "realism" as more of a worldview opposed to "idealism," one that is compatible with a variety of epistemological foundations and methodologies. In this case, the concept of a "paradigm" becomes stretched too far to be meaningful. The editors of this volume still share Smith's conclusion that IR has benefited from the emergence of alternative dis-

courses embracing a different set of assumptions about the world and the behavior of actors. See Smith, "Paradigm Dominance," pp. 7–13.

32. Waever, "The Rise and Fall of the Inter-Paradigm Debate," passim.

33. See, for example, Barry Buzan, "The Timeless Wisdom of Reorealism," in Smith et al., pp. 47–65; and Richard Little, "The Growing Relevance of Pluralism," in Smith et al., pp. 66–86.

34. Haggard, p. 432.

35. It is true, as Kuhn noted (*The Structure of Scientific Revolutions*, p. 24), that "[b]y focusing attention upon a small range of relatively esoteric problems, the paradigm forces scientists to investigate some part of nature in a detail and depth that would otherwise be unimaginable." This might constitute a reasonable proposition, but in this case, the logic for distinguishing between research traditions becomes the same as the logic informing the disciplinary specialization discussed in the previous section. In this case, there still remains a need for complementary mechanisms to integrate related strands of research bearing on similar empirical phenomena that may have been previously pursued in greater detail within different research traditions.

36. Toulmin, esp. pp. 122–166, and pp. 224–279. Toulmin's selectionist theory of gradual, evolutionary progress is also adopted by Ernst Haas (fn. 1).

37. See Paul Feyerabend, *Against Method: Outlines of an Anarchistic Theory of Knowledge* (London: New Left Books, 1975).

38. James Rosenau, "Probing Puzzles Persistently: A Desirable but Improbable Future for IR Theory," in Smith et al., p. 313.

39. The term "inter-discursive communities" is from James Der Derian, "A Reinterpretation of Realism: Genealogy, Semiology, Dromology," in Der Derian, ed., p. 37.

PART ONE

CONSTRUCTING INTEGRATIVE FRAMEWORKS

2

NEGOTIATING ACROSS DISCIPLINES

The Implications of Judgment
and Decision-Making Research
for International Relations Theory

EILEEN M. DOHERTY

Everything that is beautiful and noble is the product of reason
and calculation.
—Charles Baudelaire, "The Painter of Modern Life"

It was not reason that besieged Troy; it was not reason that sent
forth the Saracen from the desert to conquer the world; that
inspired the crusades; that instituted the monastic orders; it was
not reason that produced the Jesuits; above all, it was not reason
that created the French Revolution. Man is only great when he
acts from the passions; never irresistible but when he appeals to
the imagination.
—Benjamin Disraeli, *Coningsby*

The evolution of international relations theory has been characterized by
explicit attempts to draw insights from other disciplines. International
political economy (IPE) has been most heavily influenced by economics,
and more recently, as Clunan notes in this volume, by sociology. This chapter focuses on the insights of cognitive psychology for theories of international political economy. The chapter explores the ways that two research
traditions in the field of judgment and decision making (JDM)—prospect
theory and social judgment theory (SJT)—further inform the study of international political economy generally, and international negotiations specifically. Both these traditions offer separate and valuable insights about the
factors that shape human cognition.[1] As will be discussed, prospect theory
has already had a significant impact on international relations theory, not

31

least because it has highlighted important new areas of inquiry for students of international negotiations. Social judgment theory, by contrast, has made virtually no inroads in the study of international relations, although it has had a significant impact on a range of other fields, including medicine,[2] business,[3] public policy,[4] education,[5] and social work.[6]

The chapter begins by discussing rational choice theory and some criticisms thereof. It then discusses the ways in which prospect theory and social judgment theory stand as a challenge to rational choice theories of human behavior. Prospect theory emerged from within (and as a reaction to) the tradition of rational choice. The research findings regarding the importance of problem framing for human risk tolerance have already prompted international relations scholars to reconsider a range of existing international relations theories, including deterrence theory and bargaining theory. Social judgment theory started with different assumptions, methodological techniques, and criteria for evaluating human decision making.[7] This research tradition offers a range of important insights regarding the ways that task characteristics affect decision making behavior, the role of intuitive cognition in human behavior, and the difficulties that humans have in fully understanding, hence, articulating, the thought processes leading to particular judgments. These are important insights for our understanding of the dynamics of international negotiations, particularly the danger that bargaining impasses may emerge and be sustained because of cognitive rather than material conflicts.

"Rationality," "Bounded Rationality," and Incrementalism in Decision Making

The "political psychology" approach to international politics is premised on the notion that factors at the individual level of analysis significantly affect international outcomes.[8] In short, human cognition matters.[9] Some political psychology research focuses on the way that the cognitive beliefs or thought processes of particular individuals matter; other research focuses more generally on the ways that patterns of human cognition affect policy outcomes. Yet the impact of psychological research in international relations theory remains more limited than is warranted. Two points in particular must be made. First, while there is certainly a broad array of cognitive approaches in international relations,[10] "psychological" approaches to international relations have generally focused on the cognitive processes that do not conform well to purely "rational" standards of behavior.[11] Second, to the extent the political psychology has been integrated into the study of international relations, it has been almost exclusively in the area of foreign policy. There exists a rich literature on the role of cognitive factors in such areas as elite decision making, crisis-management, deterrence, the emergence of the Cold War, and international conflict.[12] But until recently, there has been little crossover into international political economy.

The dearth of psychological approaches to international political economy stems at least partly from the long-standing assumption that psychological and economic approaches to the study of IPE are fundamentally incompatible. Because IPE has been predominantly influenced by economics, there has been little room for cognitive analysis. Testimony to the perceived tension between these two disciplines can be found in the prominence of round table discussions on "psychology versus economics" in recent years at annual meetings of the International Studies Association and the American Political Science Association. Debates have raged as to whether "economic" approaches and "psychological" approaches are alternative or complementary theories. Much of this debate has hinged on the assumptions we make about human cognition. Do assumptions of "rationality" apply—and if so, what exactly does "rationality" mean? How does intuitive thought fit, if at all, into our understanding of "rational" or competent decision-making behavior?

There is perhaps no concept that is more central—or more contested—in studies of decision making than that of "rationality." In a 1954 pathbreaking paper, Ward Edwards introduced Bayesian analysis to the field of psychology. In that paper, he argued that "the crucial fact about economic man is that he is rational . . . [E]conomic man must make his choices in such a way as to maximize something."[13] Since that time, decision theory has proceeded on the basis of that assumption. For decision theorists, rational behavior entails making a decision that maximizes one's utility. To make a utility-maximizing decision, an actor must know the full set of options available to him or her, apply a set of causal beliefs about actions and outcomes, and be able to evaluate the utilities associated with various outcomes.[14] Decisions are made by calculating the expected utility of various alternatives (defined as product of the probability of a given outcome and the utility associated with that outcome). Actors maximize utility by choosing the options that yield the greatest expected value. One key to this conception of rationality is Bayes' theorem, which rests on the assumption that decision makers can perform probabilistic calculations necessary to assess the expected utility of various choices. Moreover, in situations of incomplete information, decision makers will rely on Bayesian updating in their decision processes, that is, they will revise their expected utility estimations, after combining prior probabilities with the probabilities associated with new information.

Herbert Simon and others have argued that the assumptions implicit in expected utility models are unrealistic and should be revised to reflect the constraints that characterize decision making.[15] Simon argues that individuals cannot feasibly know—much less rank order—the full set of actions and outcomes that are associated with any given decision. To do so for every decision would obviously require too much time and energy. Moreover, even if an individual were willing to expend the time and energy associated with a full examination of options, it is unlikely that he or she could do so. This is for two reasons. First, in an environment of limited information, the uncertainty associated with various decisions precludes a complete rank-ordering of various options. Second, even in an environment of complete information, the complexity associated with "informational overload" is likely to overwhelm an individual's ability to process and integrate various informational signals. In short, utility maximizing decision making is hampered by the existence of not enough information (uncertainty), as well as human limitations to understand and integrate an abundance of information (complexity).

Because of these constraints, individuals do not engage in "maximizing" behavior, but rather "satisfice" by examining decision alternatives sequentially, stopping when a minimally acceptable alternative presents itself. As Simon argues:

> The term ["bounded rationality"] was introduced . . . to focus attention upon the discrepancy between the perfect human rationality that is assumed in classical and neoclassical economic theory and the reality of human behavior as it is observed in economic life. The point was not that people are consciously and deliberately irrational, although they sometimes are, but that neither their knowledge nor their powers of calculation allow them to achieve the high level of optimal adaptation of means to ends that is posited in economics. . . . We know today that human reasoning, the product of bounded rationality, can be characterized as selective search through large spaces of possibilities. The selectivity of the search, hence its feasibility, is obtained by applying rules of thumb, or heuristics, to determine what path should be traced and what ones can be ignored. The search halts when a satisfactory solution has been found, almost always long before all alternatives have been examined.[16]

Note, however, that Simon is stressing the limits of human rationality, not fundamentally "irrational" components to human behavior.

Simon's notions of bounded rationality and satisficing have been used by others to analyze the policy-making sphere. One type of satisficing behavior, for example, has been termed "muddling through"—or the act of making minor changes in current policy while at the same time avoiding a commitment to irrevocable actions or decisions that might have serious negative unforeseen consequences. This incrementalism serves as a hedge against the uncertainty surrounding the decision. This approach to decision making is not necessarily a negative thing; indeed several organizational theorists have suggested that it can be a way of getting to desirable policy outcomes. Braybrooke and Lindblom have argued, for example, that policy makers are likely to prefer to separate decision tasks into small segments that will allow them to address problems incrementally rather than in ways that are far-reaching and perhaps irreversible.[17] If policy makers embrace incrementalism consciously and carefully, they can use this decision-making strategy to take minor steps toward a goal, to consider the impact of those minor steps, and if need be, to make corrections when mistakes are made.[18]

Yet incremental decision making, employed poorly or unconsciously, may also have serious negative consequences. What is desirable from a short-term perspective is not necessarily desirable—in the sense of utility-maximizing or satisficing—in the context of a longer time frame. The cumulative effects of short-term decisions may fall far short of those that decision makers would have stated as optimal, or even satisfactory, at the beginning of the decision process. Consider the United States' involvement in Vietnam—a foreign policy debacle that some analysts have attributed at least partly to the pitfall of incremental decision making. The increase in U.S. troops in Southeast Asia came gradually, without a grand strategy or well-thought-out U.S. commitment. Alexander George has distinguished two types of incremental decision making: "calculated" and "defensive" procrastination. The former entails a conscious effort to postpone a decision or some elements of a decision in order to use the extra time to gather more information. The latter refers to the simple postponement of a decision when there is no deadline facing the policy maker.[19] According to George, the primary difference is that the strategy of calculated procrastination is aimed at devising ways to reduce the uncertainty that surrounds the decision, while the tactic of defensive procrastination is aimed at escaping the unpleasantness of the uncertainty surrounding the decision.[20]

Consider again the issue of rationality. How are we to interpret these two very different notions of incrementalism in terms of "rational" underlying behavior? Both are consistent with Simon's notion of bounded rationality. What George calls calculated procrastination assumes that decision makers recognize the informational constraints—and either (1) delay a decision or (2) take the minimal action necessary—while they attempt to increase their understanding of the available options and likely consequences of various decisions. In other words, decision makers employ something akin to Bayesian updating techniques in their decision process. The process of defensive procrastination assumes that decision makers delay action or take minimal action in order to avoid a negative outcome in the short term. Using a short-term time frame, the preferences and utilities of decision makers may well differ substantially from the those viewed in a longer-term perspective. Again, this kind of short-term decision making behavior would fit the definition of bounded rationality—even though the long-term result may well be viewed as decidedly suboptimal.

These notions of bounded rationality and incremental decision making are variations of decision theory's utility maximization model. The point is not the definition of rationality per se, but rather whether humans are capable of fully considering all their options in an uncertain and complex world. In this sense, bounded rationality and incrementalism can be thought of as a kind of constrained utility maximization. Should we assume, then, that some kind of rational actor model, whether it assumes maximizing or satisficing behavior, is an appropriate conceptual model by which to view individual decision-making behavior? Are the only relevant questions centered around the constraints under which actors increase their utility? Or are there other ways to conceptualize "competent" decision-making behavior?

As will be discussed below, both prospect theory and social judgment theory create new challenges for rational actor models of decision making. Prospect theory starts with the same utility-maximization definition of rationality as does decision theory. However, empirical findings, such as those concerning the impact of framing on judgment, create a serious challenge for rational choice models of human behavior. Social judgment theory, by contrast, starts with an entirely different definition of judgment competence than does decision theory or prospect theory. In doing so, SJT research suggests that an excessive focus on the issue of "rationality" may itself obscure important insights about what constitutes "good" decision making. By moving away from a strict focus on rationality, the SJT research agenda expands to encompass the characteristics of intuitive as well as analytical cognition.

Challenges to Rational Choice Theory:
From the Decision Theory Camp

The single biggest crossover from JDM research into political science is prospect theory. During the last ten years, political scientists have focused increasingly on the insights that prospect theory may have for political scientists' understanding of decision making. As Kahneman and Tversky have argued, empirical evidence suggests that people make decisions in ways that are systematically different than expected utility theory suggests. Specifically, decision makers assess their options from a reference point—evaluating *changes in assets* (i.e., gains and losses), rather than forming preferences across a range of final asset levels.[21] Referent-dependent decision making yields very different results than those postulated by classical decision theory. For example, experimental evidence suggests that people tend to be loss averse: they place more value on the possibility of losing existing assets than the possibility of achieving comparable gains. Further, people behave in ways that are more risk acceptant in the domain of losses, and more risk averse in the domain of gains.

These differences have dramatic effects on human behavior. For example, whether a question is framed as a potential loss or a potential gain can affect people's judgments. One well-known experiment uses medical treatment options to demonstrate this difference:[22]

Problem 1

Imagine that the United States is preparing for the outbreak of an unusual Asian disease, which is expected to kill 600 people. Two alternative programs to combat the disease have been proposed. Assume that the exact scientific estimates of the consequences of the programs are as follows. Which of the two would you favor?

—If Program A is adopted, 200 people will be saved. (Chosen by 72% of respondents)

—If Program B is adopted, there is a one-third probability that 600 people will be saved and a two-thirds probability that no people will be saved. (Chosen by 28% of respondents)

Problem 2 (Same cover story)

—If Program C is adopted, 400 people will die. (Chosen by 22% of respondents)

—If Program D is adopted, there is a one-third probability that nobody will die and a two-thirds probability that 600 people will die. (Chosen by 78% of respondents)

The responses for Problem 1 and Problem 2 vary dramatically, even though there is no mathematical difference in the expected value of the A/B and C/D sets of options. All four options have an expected value that equals 200 saved lives out of 600 (in the first problem) or 400 lost lives out of 600 (in the second problem). However, the options in the first problem use as the reference point a situation in which the disease kills 600 people. The options are therefore posed as the number of lives that will be saved—

a gain. Faced with a choice between a "sure thing" gain of 200 lives versus a gamble that might result in 600 saved lives, the majority of respondents opted for the sure thing—a risk-averse decision posture.

But change the framing of the question. Assume, as does Problem 2, that the reference point is a situation in which no one dies. The options, then, are posed as the number of lives that will be lost as a result of the medical treatment. When faced with a "sure loss" of 400 people, or a gamble that might result in no deaths, respondents embraced a risk-oriented posture, opting for the gamble of Program D. Thus, changes in framing can lead decision makers to reverse their preferences. This finding poses a challenge to traditional decision theory. According to the invariance axiom of rational choice theory, two equivalent options (Problem 1 and Problem 2) should yield identical results. That they do not is a violation of rational choice assumptions regarding consistent, transitive preferences.[23]

Implications of Prospect Theory for International Relations

The implications of prospect theory research for international relations has been a topic of debate in the discipline—with some scholars going so far as to argue that prospect theory may stand as a paradigmatic alternative to rational choice theory.[24] Drawing from this body of research, Levy has suggested a series of hypotheses for international relations research:

- Leaders are likely to take greater risks in order to maintain their international position, reputation, and domestic political base than they will in order to enhance them.
- Leaders are likely to take excessive risks (defined as risks that are not justified by predictions based on expected value) in order to recoup losses in such things as territory, reputation, and domestic political base.
- Because leaders are likely to be slow in accommodating to losses, they are likely to be influenced by sunk costs in making decisions.
- It is easier to deter another leader from taking an objectionable action than it is to persuade him to terminate or reverse such an action.
- It is easier for states to cooperate in distributing gains than in distributing losses.
- In cooperation problems such as the prisoner's dilemma, cooperation will be more likely if it entails an agreement to restrain taking from the commons than if it entails an agreement to contribute to a public good.[25]

Some of these hypotheses map well with existing international relations theory. If states are willing to run high risks in order to defend against a possible loss, then states that are defending the status quo should have a bargaining advantage. This complements a well-established premise of bargaining theory: deterrence (Actor A is maintaining the status quo, or in other words, defending against a possible loss) is easier than compellence (Actor A is forcing Actor B to take new actions or reverse an objectionable action, a gain for Actor A).[26] As Jervis points out, however, this hypothesis assumes that both states know which of them is the defender of the status quo and which, the challenger. This is not always the case—and leads to another hypothesis: international conflict (and by implication, bargaining breakdown) is more likely when each actor believes that it is defending the status quo.[27]

Framing issues also have strong implications for international bargaining theory. If actors are more risk-averse in the domain of gains, then influence attempts may be more successful if the adversary sees itself as negotiating about possible gains. By contrast, if the adversary believes itself to be negotiating to avoid losses, it may more willing to take risks (such as inflexible bargaining positions) in order to preserve the status quo. Similarly, deterrence-oriented threats may be more likely to fail if an adversary's actions are motivated by a fear of losses; in such cases, threats may produce a spiral of increasing tension rather stability.[28]

Moving from the issue of international conflict to cooperation, an important insight stemming from prospect theory is that it may be easier to reach a consensus on dividing gains than on distributing losses. Stein has suggested that most recent theories of international cooperation focus on attempts to distribute gains. This has led to a systematic bias in the political science literature, which can only be resolved by expanding research with regard to cooperation in the distribution of losses. This suggests the need for students of international relations to expand their research agenda with regard to the emergence of cooperation in the distribution of losses.[29]

Challenges to Rational Choice Theory: Social Judgment Theory

Another challenge to rational choice theory emerges from social judgment theory. Unlike prospect theory, SJT is characterized by a reliance on correlational statistics rather than axiomatic or deductive approaches to the study of human decision behavior. But the difference between these two approaches is much more profound than simple choice of analytic method. Decision theory and SJT reflect fundamentally different assumptions regarding the proper way to evaluate human decision competence; these assumptions relate directly to the issue of whether human "rationality" should be the defining notion of competent decision making.

Specifically, decision theory relies on *coherence* models of competence; SJT research is predicated on *correspondence* models.[30] Coherence approaches rely heavily on the concept of rationality in that they evaluate decisions according to the internal logical consistency of the process, as defined by a comparison with a perfectly coherent logical or mathematical model. A judgment or prediction may not be empirically accurate, yet be rational in this sense. There may in fact be no empirical test available to measure the accuracy of judgment. But for the coherence model, whether or not empirical evidence exists is not the point; decisions are measured against a formal, not empirical, standard of rationality.

Note that Kahneman and Tversky's work falls firmly within this tradition of research. This is often overlooked, since prospect theory has challenged much traditional decision theory. Kahneman and Tversky argue that while much human decision making behavior is rational, individuals demonstrate systematic biases and errors in their cognitive abilities. Further, framing effects means that humans do not have consistent and transitive preferences. The notion of consistent preferences implies that individuals would have the same preference for alternatives with the same expected utility such as treatments A/B and C/D in the example above. In other words, the assumptions of many rational choice models do not hold up; no purely axiomatic system can account for inconsistent preferences in formally identical circumstances. Note again that the battle is fought entirely in the territory of decision theory—and that the language of the dispute reflects a coherence approach to decision competence.

Correspondence models, including the social judgment theory model, start from different premises. The question is not whether a judgment is "rational," but whether that judgment is empirically accurate. In other words, how well does the judgment correspond to some external standard of accuracy? By this standard, the logical consistency of the thought process is not taken into account in assessing the competence of the decision maker. A decision maker may not know, or may not be able to articulate, the reasons behind her judgment. But in a fundamental sense, the reasons behind the judgment are irrelevant if the judgment yields empirically accurate results.

The differences in these two approaches stem partly from their roots. Whereas decision theory has its roots in economics and Bayesian statistical theory, SJT has its roots in the psychology of perception, specifically Egon Brunswik's probabilistic functionalism.[34] Brunswik developed a Lens Model as a heuristic for understanding a range of issues related to human cognition. The Lens Model, depicted in Figure 2.1, is not simply a representation of an individual, but rather of an individual in the environment.[32]

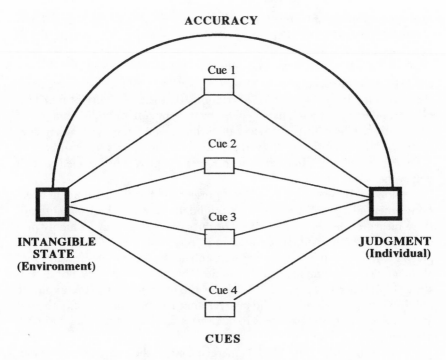

Figure 2.1
The "Lens Model"
Schematic depiction of Brunswik's lens model that illustrates how a person's judgment of an intangible object, event, or state is made on the basis of multiple fallible indicators (or cues). The left side of the lens indicates the environment. The right side of the lens shows how individuals make judgments based on the indicators.

In this model, the decision maker is on one side, the physical environment on the other. The task facing the decision maker is to understand or "know" the environment. In order to do so, he or she makes use of multiple, fallible (i.e., probabilistic) sources of information (cues). These cues are intersubstitutable; that is, the decision maker selects and aggregates the multiple sources of information in order to make inferences about the external environment.[33]

A fundamental tenet of social judgment theory is that judgments must be probabilistic, given the existence of irreducible uncertainty in the external environment. An individual cannot know his or her environment with absolute certainty. Rather, he or she attempts to understand the environment by relying on partial relationships—focusing on multiple, partially redundant cues to achieve perception. The result, generally, is highly accurate perception and adaptive human behavior.[34] (Consider the range of perceptual abilities that we take for granted: ability to perceive details, depth perception, and so forth.)

Extending this notion from physical perception to social judgment and to action in social situations was not difficult. Social judgment theorists stress the idea of vicarious functioning, that is, the ability of individuals to understand their environment by relying on multiple sources of information. Consider the process of hiring a new employee. What cues matter? College grade point average? Reputation of university attended? Prior job experience? Interview attire? Eye contact? The frequency with which the candidate smiles?

None of these cues is a perfect representation of the attribute in question: potential for job success. The candidate may rate high on some of these measures, but low on others. The cues themselves may be highly predictive for some individuals or situations, but not others. The task for the person making the judgment is to select and aggregate the cues in ways that allow an accurate judgment to be made. This process may be not a conscious one. Indeed, it may be difficult for the interviewer to later explicate the reasons she rated one candidate over another, much less specify the relative weights that she attached to various attributes in making the final decision.

Recall that the Lens Model emerged first in the study of perception. Human physical perception is highly accurate, but the processes involved are also largely subconscious. Similarly, different types of cognition can be employed in drawing inferences about the physical and social environments. Consequently, it is important to move away from notions of "rational" and "irrational" thought—and to consider the range of cognitive modes that are employed in human inference as well as actions based in part on those inferences.

In short, coherence researchers investigate human cognition in relation to the way that cognition *ought* to work; correspondence researchers investigate human cognition in relation to the way the *world* works (or in other words, in relation to empirical outcomes).[35] In the job interview example, a coherence researcher would evaluate the quality of the interviewer's decision process in terms of its underlying logic as defined by a given deductive model. By contrast, a correspondence researcher would assess the quality of the decision by examining the extent to which the interviewer's choices correlated with various candidates' job success.

In the SJT tradition, then, the assessment of competent decision making moves beyond the question of "rational" or "irrational" styles of thinking. Accurate judgments need not be logically derived judgments. In and of itself, this is hardly a surprising insight. Who has not heard the phrase,

"[My] gut instinct is . . ."? Or the self-flagelating, "I should have trusted my gut!"? Who has not heard the distinction between left-brain and right-brain modes of thinking? Who would deny the role of intuitive thought in human behavior? Intuitive thought stands as an alternative to analytical thought, and has been viewed as the opposite of analysis. Whereas analytical thought relies on building a logical, verbally defensible position in a step-by-step manner, intuitive thought implies no conscious reasoning, no step-by-step process, and no logical defenses of the "answer" that emerges.[36] One who makes an intuitive judgment is often unable to articulate the process of the judgment, much less defend that judgment in logical terms. Hammond offers some compelling examples of intuitive modes of thinking:

- Nikos Kazantzakis, in his classic novel, *Zorba the Greek*, offers a dialogue between the Zorba and his English employer. After Zorba spends the money that was entrusted to him on wine, women, and song, the Englishman attempts rationally to communicate the reasons why Zorba had acted so wrongly. Zorba listens, then responds: "Ah Boss, if you could only dance that for me!"[37]
- Mark Twain, in Life on the Mississippi, writes of the way an experienced river boat pilot attempted to explain the way he could distinguish between dangerous bluff reefs and harmless wind reefs in the river:

  Now don't you see the difference? It wasn't anything but a wind reef. The wind does that.

  So I see. But it is exactly like a bluff reef. How am I ever going to tell them apart?

  I can't tell you. It is an instinct. By and by you will just naturally know one from the other, but you will never be able to explain why or how you know them apart.[38]

- Freeman Dyson describes the way that Nobel laureate Richard Feynman approached physics:

  The reason Dick's physics was so hard for ordinary people to grasp was that he did not use equations. The usual way theoretical physics was done since the time of Newton was to begin by writing down some equations and then to work hard calculating solutions of the equations. This was the way Hans and Oppy and Julian Schwinger did physics. Dick just wrote down the solutions out of his head with-

out ever writing down the equations. He had a physical
picture of the way things happen, and the picture gave him
the solutions directly, with a minimum of calculation. It
was no wonder that people who had spent their lives solving equations were baffled by him.[39]

Intuitive judgments may be highly competent judgments, according to
the correspondence model. So, too, may analytical judgments. Traditionally, psychologists have viewed analytical and intuitive thought as rival patterns of thought. According to the definitions above, there can be no
overlap in these two modes of thought. As Bruner argued:

There are two modes of cognitive functioning, two modes of
thought, each providing distinctive ways of ordering experience,
of constructing reality. The two (though complementary) are
irreducible to one another. Efforts to reduce one mode to the
other or to ignore one at the expense of the other inevitably fail
to capture the rich diversity of thought.[40]

Is there room for compromise? Hammond argues that rather than conceptualizing human cognition as either intuitive or analytical, it would be more
useful to view the two modes as opposite ends of a spectrum—with a range
of cognitive modes falling between those two poles. These "in-between"
modes of thinking can be termed "quasi-rational."[41] While it is difficult to
give a precise definition of quasi-rational cognition, most people would probably agree that there are such "in-between" modes of thought: cognition that
involves some kind of "soft" reliance on deductive principles or formulae,
but at the same time deviates from strict adherence to the rules of logic.

The notion of quasi-rational thought is especially relevant to the
international relations literature on cognitive heuristics.[42] The complexity
of some international issues makes it more likely that policy makers will
embrace cognitive shortcuts to help them interpret new information. For
example, reliance on historical analogies, or "lessons of history," reflects
quasi-rational cognitive behavior. Such thinking displays elements of both
analysis and intuition. There is an underlying causal logic in historical
analogies, but this logic tends be in the form of broad propositions rather
than tight logical arguments.

The fundamental idea is that human cognition moves along a continuum, with decision makers using analytical cognition sometimes, intuitive
cognition at other times.[43] One manifestation of this continuum reflects the
various ways that individuals, groups or organizations attempt to solve problems. According to Hammond, there are six basic modes of inquiry, which
map well with the analysis/quasi-rationality/intuition continuum:

Mode 1: True analytical experimentation
(Controlled experimentation such as laboratory research in chemistry)

Mode 2: Moderately strong analytical experimentation
(Experimentation that relies on control groups and statistical inference)

Mode 3: Weak analytical experimentation
(Surveys, participant-observer research, field observations, etc.)

Mode 4: Strong quasi-rational judgment
(Thought experiments by experts such as consultants; computer simulations)

Mode 5: Data-based expert judgment
(Expert interpretation of an existing database)

Mode 6: Expert judgment unconstrained by data[44]

Consider the two ends of the spectrum. Mode 1 suggests pure analytic thought. Laboratory experimentation relies on the use of controls in order to limit the number of variables (or cues) that are being studied. It relies on the application (and testing) of stringent and often abstract principles. The experiments are done in the context of a body of theoretical knowledge, with the intention of adding to that body of knowledge. Researchers are highly aware of the principles that guide their actions; indeed, they attempt to specify as precisely as possible the theories, hypotheses, and variables that are the core of their activity. Further, experimentation cannot be a rushed process; it involves checking and double-checking control conditions as well as experiment results.

Now consider Mode 6, which stands at the "intuitive" end of the spectrum. This form of cognition is not data-driven; and does not rely on manipulating the external environment through experimentation in order to gain more information about the world. Mode 6—and in fact, Modes 4–6—rely on cognitive representations of the world, rather than data-driven analysis (Modes 1–3). This implies a very different starting point: the cognitive maps that are the focus of the intuitive end of the spectrum are pictorial rather than verbal or quantitative. Little wonder, then, that it is difficult to verbalize the rationale behind intuitive judgments! Factors shaping judgments are likely to be less precise than analytical formulae; moreover, individuals are likely to be less aware of those factors. Finally, whereas true experimentation must be slow and careful, intuitive judgments are often rapid. A corollary to this is that time pressure is likely to spark intuitive rather than analytical judgment. Hammond schematizes the differences between intuition and analysis in the following way:

Properties of intuition and analysis[45]

	Intuition	*Analysis*
Cognitive control	Low	High
Awareness of cognitive activity	Low	High
Amount of shift across indicators	High	Low
Speed of cognitive activity	High	Low
Memory	Raw data or events used	Complex principles stored
Metaphors used	Pictorial	Verbal, quanitative

One particularly relevant issue for students of international relations is whether there are systematic differences in the circumstances that induce intuitive, quasi-rational, and analytical cognition. The answer, quite simply, is yes. Extensive experimental research in the field of SJT suggests that the nature of the task affects the kind of cognitive activity the decision maker embraces. Therefore, by extension, the nature of the task affects the extent to which a decision maker can articulate the logic behind that task. This means that a theory of decision making will be more complete if it incorporates task characteristics, and specifically, the relationship between cognition and task structure.

Some of the specific task characteristics that affect cognitive modes follow. While these are presented as inducing intuition or analysis, it is important to emphasize that these modes should be viewed as opposite ends of a spectrum. Intermediate levels of the following characteristics, or mixtures of intuition-inducing and analysis-inducing task characteristics, are likely to induce quasi-rational cognition.[46]

- An individual with no prior training or task information is more likely to rely on intuition, whereas an individual with such training or information is more likely to rely on analysis.
- A task with multiple (greater than five) indicators is likely to induce intuition, whereas a task with few (2–4) indicators is likely to induce analysis.
- A task in which indicators are presented simultaneously is more likely to induce intuition, whereas a task in which indicators are presented sequentially is more likely to induce analysis.
- A task in which indicators are presented as pictures is more likely to induce intuition, whereas a task in which the indicators are presented in quantitative terms is more likely to induce analysis.

- A task in which the individual measures the indicators is more likely to induce intuition, whereas a task in which the individual has objective measures is more likely to induce analysis.
- A task in which there are many judgment alternatives is more likely to induce intuition, whereas a task in which there are few alternatives is more likely to induce analysis.
- A task that requires rapid response is more likely to induce intuition, whereas a task with an open-ended response time is more likely to induce analysis.
- A task for which there is no organizing principle is more likely to induce intuition, whereas a task for which there is an available organizing principle is more likely to induce analysis.
- A task in which equal weight is placed on indicators is more likely to induce intuition, whereas a task in which some indicators are weighted more heavily than others is more likely to induce analysis.
- A task that yields minimal or no feedback is more likely to induce intuition, whereas a task that yields feedback is more likely to induce analysis.

One theme that emerges from the above exposition of task characteristics is that individuals have difficulty making analytically based judgments in environments of extreme complexity. For example, combine five of the intuition-inducing task characteristics above. Imagine a situation in which an individual is told that a large number of factors is relevant to a particular problem; that he or she will see all these factors at the same time (as opposed to sequentially); that all of these factors appear to be equally relevant to the problem, that no organizing principle or well-established set of principles is available by which to evaluate the relevant information, and that there are multiple decision alternatives. The complexity of this task renders it nearly impossible for that individual to seize on a decision rule that is orderly and verbally defensible. It is likely that the response will be drawn more from a "gut feel" than from a logical analysis and evaluation of the cues.

Implications of Social Judgment Theory for International Relations

Social judgment theory research was initially focused on understanding more about the ways in which people made judgments about particular empirical problems. For example, which of several symptoms do physicians use most heavily in making a medical diagnosis regarding a particular disease? To answer that question, SJT researchers typically use correlational statistics and multiple regression analysis, but in a way that differs from most other social science research.[47] Rather than tracking the performance of a sample of physicians with regard to one task, SJT researchers track one individual at a time over a sample of tasks, each of which has a common set of cues. For example, a physician may be asked to look at 100 cases, each with varying values on a certain number of symptoms, and make 100 diagnostic judgments regarding the presence or absence of a particular disease. The physician's responses are then correlated with the "true" values for the 100 cases, in this example, whether the patients actually had the disease in question. Given a sufficient sample of cases, a "policy model" of the environment—reflecting the relationship between particular symptoms and the presence of the disease—can be built via multiple regression. A policy model of each subject—how each subject weights various symptoms in making her judgment—can also be built via multiple regression. This research provides insights to a number of questions about the decision process:[48]

- Do people use information (cues) that are generally recognized as important?
- Do they use information that is generally not thought relevant to the task?
- Do people use information similarly to each other?
- Do people use all of the information available in making judgments, or do they rely on a subset of cues?
- How do the statistical weights associated with people's judgments compare with their self-described strategies?
- Can judgment strategies be grouped into meaningful categories? Are there subsets of decision makers with similar strategies?
- Are people consistent in their judgments from one time period to another?

An interesting theme emerges from comparing statistical weights (policy models) with subjective weights (self-reports regarding a decision process). SJT research suggests that, for complex tasks, people can rarely give accurate descriptions of their own judgment processes.[49] A major finding relates to the importance of unexpected, and sometimes irrelevant, cues in decision making. Some studies of physicians have revealed, for example, that the most statistically significant factor affecting the decision to recommend a treatment is a patient's desire for that treatment.[50] Another major finding is that people tend to overestimate the number of informational sources they use in complex decision tasks.[51] For example, if a subject is asked how many of fifteen variables she utilized in making a diagnosis, she is likely to report a number that is higher than the number of cues with statistically significant weights. The broader insight is that decision makers are sometimes unaware of the factors that motivate them.

Consider the implications of these two findings for our understanding of international negotiations. First, people often are unaware of, or unable to articulate, the most important factors that motivate their decision processes. This creates a potential for miscommunication and for distrust to emerge if each side attributes the other's vagueness or inconsistency to bad faith. Recall that the more complex a decision task or issue, the more likely that people will rely on intuitive rather than analytical cognition. This potential for miscommunication and distrust is exacerbated by another fundamental finding in the SJT literature; people's judgments in the face of uncertainty are often far from perfectly consistent. Obviously, such inconsistent behavior may very easily be attributed to bad faith rather than to cognitive factors by a bargaining opponent.[52] Second, if people tend to overestimate the number of issues (cues) that are important to them in making a given judgment, negotiators may also be likely to overestimate the number of concessions that are necessary for a satisfactory agreement. In complex negotiations, then, there exists a cognitive bias for miscommunication toward overstating demands and, in doing so, narrowing the window of opportunity for cooperation.

Confirming evidence for this hypothesis is reflected in a study that is now a classic in the field of SJT research.[53] In assessing a set of labor-management negotiations, researchers found an important divergence in (1) the statements that each side made regarding the necessary concessions for an acceptable agreement and (2) the ways that each side evaluated sample contracts. Specifically, both sides insisted that four issues were critical components of any acceptable contract: contract duration; wage increases; number and use of machine operations; and number of strikers to be recalled. At the same time, each side privately ranked a range of 25 sample contracts on a scale of 1 (recommend rejection) through 7 (recommend acceptance). The statistical analysis revealed a very different story. The only statistically significant variable in the union negotiators' judgment policies was the recall issue, and the only statistically significant variable in the management negotiators' judgment policies was the wage issue! Moreover, when negotiators predicted the way the other side would evaluate the sample contracts, it was revealed that both sides were highly inaccurate. This was the case even though both sides had initially been confident that they understood each other's preferences well because of repeated association and negotiation experience. These findings suggest that there may have been more underlying room for agreement than either side realized.

Certainly, negotiators often have important strategic reasons for obscuring their priorities or for overstating their demands. It is critical, however, to distinguish between a bargaining strategy of obscuring priorities or consciously overstating demands, on the one hand, and a less conscious overstatement due to cognitive limitations, on the other. The major point is that, especially for complex issues, actors are likely to have difficulty articulating the relative importance they attach to various aspects of a satisfactory agreement—and may inadvertently send misleading signals to each other during the course of negotiations.

In short, the experimental findings associated with SJT research suggest that more attention should be paid to the cognitive obstacles to successful negotiation. Much bargaining theory focuses on the material or ideological factors underlying conflicts. However, SJT suggests that certain aspects of the normal human judgment process can themselves be a source of conflict, particularly when judgment moves more toward the intuitive end of the cognitive continuum. If we limit our analyses of international negotiations to an exclusive focus on material and ideological issues, we risk overlooking some of the cognitive factors that might exacerbate these conflicts. Moreover, more attention to cognitive sources of conflict may lead theorists or policy makers to identify windows of opportunity that do exist for cooperation and that might otherwise be obscured.

Conclusion

This chapter has briefly examined the challenges that have emerged to rational choice theory. Theories of bounded rationality and incremental decision making suggest that we look past assumptions of "utility maximizing" behavior—and focus instead on the impact of satistificing behavior and the tendency of decision makers to adopt short-term time frames in situations of uncertainty. Prospect theory suggests new hypotheses about the ways that the framing of issues can affect negotiation success. Among these hypotheses is the premise that actors who negotiate in the domain of losses are likely to have a bargaining advantage, as well as the premise that negotiations about distributing gains are more likely to be successful than negotiations about distributing losses. Social judgment theory suggests that cognitive sources of conflict may emerge as a result of the limited insight that actors have into their own judgment processes. The idea is simple, but may have profound implications. Too often, we see conflict as resulting from differences in material or ideological objectives. SJT research suggests that people (and states) may also engage in conflict when motives in fact coincide, but cognitive limitations prevent them from knowing so. In short, the research findings both in the field of prospect theory and of social judgment theory suggest new areas for research in the field of international bargaining. These insights also reinforce the premise that our understanding of international relations will be enriched by a deeper understanding of human judgment and decision-making behavior.

Acknowledgments

The author gratefully acknowledges the comments of John Aram, Michael Doherty, Kenneth Grundy, Kenneth Hammond, Steven Weber, participants of the International Relations Colloquium at the University of California, Berkeley, and participants of the 1997 International Invitational Meeting of The Brunswik Society.

Notes

1. The landmark paper introducing decision theory in psychology is W. Edwards, "The Theory of Decision Making," *Psychological Bulletin,* 51, 1954, pp. 380–417. Social Judgment Theory was inspired by the work of Egon Brunswik; the landmark paper for this approach was written by Brunswik's student, Kenneth Hammond, "Probabilistic functionalism and the Clinical Method," *Psychological Review,* 62, 1955, pp. 255–262. In 1971, another landmark paper comparing the two approaches sparked the creation of the field of Judgment and Decision Making in psychology. See P. Slovic and S. Lichtenstein, "Comparison of Bayesian and Regression Approaches to the Study of Human Information Processing in Judgment," *Organizational Behavior and Human Performance,* 6, 1971, pp. 649–744.

2. See D. G. Smith, D. G., and R. S. Wigton, "Research in Medical Ethics: The Role of Social Judgment Theory" in *Human Judgment: The SJT View,* B. Brehmer & C. R. B Joyce, eds. (Amsterdam: North Holland Elsevier, 1988); R. S. Wigton, "Applications of Judgment Analysis and Cognitive Feedback to Medicine," in Brehmer and Joyce, 1988; and R. S. Wigton, "Social Judgment Theory and Medical Judgment. *Thinking and Reasoning* 2/3, 1996, pp. 175–190.

3. See J. J. Martocchio, "Employee Decisions to Enroll in Microcomputer Training: A Policy Capturing Study." *Human Resource Development Quarterly* 4, 1993, pp. 51–69; R. L. Wilsted, T. Henrick, and T. Stewart, "A Judgment Policy-Capture of Bank Loan Decisions: An Approach to Developing Objective Functions for Goal Programming Models." *Journal of Management Studies* 12, 1975, pp. 210–215; W. F. Wright, "The Lens Model Applied to the Study of Financial Information Processing" in *Realizations of Brunswik's Representative*

Design, K. R. Hammond and N. Wascoe, eds. (San Francisco: Jossey-Bass, 1980); and I Zimmer, "A Lens Study of the Prediction of Corporate Failure by Bank Loan Officers," *Journal of Accounting Research* 18, 1980, pp. 629–636.

4. D. Brady and L. Rappoport., "Policy Capturing in the Field: The Nuclear Safeguards Problem," *Organizational Behavior and Human Performance* 9, 1973, pp. 253–266; K.R. Hammond, ed., *Judgment and Decision in Public Policy Formation* (Boulder, CO: Westview Press, 1978); R. J. Holzworth, R. J and C. B. Pipping, 'Drawing a Weapon: An Analysis of Police Judgments," *Journal of Police Science and Administration* 13, 1985, pp. 185–193; J. L. Mumpower, S. Livingston, and T. J. Lee, "Expert Judgments on Political Riskiness," *Journal of Forecasting* 6, 1987, pp. 51–65; and T. R. Stewart, and C. M. Lusk, "Seven Components of Judgmental Forecasting Skill: Implications for Research and the Improvement of Forecasts," *Journal of Forecasting* 13, 1994, pp. 579–599.

5. B. A. Browne and J. S. Gillis, "Evaluating the Quality of Instruction in Art: A Social Judgment Analysis," *Psychological Reports,* 50, 1982, pp. 955–962; R. W Cooksey, P. Freebody, and A. J. Bennett, "The Ecology of Spelling: A Lens Model Analysis of Spelling Errors and Student Judgments of Spelling Difficulty," *Reading Psychology: An International Quarterly* 11, 1990, pp. 293–322; R. W. Cooksey, P. Freebody, and G. Davidson, "Teacher's Predictions of Children's Early Reading Achievement: An Application of Social Judgment Theory," *American Educational Research Journal* 23, 1986, pp. 41–64; and J. E. Heald, "Social Judgment Theory: Applications to Educational Decision Making," *Educational Administration Quarterly* 27, 1991, pp. 343–357.

6. L. I. Dalgleish, "Decision Making in Child Abuse Cases: Applications of Social Judgment Theory and Signal Detection Theory," in Brehmer and Joyce, 1988.

7. Recent works discussing the foundations and implications of Social Judgment Theory include K. Hammond, *Human Judgment and Social Policy* (New York: Oxford University Press, 1996) and M. Doherty and E. Kurz, "Social Judgment Theory," *Thinking and Reasoning*, 2/3, 1996, pp. 109–140. The latter is part of a special issue devoted entirely to that topic.

8. For the classic statement on levels of analysis issues, see Kenneth Waltz, *Man, the State and War* (New York: Columbia University Press, 1959).

9. "Political psychology" is, of course, not limited to the study of international relations in political science. Students of American politics have a long tradition of focusing on "political psychology" to understand such issues as political leadership, group behavior, and public opinion.

10. Tetlock and McGuire distinguish two types of "cognitive strategies" that have received considerable attention in the study of political cognition as it relates to international relations: (1) reliance on knowledge structures based on past experiences in order to evaluate new information or to choose among policy alternatives (belief systems, operational codes, cognitive maps, etc.); and (2) reliance on judgmental and choice "heuristics" as cognitive aids or shortcuts in evaluating information. See Philip E. Tetlock and Charles McGuire, Jr., "Cognitive Perspectives on Foreign Policy" in S. Long, ed., *Political Behavior Annual* (Boulder, CO: Westview Press, 1985).

11. See, for example, Robert Jervis, *Perception and Misperception in International Politics* (Princeton: Princeton University Press, 1976); I. Janis and L. Mann, *Decision Making: A Psychological Analysis of Conflict, Choice and Commitment* (New York: The Free Press, 1977); and R. Jervis, R. N. Lebow and J. G. Stein, *Psychology and Deterrence* (Baltimore, MD: Johns Hopkins University Press 1985).

12. In addition to the works cited in footnote 11, illustrative examples include Ole R. Holsti, "Cognitive Dynamics and Images of the Enemy: Dulles and Russia" in *Image and Reality in World Politics*, John C. Farrell and Asa P. Smith, eds. (New York: Columbia University Press, 1967); Alexander George, "The 'Operational Code': A Neglected Approach to the Study of Political Leaders and Decision-Making," *International Studies Quarterly* 13, 1969, pp. 190–222; Irving Janis, *Groupthink: Psychological Studis of Policy Decisions and Fiascoes* (Boston: Houghton Mifflin, 1982); Deborah Larson, *Origins of Containment: A Psychological Explanation* (Princeton: Princeton University Press, 1985); and George Breslauer and Philip Tetlock, eds., *Learning in U.S. and Soviet Foreign Policy* (Boulder, CO: Westview, 1991).

13. Edwards, 1954.

14. See Jon Elster, "Introduction" in *Rational Choice*, J. Elster, ed. (New York: New York University Press, 1986). On page 4, Elster phrases the second of these three conditions even more stringently, arguing that utility maximization requires "(a set of rational beliefs about) the causal structure of the situation, which determines what course of action will lead to what outcomes."

15. Herbert Simon, *Administrative Behavior* (New York: Macmillan, 1958) and "A Behavioral Model of Rational Choice," *Quarterly Journal of Economics*, 69 (Feb.) 1955.

16. Herbert Simon, *Economics, Bounded Rationality and the Cognitive Revolution* (Brookfield, VT: Edward Elgar, 1992), pp. 3, 4.

17. Davide Braybrooke and Charles E. Lindblom, *A Strategy of Decision* (New York: Free Press, 1963).

54 Doherty

18. See also T. Connolly, "Hedge-Clipping, Tree-Felling and the Management of Ambiguity: The Need for New Images of Decision-Making," in L. Pondy, R. Boland Jr., and H. Thomas, *Managing Ambiguity and Change* (New York, John Wiley and Sons, 1988).
19. This is similar to Janis and Mann's (1977) discussion of defensive avoidance.
20. The distinction between strategy and tactic is also George's. See A. L. George, *Presidential Decision Making in Foreign Policy* (Boulder, CO: Westview Press, 1980), p. 36. George goes draws the following conclusion about incremental decision making: "Incrementalism is not a substitute for policy analysis that encompasses longer-range considerations and generates a planning context within which, then incremental decisions are made." Ibid, p. 41.
21. D. Kahneman and A. Tversky, "Prospect Theory: An Analysis of Decision Under Risk," *Econometrica*, 47, 1979, pp. 263–291. For a broader discussion of the "irrational" components of human cognition—that is, the role of heuristics and biases in decision making—see D. Kahnman, P. Slovic and A. Tversky, *Judgment under Uncertainty: Heuristics and Biases* (New York: Cambridge University Press, 1982).
22. The example is from D. Kahneman and A. Tversky, "Choices, Values and Frames," *American Psychologist,* 39, 1984, p. 343, as discussed in Hammond, 1996, pp. 106–109.
23. See the discussion in Jack S. Levy, "Prospect Theory, Rational Choice and International Relations," *International Studies Quarterly* 41, 1997, pp. 92–93.
24. For a good discussion of the role of prospect theory in informing international relations theory (including an argument against portraying rational choice and prospect theory as paradigmatic alternatives), see Levy, 1997, pp. 87–112.
25. Levy, 1997, p. 93. See also J. Levy, "Loss Aversion, Framing and Bargaining: The Implications of Prospect Theory for International Conflict," *International Political Science Review*, 17, 1996, pp. 177–193. Levy stresses, however, that the insights associated with prospect theory are in no way automatically transferable to international relations theory. For example, it is an open question as to whether a theory of individual decision making is an accurate representation of group behavior or institutional decision making. It should be noted that the same aggregation problem applies to rational choice theory.
26. T. Schelling, *Arms and Influence* (New Haven: Yale University Press, 1966) and R. Jervis, *The Meaning of the Nuclear Revolution* (Ithaca, NY: Cornell University Press, 1989).

27. R. Jervis, "Political Implications of Loss Aversion," in *Avoiding Losses/Taking Risks: Prospect Theory and International Conflict*, B. Farnham, ed. (Ann Arbor: University of Michigan Press, 1994).

28. Jervis in Farnham, 1994, pp. 28–29.

29. J. Stein, "International Cooperation and Loss Avoidance: Framing the Problem" in J. G. Stein and L. Pauly (eds.), *Choosing to Cooperate: How States Avoid Loss* (Baltimore: Johns Hopkins University Press, 1992), as discussed by Levy in Farnham, 1994, p. 127. Other important applications of prospect theory include B. Farnham, *Roosevelt and the Munich Crisis* (Princeton: Princeton University Press, 1997) and R. McDermott, *Risk-Taking in International Politics* (Ann Arbor: The University of Michigan Press, 1998).

30. See Slovic and Lichtenstein, 1971. Hammond (1996) develops an extensive discussion of the implications of these different "metatheories," as he refers to the two approaches.

31. See M. Doherty and E. Kurz, 1996.

32. In other words, SJT is an explicitly ecological approach to human behavior. The figure is adapted from Hammond (1996), p. 87.

33. As will be discussed below, in order to study this process of aggregation, social judgment theorists typically use multiple regression techniques. However, the methodology is not intrinsic to the theory.

34. See discussion in M. Doherty and E. Kurz, 1996. The inclusion of intuitive perceptual abilities is one reason that SJT research tends to focus more on cognitive success than does prospect theory. Indeed, Hammond argues that JDM literature overemphasizes cognitive error: "[H]uman judgment is susceptible to error . . . [But] error-finding is a large part of the culture of psychology; findings that denigrate human capability are prized by psychologists . . . [D]iscovering that human beings can do certain things is not interesting; discovering that they cannot do what is generally thought they can do is interesting. Bad news is news—good news is not news." K. Hammond, "Upon Reflection," *Thinking and Reasoning*, 2/3, 1996, pp. 243–244.

35. Hammond, 1996, p. 106.

36. Hammond, 1996. See chapter 3 for a discussion of the "rivalry" between intuition and analysis.

37. Quoted in Hammond, 1996, p. 81.

38. Mark Twain, *Life on the Mississippi* (Toronto: Bantam Books, 1896/1985), p. 47 as quoted in Hammond, 1996, p. 82.

39. F. Dyson, *Disturbing the Universe* (New York: Harper and Row, 1979), pp. 55–56, as quoted by Hammond, 1996, p. 65.

40. J. Bruner, *Actual Minds, Possible Worlds* (Cambridge, MA: Harvard University Press, 1986), p. 11.

41. The concept of quasi-rationality also has its roots in Brunswik's model of human perception. For an explanation, see Hammond, 1996, p. 161.

42. See Jervis 1976; Larson 1985; Jervis, Lebow, and Stein, 1985; and Y. F. Khong, *Analogies at War: Korea, Munich, Dien Bien Phu, and the Vietnam Decisions of 1985* (Princeton: Princeton University Press, 1992).

43. See Michael E. Doherty, "The Many Camps on Rationality," Paper presented at the Third International Conference on Thinking, London, August 1996, p. 15.

44. The modes of inquiry are Hammond's. See K. R. Hammond, "Toward Increasing Competence of Thought in Public Policy Formation," in Hammond (ed.), 1978. See also M. Doherty, 1996, for an exposition and discussion of these modes of inquiry.

45. Hammond, 1996, p. 182.

46. See the discussion in M. Doherty and E. Kurz, 1996.

47. For an excellent introduction to the methodological issues, see R. W. Cooksey, *Judgment Analysis: Theory, Methods, and Applications* (San Diego: Academic Press, 1996).

48. See Wigton, 1996.

49. See Slovic and Lichtenstein, 1971; W. M. Balke, K. R. Hammond, and G. D. Meyer, "An Alternative Approach to Labor-Management Relations," *Administrative Science Quarterly* 18, 1973, pp. 311–327; and B. Brehmer, and A. Brehmer, "What Have We Learned About Human Judgment from Thirty Years of Policy Capturing?" in Brehmer and Joyce, 1988. Other researchers have suggested that the problem may not be so much poor self-insight as it is difficulty in *articulating* judgment processes. See B. A. Reilly and M. E. Doherty, "The Assessment of Self-Insight in Judgment," *Organizational Behavior and Human Decision Processes*, 53, 1992, pp. 285–309.

50. D. G. Smith et al., "Pleasing Patients and the Decisions to Use Antibiotics for Sore Throat," [Abstract]. *Medical Decision Making*, 6, 1966, p. 269. See also M. L. Rothert et al., "Differences in Medical Referral Decisions for Obesity among Family Practitioners, General Internists, and Gynecologists." *Medical Care*, 22, 1984, pp. 42–53.

54. Brehmer and Brehmer, 1988.

55. K. R. Hammond and B. Brehmer, "Quasi-Rationality and Distrust: Implications for International Conflict." In *Human Judgment and Social Interaction*, L. Rappaport and D. Summers, eds. (New York: Holt, Rinehart and Winston, Inc, 1973).

56. Balke, Hammond, and Meyer, 1973.

3

CONTEXTUAL INFORMATION AND THE STUDY OF TRADE AND CONFLICT

The Utility of an Interdisciplinary Approach

NORRIN M. RIPSMAN
AND
JEAN-MARC F. BLANCHARD

In the political economy of international conflict, a central research question is the relationship between economic interdependence and international conflict. Commercial liberals have long maintained that international trade and investment forges economic bonds between states that restrain them from going to war.[1] Empirical investigations of this important claim by political scientists and economists, however, have yielded incomplete and conflicting results.[2] We argue that to reach definitive judgments about the commercial liberal argument researchers must address two underlying methodological issues. First, they must tackle the question of how researchers should evaluate the putative pacifying effect of economic interdependence. Second, they must determine how best to measure economic interdependence. On both counts, we suggest, commercial liberals provide incomplete accounts because they have restricted themselves to concepts, tools, and methods of traditional political science and economics.

This is clearly evident in attempts to define and measure interdependence where commercial liberals have tended to focus solely on standard quantitative measures such as the volume of bilateral trade, trade as a percentage of GNP, and the transmission of inflation. Such "measures" ignore important contextual information about international trade—for example, the material composition of trade and its importance to each state as a function of its geographical location and access to strategic resources—that is essential to a meaningful determination of national dependence/international independence. We contend that political scientists and economists must borrow relevant concepts from political geographers and geopoliticians in order to develop more meaningful and useful measures of interdependence.

The more general argument concerning the systemic effects of this interdependence on multiple units is also rendered more problematic by the lack of attention to tools and methods of other disciplines that would allow us to more accurately trace these effects. In order to assess whether economic interdependence actually influences the national security decisions of individual states in the manner posited by commercial liberals, it is necessary to examine the extent to which decision makers perceived the constraints of interdependence and subsequently whether this knowledge actually affected their policy choices during international crises. Quantitatively oriented political scientists are ill-suited to answer this question unless they supplement their work with insights gained from the historian's method of primary source, decision-making analysis.

In this essay, we adapt salient tools and insights from historians, political geographers, and economists, to develop a comprehensive framework for the qualitative analysis of economic interdependence and its effect on national-security decision making. We present two contextual schemes for measuring interdependence that are conducive to rich, contextual, primary source decision-making case studies that assess if national leaders perceived the constraints of interdependence and the impact, if any, that interdependence had on national security decisions in crisis situations. The first method, our Strategic Goods Test (SGT), appraises the level of a state's vulnerability to a disruption of trade relations with an adversary and the adversary's potential supporters in the event of war by considering whether it would be able to access sufficient quantities of the goods that are essential for the pursuit of national objectives if these links were terminated. Inspired by political geographers and geopoliticians, our SGT considers the nature and importance of the goods traded and the ability of each relevant state to acquire alternative suppliers, substitute, expand domestic production, tap strategic goods stockpiles, and conserve. Our second method, the Contextual Sensitivity Estimator (CSE), gauges sensitivity by measuring a state's trade with its potential adversary and the adversary's allies as a percentage of total trade and national income, the state's short- and long-term investment in the potential adversary and its supporters, and its exposure to international capital market movements. We draw on our research on Anglo-German decision making in 1914 and English and French decision making during the Rhineland Crisis of 1936 to illustrate the utility of our approach.

The application of our interdisciplinary analytical framework has led to three significant findings. First, previous measures of interdependence have led to incomplete judgments of international interdependence. The conventional wisdom, based on traditional quantitative measures of interdependence, is that all states were highly interdependent prior to the First World War and not interdependent during the 1930s.[3] Using our SGT, however, we determined that in 1914, while Germany was highly vulnerable to a disruption of trade with England and its allies, England was not heavily dependent on trade with Germany and German allies.[4] During the interwar years, our CSE reveals that, in spite of the depressing effect of the economic crises of the late 1920s and early 1930s, both Great Britain and France were sensitive to a disruption of economic relations with Germany. Our second finding is that in both 1914 and 1936 decision makers were well aware of the constraints of their dependence, an observation that quantitative methods could not have confirmed. This finding lends added significance to our third finding that, despite their awareness, policy makers deemed economic interdependence to be far less significant than strategic and domestic political concerns when selecting their policy options in times of crisis.[5]

In sum, a more contextual, decision-making analysis—one that reaches beyond the confines of political science and economics—renders a more accurate picture of international patterns of interdependence and casts doubt on the commercial liberal argument that economic interdependence restrains national security decision makers. The remainder of this essay (1) evaluates existing methods of measuring economic interdependence and explains why an interdisciplinary approach is necessary, (2) presents our own methods for evaluating interdependence, (3) applies these techniques to British and German economic relations on the eve of the First World War and to British and French economic relations prior to the Rhineland Crisis of 1936, and (4) summarizes our case studies of crisis decision making by the interdependent states in 1914 and 1936.

Measuring Interdependence: A Critique

Interdependencies exist between states when they run the risk of incurring economic and military costs if they disrupt their trade and investment ties with one another.[6] There are two types of economic interdependence, sensitivity and vulnerability.[7] States are *sensitive* to changes in trade and investment relationships if they suffer costs in the short run, but would be able to recover over the long run through policy measures such as seeking new suppliers, developing substitutes, or locating alternative investment opportunities. They are *vulnerable* if they would be unable to mitigate any disruption of existing economic arrangements with appropriate policy changes. Vulnerability interdependence is likely to characterize economic relations between states when they rely on one another for what political geographers and geopoliticians call "strategic goods," which are materials that are essential for national survival or defense.[8] As a result, the costs associated with vulnerability interdependence are likely to be much greater than those associated with sensitivity,[9] although both types of interdependence can have important policy consequences and need to be measured. To measure them, we need to take into account more than simply aggregate measures of international trade; we must also consider the geopolitical context of that trade.

The Importance of Contextual Information

Quantitative methods have a comparative advantage in discerning patterns of interaction between many different actors and groups of actors at a multiplicity of points in time. The inclusion of contextual information, however, presents a problem for quantitative analysis. To make the search for correlation patterns manageable, researchers must simplify their data as much as possible, thereby shedding much of the contextual information that would help in grouping like situations or rejecting inappropriate cases which may bias the results of the study. The larger the sample being studied, the more difficult it is to retrieve the relevant information and verify it, and the simpler each individual datum must become in order to be easily manipulable.[10] Traditional quantitative measures of interdependence, therefore, have relied on aggregate trade statistics and other readily obtainable, easy-to-process indices, without considering the material composition of that trade. They also have difficulty incorporating the strategic context of trade, namely the degree to which states are dependent on trade with potential adversaries and their likely alliance partners. Finally, they cannot capture the extent to which states can mitigate the effects of the termination of trade by making policy changes such as finding alternate suppliers or increasing domestic production, which relates *inter alia* to their geographical location and their natural resource endowments.[11] Consequently, they are unable to differentiate between mere interconnectedness—as would be the case if states traded with each other primarily for relatively unimportant goods, such as clothing or jewelry, or if they could find an alternative supply of any strategic goods traded—and genuine interdependence. And they cannot distinguish between sensitivity and the more strategically significant vulnerability interdependence. Case-specific measures, in contrast, can accommodate greater complexity.[12] Qualitative analysis has the added advantage of being able to select crucial test cases, whereas researchers employing large-N studies cannot ensure that they are choosing the most appropriate cases to study.[13]

A second weakness of quantitative analysis is its inability to prove definitively that a causal relationship exists between two variables in the analysis of interstate politics. Although large-N studies are ideally suited to find important correlations, they cannot conclusively demonstrate that the values of the relevant independent variables were responsible for policy outcomes in the cases being studied. This is so for two related reasons. To begin with, correlative studies are not geared for the cumbersome task of determining in a large number of cases if decisionmakers correctly perceived the objective interdependence situation.[14] This determination is essential since the mere objective existence of interdependence does not mean that decision makers were aware of it. In addition, quantitative methods cannot possibly assess the decision-making process in each state included in the study to determine if the level of national dependence truly influenced policy decisions.[15] In order to answer these more difficult questions of perception and influence, the researcher must peer inside the decision-making process to the best of his or her abilities. The difficulties of such an enterprise cannot be understated, but they can be surmounted, to some extent, by using the historical method of primary source analysis—that is, employment of documentary materials and memoir literature—supplemented by a survey of the secondary literature.[16] We are, thus, advocating something akin to what has been termed decision-making "process tracing" or the analysis of the procedure through which decision makers transform objective circumstances into political outcomes.[17] Nonetheless, unlike many other process tracers, we argue that the analysis cannot restrict itself to the secondary historical literature, since (1) historians rarely address exactly the same theoretically-inspired questions as political scientists and do not always pursue them in as rigorous a manner to meet social scientific standards of inquiry, and (2) it is difficult to choose between conflicting secondary source accounts in anything approaching an objective manner without reference to primary source accounts.[18] Therefore, the political scientist must be at least part historian in order to render comprehensive judgments about the trade-conflict relationship.[19]

In order to reach definitive conclusions about the impact of economic interdependence on national-security decision making, then, researchers must necessarily supplement quantitative research methods, which are essential for uncovering general trends, with two more qualitative research tools.[20] Specifically, they must use: (1) qualitative or mixed qualitative/quantitative measures of interdependence that take into account the contextual nature of economic interdependence; and (2) a detailed contextual case study approach that analyzes as much documentary material as possible in order to reach a reasonable judgment regarding the impact of interdependence on national-security decision making. Only then can we arrive at meaningful conclusions about the validity of the commercial liberal argument.

To this end, the next section examines previous efforts to measure interdependence and explains why they are insufficient to capture the contextual information that is required to render judgment on interdependence levels or to inform decision-making case studies on the effect of economic interdependence on international conflict. Subsequently, we propose two interdisciplinary mixed qualitative/quantitative measures that can assist researchers in incorporating this vital information.

Existing Measures of Interdependence and Their Limitations

Until now, researchers investigating the impact of economic interdependence on national policy have chosen to focus solely on three types of interdependence: (1) vertical, (2) horizontal, and (3) limited vulnerability.

Vertical interdependence refers to "the direct and positive linkage of interests of states such that when the position of one state changes the position of others is affected *and in the same direction.*"[21] Researchers concentrating on vertical interdependence have constructed indices that assess the convergence of prices and interest rates as well as the transmission of inflation.[22] Such measures offer no means to identify those states that are completely dependent on international exchanges for the supply of strategic goods. In other words, they do not provide any means to capture the strategically significant constraint of vulnerability interdependence. Although measures of vertical interdependence are undoubtedly useful for assessing particular types of sensitivity, they do not supply an adequate method for the comprehensive measurement of sensitivity. They are not designed for interdependence relationships that are not directly and positively linked. They also do not contain any method for assessing whether the convergence of prices and interest rates between two states is spurious. Furthermore, they do not take into account the economic and political context in which sensitivity relationships exist.

Indices of *horizontal interdependence* emphasize transnational trade and investment flows as well as the number of transactions between states. Analysts gauging the level of horizontal interdependence between states have employed measures that calculate, *inter alia*, the dollar values of a state's exports and imports, total trade and total exports as a percentage of Gross Domestic Product, foreign investment as a percentage of national income, and the share of foreign currencies as percentage of a state's total reserves.[23] These measures provide an excellent means for assessing the level of interdependence present in the international system and for conducting the coding operations that are a basic part of large-N statistical analyses. These indices do not, though, yield data on the composition of bilateral economic transactions. In addition, they do not incorporate information on each state's ability to limit or eliminate its exposure to a disruption of bilateral flows, particularly exchanges of strategic goods; therefore, they cannot be utilized to measure vulnerability. They do, however, provide good starting points for a study of sensitivity.

In addition to the larger communities of researchers who examine vertical and horizontal interdependence, there are a handful of analysts who have developed measures designed to gauge vulnerability. Most notable among these is Albert Hirschman who created the trade partner concentration index, which is grounded in the logical assumption that a state with fewer trading partners is more vulnerable than one with many.[24] Similarly, Richard Rosecrance and Arthur Stein developed a method, called the commodity concentration of exports, which assesses the extent to which a state is dependent on the export of a limited number of goods.[25] These measures move us closer to capturing the costs associated with vulnerability, but ultimately fall short of this objective.[26] On the one hand, the trade partner concentration index is of limited value because it does not account for the material composition of trade. On the other hand, the commodity concentration of exports measure is deficient because it does not provide any way to account for imports, especially imports of strategic goods. In addition, neither measure recognizes that their geographical location and resource endowments may allow states to undertake policies designed to address trade or commodity concentration problems and that these policy options (or the lack thereof) have important implications for national security decision making. As measures of sensitivity, these indices also have their limitations since they only provide information on particular types of sensitivity.

In sum, existing measures are insufficient for a contextual analysis of economic interdependence. Other more robust measures are necessary to provide a richer picture of the true costs associated with a potential disruption of international trade. Before proposing these more appropriate (and new) contextual measures, one more substantive issue must be addressed. Arthur Stein has observed that researchers who measure interdependence face a level of analysis problem regardless of whether they are trying to measure vulnerability or sensitivity.[27] In short, they need to decide if they should use methods that assess the extent to which all countries are linked or if they should employ techniques that solely emphasize dyadic interdependence relationships. We argue that a *mixed* measure for calculating interdependence, rather than the bilateral indices favored by traditional analysts, most accurately represents the strategic context of international trade because it can account for two important facts.[28] First, a state might be sensitive or vulnerable to a severance of its trade and investment relations with another state *as well as that state's allies.* Second, the latter state's supporters might interfere with the former state's global economic activities through such actions as blockades or economic sabotage. In short, we advocate a modified dyadic measure that assesses the ability of a potential adversary and its allies to cut off their economic linkages, particularly their strategic goods sales, with a target state and to disrupt that state's involvement in international trade and investment activities. In the next section, we offer two mixed measures: one that measures vulnerability and another that gauges sensitivity.

Two Contextual Measures of Interdependence

The Strategic Goods Test

To measure vulnerability, we must assess the degree to which states depend on each other for the supply of strategic goods.[29] The universe of strategic goods, however, does not remain static. Whether or not a specific material deserves classification as a strategic good is historically contingent not only on the nature of military and industrial technology, but also on the definition of national security during the period under study.[30] Actual vulnerability interdependence exists when states import significant amounts of strategic goods *and* when they would find themselves unable to replenish shortfalls in strategic goods supplies through compensatory policy measures. In order to determine the vulnerability of particular states, it is necessary both to identify the goods that these states acquire from abroad and to evaluate their options for addressing any disruptions in their strategic goods supplies.

Political geographers and geopoliticians have highlighted a number of measures that are available to states that face cut-offs of these vital goods: (1) the use of alternative suppliers; (2) increased domestic production; (3) substitution; (4) conservation and recycling; and (5) drawdowns of strategic goods stockpiles.[31] It is wrong to assume, however, that any or all of these methods will be adequate, viable, cost effective, or readily available.[32] First, it may not be possible to increase domestic production unless the infrastructure already exists to exploit available strategic goods reserves.[33] Second, substitution may create new strategic goods dependencies. The substitution of aluminum for copper, tin, or light steel dramatically increases the need for coal and electricity not to mention bauxite.[34] Furthermore, substitution may be cost ineffective. Around the time of the First and Second World Wars, synthetic oil was not an economically viable substitute for oil.[35] Third, recycling and conservation programs may not yield an adequate recovery of strategic goods and may take many years to establish. During the First World War, for example, it took Germany three to four years to create meaningful copper and aluminum recycling programs.[36] Moreover, recycled materials—such as rubber reclaimed from discarded tires—might be of inferior quality and, therefore, might entail a loss of efficiency.[37] Fourth, stockpiles may decay if there is insufficient care devoted to such reserves. In the absence of proper care, grains will spoil, magnesium will oxidize, and asbestos may become contaminated.[38] In short, the analyst must consider a broad range of contextual geostrategic factors to arrive at a reasoned assessment of a particular state's compensatory policy options.

We argue that our Strategic Goods Test is the best procedure for measuring vulnerability because it accounts for the material composition of trade and its strategic context. It involves four basic steps: (1) the identification of strategic goods in the period under investigation; (2) an examination of trade data to determine the relevant states' dependence on external supplies of these goods; (3) a determination of the effect that war would have on supplies of these valuable materials; and (4) an analysis of the ability of each of the relevant states to cope with a disruption of strategic goods flows through policy changes such as the acquisition of new suppliers, increased domestic production, the development of substitutes, national conservation, or the use of stockpiles.[39]

Following these steps, we generate two lists of strategic goods: those for which a state's supply is independent of adversary interference and those whose supply is vulnerable to adversary interference. This division alone does not tell us if a state is vulnerable. We must also have a means of ranking the relative importance of strategic goods. For this purpose, we divide the universe of strategic goods into two categories: *Class I Goods*, materials whose cut-off will have rapid and negative effects on a wide range of economic and military activities or a narrow range of key activities; and *Class II Goods*, materials whose supply disruption would have adverse consequences over a longer term or would affect a narrower range of still important, but less essential activities. On the eve of the First World War and the Rhineland Crisis, oil and foodstuffs clearly represented Class I Goods since shortages of these materials would have had a bearing on all aspects of a state's productive and military activities. Class II Goods include materials such as rubber. A termination of rubber supplies would have affected significant portions of industry and wartime military functions such as troop and equipment transportation. It would not, however, have had harmful consequences for many other national activities. Moreover, its effects would not have been felt immediately. We determine a state's composite vulnerability depending on the number of Class I and Class II goods in which it is dependent.

We label a state "vulnerable" when it would be unable to compensate for shortages of any one or more Class I Goods. Since denial of a Class I Good could paralyze a state's military and industrial effort, it would not be reasonable to consider states that depend on adversaries for any one Class I Good to be invulnerable. We require states to be unable to compensate for a disruption in the supply of two or more Class II Goods before we classify them as vulnerable. Shortages of Class II goods do not have as immediate or crippling affect on national activities; therefore, it would require more than one of these dependencies to render a state vulnerable.

This kind of objective benchmark of vulnerability is particularly helpful for case study analysis where researchers may need to know if the cases they select reflect meaningful vulnerability. The categorical data emerging from our SGT may also be of use to quantitative researchers who could employ it in multiple regression analyses employing dummy variables to identify correlations between situations entailing vulnerability and political behavior.

There are two noteworthy limitations to the SGT. First, it is extremely labor-intensive. In order to gauge vulnerability, the researcher must identify *inter alia* all the strategic goods of the period under study, sift through a large amount of trade and production data to identify raw dependence levels, and evaluate the ability of a variety of policy instruments to mitigate supply shortfalls. Detailed analysis of this sort would make large-sample research a prohibitively time-consuming endeavor. Second, our SGT yields categorical data about whether a state is vulnerable or not, rather than a more versatile scaled measure of vulnerability.[40] This is necessarily the case, since a scaled measure would require intensely complex and debatable judgments about the relative importance of strategic goods within each class of goods. For example, would a dependence on oil be more debilitating than a dependence on foodstuffs? Certainly, both would have serious consequences for all aspects of a state's economy and defense efforts, but it would be impossible to make a definitive judgment about their relative importance. Similarly, it would be difficult to compare the effects of chromium and nickel dependence. These difficulties undermine the utility of the Strategic Goods Test as a tool for quantitative researchers.

Our SGT is, however, ideally suited to case study analysis. When selecting cases, qualitative researchers need a method that allows them to determine whether particular cases are appropriate selections. In such circumstances, categorical data is ideal. Moreover, when the number of cases studied is small, the labor demanded by the SGT is quite manageable. Qualitative analysts will prefer to employ this method, then, because the extra work required by the SGT provides a wealth of relevant contextual information that quantitative measures cannot manage. Therefore, the judgments reached with our method will be more complex and more accurate because it can consider the importance of the goods traded, the strategic context of trade, and policy instruments available to states.

Even if there is no vulnerability, it is still important to analyze if sensitivity exists. After all, sensitivity also imposes costs and can serve to restrain leaders who are contemplating aggressive action against other states. In the next section, we discuss our method for measuring sensitivity, the Contextual Sensitivity Estimator, which incorporates traditional variables in a nontraditional way by adopting a modified dyadic perspective to study potential trade and investment losses and which also accounts for nontraditional variables such as currency/financial factors.

The Contextual Sensitivity Estimator

Typically, scholars have employed a wide variety of techniques to measure sensitivity. They have looked at the transmission of inflation, calculated the ratio of foreign trade to a base such as total trade, measured the volume of total trade and Foreign Direct Investment levels, and gauged the commodity concentration of exports. We too believe it is worthwhile to look at trade and investment indicators to assess whether a particular state is sensitive (cf. 23). Unlike most other scholars, however, we consider the strategic context of trade to calculate the *total* loss of trade and investment that would be sustained in the event of hostilities. It is essential to examine the strategic context of trade because a conflict not only can affect a state's trade with and investment in its prospective adversary, but also can disrupt that state's economic linkages with the adversary's supporters. For example, during the Cold War, a war in Europe would have adversely affected West Germany's extensive trade with and loans to the Soviet Union as well as West German economic ties with Moscow's Warsaw Pact allies.

We also depart from traditional practices for measuring sensitivity by considering each state's financial sensitivity. We do this because states can be linked in indirect and consequential ways through the operation of international capital markets. In the 1990s, the Board of Governors of the U.S. Federal Reserve was deeply concerned about the financial and real estate situation in Japan because of the very real possibility that declines in Japanese asset values would be channeled through international capital markets with adverse consequences for exchange and interest rates as well as the global and American banking systems. In 1994, the collapse of the

Mexican peso led to capital flights from lower-tier currencies around the world and resulted in a massive loan from the American Treasury Department, where leading officials had argued that it was essential to stabilize the Mexican currency in order to protect the world and American economy. During times of crises, the indirect, financial interdependence of states may become even more obvious as investors shun the currencies of potential belligerents due to the inflationary pressures of conflict and demand higher interest-rate risk premiums for investing in the assets of prospective combatants.

To summarize, our CSE entails three basic steps to gauge a state's sensitivity: (1) the measurement of the state's trade (exports and imports) with an adversary and the adversary's supporters as a percentage of total trade and national income; (2) an assessment of the state's long- and short-term investments in the assets of a potential adversary and the adversary's allies; and (3) an examination of the state's exposure to international capital market movements.

The first two steps of the CSE yield one ratio pertaining to trade and another ratio pertaining to investment. Although these ratios are a useful starting point for analysis, they have no meaning on their own. In other words, they cannot tell us whether or not a state is truly sensitive. In order to determine the significance of these ratios, it is necessary to evaluate them in their contextual setting. A contextual approach enables researchers to focus on the economic sectors that, if affected by a disturbance of existing trade and investment relationships, would obtain the greatest attention from key decision makers. It also permits analysts to take into account the fact that certain economic sectors have an importance far beyond their own narrow domain. For instance, the default of an adversary and/or its allies not only could seriously reduce the profitability of the domestic banking sector, but also could severely constrain the banking sectors' ability to provide credit to other domestic economic sectors and thereby dampen these sectors' economic growth.

Economic Interdependence in 1914 and 1936

In this section, we apply the Strategic Goods Test and Contextual Sensitivity Estimator to determine if England and Germany were meaningfully dependent on each other prior to the First World War and whether Britain and France were meaningfully dependent on Germany at the time of the Rhineland Crisis.[41] We then summarize our decision-making studies of both periods to demonstrate that a qualitative approach reveals valuable information about the impact of economic interdependence on national security decisions that a quantitative approach cannot.

Vulnerability in 1914

In the period prior to the outbreak of the First World War, economic and defense activities required the following strategic goods: Chromium, coal, copper, foodstuffs, iron ore, lead, manganese, money, nickel, nitrates, oil, rubber, and sulphur/pyrites. Table 3.1 summarizes our classification of these essential materials into the Class I and Class II Goods categories.

Table 3.1 A Typology of Strategic Goods	
Classification Category	*Items*
Class I Goods	Coal, copper, foodstuffs, iron ore, lead manganese, nitrates, oil, and sulphur/pyrites
Class II Goods	Chromium, money, nickel, and rubber

German Dependence on the Eve of the First World War. Our first step, after identifying the universe of strategic goods in 1914, was to identify the states with whom German leaders could have expected to continue trading in the event of a war with England and, by implication, the Triple Entente. Due to the threat of a British naval blockade, obvious supply-line problems in getting goods through France and Russia, and German doubts about the reliability of so-called allies Italy and Bulgaria, we concluded that German leaders could have only expected to continue uninterrupted trading with Sweden and Austria-Hungary. Examining, on a good-by-good basis, all the compensatory policy instruments available to Germany, we determined that Germany would be vulnerable if it went to war against the Triple Entente. Specifically, it would experience damaging shortages of foodstuffs and oil, both Class I Goods, as well as chromium and rubber, both Class II Goods. Below, we present a summary of our analysis of the German position with respect to each of these goods.

Foodstuffs—Due to its large and growing population, Germany could not meet its food needs through domestic production. As a result, it had to import substantial quantities of foodstuffs from Eastern Europe, particularly Russia, South America, the United States, and members of the English Commonwealth. Prior to the outbreak of the First World War, the Germans purchased a significant percentages of cereals (e.g., up to 40 percent of their wheat, 55 percent of their barley, and 100 percent of their maize) from foreign suppliers. The Germans also satisfied half of their dairy and two-thirds of their fish needs with foreign purchases.[42] The Germans would have had great difficulty recovering from interference with their food imports. They could not obtain food from their ally Austria-Hungary since Austria-Hungary needed all its own food production to meet internal requirements.[43] They could not have increased the production of foodstuffs dramatically since they needed labor for the war effort and they needed fertilizers to make explosives. Indeed, German food production significantly dropped during the fighting. They also could not have conserved sufficient amounts of foodstuffs since they had to maintain nutrition levels among soldiers and laborers. Furthermore, they could not have relied on stockpiles since long-term storage was not a viable option at the time.[44] The extremely unfavorable German situation vis-à-vis foodstuffs is clearly shown by the large number of German deaths that occurred during the War because of malnutrition.[45]

Oil—Prior to 1914, the Germans bought almost all of this critical strategic good from Austria-Hungary, the United States, Romania, and Russia. A disruption of American, Romanian, and Russian imports would be a disaster for the Germans because they had no options for compensating for a shortfall of oil imports. Due to capacity and production limitations, Austria-Hungary could not produce additional oil to sell to the Germans. In addition, the Germans could not increase their own production since they did not have significant reserves of oil. Moreover, the Germans could not realistically expect to conserve oil given their increased wartime oil needs. The Germans also had no access to any oil substitutes; nor did they have adequate stockpiles of this important material.[46] German oil dependence is vividly shown by the fact that one of the first items added to Germany's wartime deficiency materials list was oil.[47]

Chromium—Before the First World War, Germany purchased all of its chromium from abroad. If its chromium purchases were disrupted, Germany would have faced shortages of this valuable metal alloy. First, Austria-Hungary and Sweden could not have served as alternative suppliers for Germany since they did not mine chromium. Second, the Germans did not have the option of increasing their own production because they lacked reserves of chromium. Third, there is no credible evidence that the Germans stockpiled chromium.[48]

Rubber—The Germans acquired all of their rubber supplies from foreign producers. In the event that these supplies were disrupted, the Germans could not have turned to Austria-Hungary or Sweden since neither state produced rubber. The Germans had the ability to conserve rubber by recycling old tires, but recycled rubber, given the technology of the period, simply was not suitable for military use. The Germans also did not have any technology available to them before the war that would have allowed them to produce a viable rubber substitute.[49] German dependence on imports of rubber is strikingly shown by their use of iron tires in lieu of rubber ones during the war.[50]

English Independence in 1914. The English were not vulnerable. Although a war with Germany would disrupt English imports from Austria-Hungary, France, Germany, Italy, Romania, Russia, Serbia, and Turkey, the English would still retain open supply lines to top strategic goods producers like Australia, Canada, India, the Dutch East Indies, Latin America, New Caledonia, Portugal, Spain, and the United States. Not surprisingly, then, our good-by-good analysis revealed that England was not vulnerable to a disruption of its trade in 1914. To illustrate this fact, we present a summary of the British supply situation with respect to the same four goods in which Germany was vulnerable.

Foodstuffs—Before the outbreak of the First World War, the English imported large percentages of their domestic food requirements. From 1911–1913, the British obtained almost 80 percent of their wheat, up to 50 percent of their barley, 25 percent of their oats, all of their maize, 80 percent of their beef, and 83 percent of their fruit from foreign sources who were predominantly friendly, non-European states. The English did not have to fear that a war with Germany might disrupt their food supplies because during a war the English would retain access to the world's top foodstuffs producers including Australia, Canada, and the United States.[51]

Oil—The English imported almost all their oil. They were able to produce some oil from oil shale in the years before the First World War; nevertheless, this production only met a small percentage of domestic needs. Indeed, the English had to obtain 80–90 percent of their oil from foreign suppliers. Fortunately for the British, they acquired the majority of their oil from the United States. They also obtained important amounts of lamp oil, motor spirits, and lubricating oil from the Dutch East Indies, India, Mexico, Romania, and Russia. A conflict with the Germans would affect Romanian and Russian oil imports, though the data do not tell us exactly how badly the English would have suffered. Even in the worst case, the English could still tap into their traditional suppliers who provided at least 70 percent, and perhaps more, of their oil needs. Furthermore, the English could have turned to the United States for additional supplies of this critical strategic good.[52] It is clear, then, that England was independent with respect to oil.

Chromium—England acquired almost all of its chromium from New Caledonia, Rhodesia, and South Africa. English control of the high seas suggested that the English would have been able to continue importing chromium from these states in the event it went to war against the Germans. Consequently, we concluded that England was not dependent on German goodwill for continued supplies of chromium.[53]

Rubber—In the years prior to 1914, Malaya and the East Indies were the dominant producers of rubber, generating almost 70 percent of the world's rubber crop.[54] As in the case of chromium, English naval dominance over the Germans meant that England could be fairly confident of its ability to continue to import rubber from Malaya and the East Indies during a war with Germany. Thus, England was in an advantageous situation with respect to this particular strategic good on the eve of the First World War.[55]

The Contextual Sensitivity Estimator and Franco-British Sensitivity in 1936

Our application of the SGT to the Rhineland period revealed that Britain and France were not vulnerable to a disruption in strategic goods supplies in the event of a war with the Nazis in 1936. Nonetheless, our application of the CSE confirmed that both countries would have suffered important economic costs if normal economic relations with Germany were to have been interrupted. We determined this by investigating three areas. First, we had to examine British and French trade with Germany and its probable allies as a percentage of total trade and national income. Second, we studied British and French long- and short-term investments in Germany and its potential supporters. Third, we examined the financial sensitivity of the French.

In the period prior to the Rhineland crisis, the British were not significant traders with the Germans or German allies. In the years before the crisis, British trade with Germany and powers friendly to Germany accounted for around 8 percent of Britain's total trade while exports to these states represented only 10 percent of national income. The French traded more extensively with Germany and its potential supporters. However, French trade with these potential adversaries represented about 12.5 percent of total French trade. Moreover, exports to Germany and German allies represented only 8 percent of national income.[56] The data indicate, then, that although the British and the French would have probably endured some disruption of their trade in 1936, they were not meaningfully sensitive to a disruption of their trade in the event of a conflict with the Germans and German allies.

The sphere of banking and finance warrants greater attention even though British investments in Germany and allied states remained extremely low as a percentage of overall long-term British overseas investment.[57] Significantly, London banks, which played a critical role in the British economy, were deeply involved in supplying short-term credits to German banks, industry, and commerce. In the event that these entities defaulted on their loans, which was likely in the event of a war, British banks would have been seriously affected. The British government would have had to rescue a number of prominent financial institutions and it is likely that the discount market in London would have collapsed.[58] The French also invested in Germany, though they did not do so in any noteworthy fashion.[59] The French were, however, indirectly tied to the Germans through international financial and currency markets as a result of their domestic financial woes, which engendered substantial borrowing needs, and their desire to stabilize the franc.[60] If the French opted to respond to Nazi maneuvers in the Rhineland with force, then they would have faced a severe capital flight problem that would have endangered their already limited access to the capital markets that provided the lifeline for the French government's day-to-day expenditures.[61] Moreover, a conflict would have pressured the French to devalue the franc from levels that leading government officials had tried so hard to defend.[62] We conclude, then, that the French were financially sensitive because a conflict with Hitler at the time would have severely disrupted their access to international capital.

In sum, the extensive lending of short-term credits to Germany in the interwar years created a situation where the British were sensitive to a German moratorium on these debts. The French were sensitive in 1936, not because of the activities of their banks, but because their access to international capital markets and the value of their franc were both linked to German actions.

Decision Making in 1914 and 1936

Having applied our measures of vulnerability and sensitivity to assess the level of Anglo-German interdependence in 1914 and the degree to which the British and French were economically intertwined with Germany in 1936, we now report our case study findings on the effect of interdependence on national security decisions. We studied the German decision to run the risks of war in 1914 and the Franco-British decisions not to challenge Hitler's remilitarization of the Rhineland in 1936.[63]

Our process tracing procedure was as follows. We studied the foreign-policy-making procedures in each country to determine who were the most important actors. Then, we scoured available documents, memoirs, and secondary accounts of the months and years preceding the conflict to judge whether these decision makers were aware of their dependence and the costs it would impose in the event of war. Finally, we analyzed the decision-making processes that led in 1914 to the German acceptance of the risks of war and in 1936 to the British and French rejection of the use of force as a viable option in order to determine what effect the fact of interdependence had on decision-maker calculations. In other words, we were not interested in the mere coincidence of interdependence with war or peace. In 1914, we wanted to determine if interdependence had any restraining influence at all on German leaders. If it did or decision-makers failed to perceive dependence, then the incidence of war might not be damning evidence against the commercial liberal argument. Similarly, the correlation of interdependence and peace in 1936, despite the existence of a *casus belli* is insufficient to disprove realists who argue that strategic considerations prevailed over economic ones, unless we confirm that leaders chose a peaceful response *because* they were economically sensitive.

July 1914: The German Decision to Run the Risks of War

The key German decision makers involved in the decision to run the risks of war with England in 1914 were Kaiser Wilhelm, Chancellor Bethmann-Hollweg, Foreign Minister Jagow, Ambassador to Great Britain Lichnowsky, and Chief of the General Staff Moltke. Our analysis of the evidence clearly indicated that all of the above, indeed the entire German government, had been painfully aware for years before the war of their vulnerability to a wide British blockade of the North Sea and the devastating effect that it would have on German access to strategic resources, especially food.[64] As a result, Moltke was quite concerned about the German ability to fight a protracted war. Moreover, despite their hope that the Schlieffen Plan could bring about a speedy German victory, German political and military leaders were well aware that the next war could be measured in years rather than months.[65]

Moreover, we concluded that at each of three critical junctures in the crisis when Germany could have pulled back from the brink of war—before issuing "the blank cheque" to Austria on July 6, allowing it to invade Serbia, prior to the Austrian mobilization against Serbia on July 28, and prior to the great power declarations of war on July 30 and 31—German leaders acknowledged that encouraging Austrian action could lead to a confrontation with England.[66] For reasons of domestic politics and strategic priorities, the Germans decided to accept the potentially severe costs of war with England. Domestically, the Kaiser wanted to allow the Austrians to punish the crime of regicide in order to prevent similar activities in Germany that could threaten his own authority. Strategically, the Germans wanted to prevent a further deterioration of Austrian power, since Austria-Hungary was their primary ally. In addition, German leaders calculated that war with the Triple Entente in 1914 would be less disastrous than it would be in 1917, after the Russian force modernization would be completed. It is particularly instructive that in two published document collections on decision making on the eve of the war, not one reference can be found to the potential economic costs of war with England.[67] The Germans were aware of their vulnerability but considered their dependence to be less important than strategic and domestic political factors when considering national security decisions.

Britain, France, and the Rhineland Crisis

The key British security policy decision makers in 1936 were Foreign Minister Anthony Eden, Chancellor of the Exchequer Neville Chamberlain, and to a lesser extent, Prime Minister Stanley Baldwin. Their French counterparts were Foreign Minister Pierre-Etienne Flandin, Prime Minister Albert Sarraut, and Chief of the French Army Maurice Gamelin. These leaders were all aware of the constraints of sensitivity. Indeed, the British Cabinet's—particularly Chamberlain's—preoccupation with the standstill debt was surpassed only by Sarraut and Flandin's overriding concern about the stability of the floundering French Treasury. Nonetheless, international economic concerns played no role whatsoever in a British and French response determined by domestic political and strategic considerations.

The British decision was primarily determined by their poor state of military preparedness. The British rearmament program started in 1935 was not yet well-advanced, which led the Cabinet to believe that a forceful response was unlikely to be successful.[68] Almost of equal importance was the overwhelming public opposition to policy options that risked war.[69] The French Cabinet would have liked to respond, but felt they could not without British support because of their poor state of military preparation and the defensive orientation of their forces.[70] The French public was also predominately pacifist and Sarraut did not want to alienate the public six weeks before a federal election.[71] We found it particularly revealing that in their postwar memoirs, when both Eden and Flandin had a powerful incentive to justify their much-ridiculed appeasement of Hitler, they did not state that economic interdependence induced any restraint with respect to the Rhineland affair.[72] We should expect that if economic interdependence played any role in the decision not to use force in 1936, they would have reported this in an attempt to vindicate themselves. But they did not. We concluded, therefore, that economic interdependence had no impact on national calculations during the crisis.

Conclusion: The Utility of an Interdisciplinary Approach

Historically, the trade and conflict studies literature has been largely quantitative in orientation and has been rooted solely in concepts and methods from the disciplines of political science and economics. It employs large data sets to investigate possible correlations between economic interdependence and national security decisions. These methods, however, have been unable to reach a definitive conclusion about how economic ties influence policy making.

In order to investigate these causal relationships, it is necessary to supplement statistical-correlative techniques with detailed decision-making case studies that assess the effect of the systemic stimulus of interdependence on specific national security choices. To conduct case studies, the qualitative researcher must first determine which cases are suitable candidates for further analysis. In other words, he or she must be able to determine whether the cases under investigation involve meaningful vulnerability or sensitivity. In this paper, we present two methods for doing this, the Strategic Goods Test and the Contextual Sensitivity Estimator, which evaluate as much relevant contextual information—political, economic, and geographical—as possible in order to formulate an accurate picture of interdependence levels. Having identified appropriate candidates for study, case study researchers must also determine if decision makers correctly perceived and were influenced by the constraints of economic interdependence. These determinations cannot be made by using statistical-correlative techniques, but only by the historical method, employing rich, contextual documentary analysis.

The interdisciplinary approach described in this essay allowed us to arrive at three important conclusions which build on the conventional understanding of the relationship between trade and conflict. First, we have shown that the received wisdom that all countries were highly interdependent prior to the First World War, but were independent prior to the 1930s is incomplete at best. In fact, while Germany was highly vulnerable to England and its likely allies in 1914, the English were not similarly vulnerable to the Triple Alliance. Similarly, although France and Great Britain were not vulnerable to Germany and German allies in 1936, they were meaningfully sensitive to a disruption of normal economic relations with Hitler. Second, it is clear that, at least in the cases we selected, decision makers had little difficulty perceiving the potential costs of interdependence. Finally, though they were aware of its constraints, decision makers in all three countries refused to allow international economic considerations to dictate national security decisions. Instead, they decided to risk war or opt for peace on the basis of strategic considerations and the exigencies of domestic politics. Therefore, our qualitative analysis fails to support the commercial liberal argument that trade reduces international conflict.

In general, we conclude, that when studying the impact of trade on conflict, context matters. Meaningful judgments about national vulnerability must incorporate the strategic, material, geographical, and technological context of international trade while judgments about sensitivity must consider the impact of alliances and financial interdependence, both direct and indirect. Moreover, when assessing the influence of interdependence on national security decisions, researchers must take into account the decision-making context and, in particular, the domestic political and international strategic context in which leaders choose policies.[73] A contextual, interdisciplinary research strategy, one that incorporates relevant insights and tools from geographers and historians, can complement existing studies on trade and conflict by more accurately and meaningfully gauging the degree to which economic interdependence causes national leaders to pursue particular national security policy options. Our research, therefore, is very much in keeping with the spirit of this book. It is the questions we ask, and not some prior commitment to particular methodologies or disciplinary boundaries, that ought to dictate the contexts of analysis and the kinds of tools we use in those contexts.

Notes

1. Early commercial liberals include Norman Angell, *The Great Illusion* (London: William Heinemann, 1933) and Baron de Montesquieu, *Spirit of Laws*, trans. by Thomas Nugent (New York: Harper Press, 1949). More recently, commercial liberal arguments have appeared in Solomon Polachek, "Conflict and Trade," *Journal of Conflict Resolution*, 24,1 (1980): 55–78; Robert O. Keohane, "International Liberalism Revisited." in John Dunn, ed. *The Economic Limits to Modern Politics* (Cambridge: Cambridge University Press, 1990), pp. 165–194; Ming Zhang, *Major Powers at a Crossroads: Economic Interdependence and an Asia Pacific Security Community* (Boulder: Lynne Rienner, 1995); and John R. Oneal and Bruce M. Russett, "The Classical Liberals Were Right: Democracy, Interdependence, and Conflict, 1950–1985," *International Studies Quarterly*, 41, 2 (June 1997): 267–294.

2. Empirical support for the commercial liberal hypothesis is provided by Solomon W. Polachek, "Dyadic Disputes," *Papers of the Peace Science Society*, 28 (1978): 67–80 and Oneal et al., "The Liberal Peace." Other researchers, though, find that interdependence can actually increase interstate conflict and violence. See, for example, Mark J. Gasiorowski, "Economic Interdependence and International Conflict: Some Cross-National Evidence," *International Studies Quarterly*, 30 (1986): 23–38.

3. See, for example, Karl Deutsch and Alexander Eckstein, "National Industrialization and the Declining Share of the International Economic Sector, 1890–1959," *World Politics*, 13,3 (January 1961):

267–299; and Richard Rosecrance et al., "Whither Interdependence?" *International Organization*, 31,3 (Summer 1977): 425–471.

4. Jean-Marc F. Blanchard and Norrin M. Ripsman, "Measuring Economic Interdependence: A Geopolitical Perspective," *Geopolitics and International Boundaries*, 1,3 (Winter 1996): 225–246.

5. Norrin M. Ripsman and Jean-Marc F. Blanchard, "Commercial Liberalism Under Fire. Evidence from 1914 and 1936," *Security Studies*, 6,2 (Winter 1996/97): 5–51.

6. Richard Cooper, *The Economics of Interdependence* (New York: McGraw-Hill, 1968); Kenneth N. Waltz, "The Myth of Interdependence," in Charles P. Kindleberger, ed. *The International Corporation* (Cambridge: The MIT Press, 1970), pp. 205–223; and Robert O. Keohane and Joseph Nye, Jr., *Power and Interdependence: World Politics in Transition* (Boston: Little, Brown, 1977).

7. Keohane and Nye, *Power and Interdependence*, pp. 11–16.

8. William S. Culbertson, *Raw Materials and Foodstuffs in the Commercial Policies of Nations,* 112 (Philadelphia: The Annals of the American Academy of Political and Social Science, 1924); Hugh B. Killough and Lucy W. Killough, *Raw Materials of Industrialism* (New York: Thomas Y. Crowell, 1929); Brooks Emeny, *The Strategy of Raw Materials* (New York: Macmillan, 1936); Eugene Staley, *Raw Materials in Peace and War* (New York: Council of Foreign Relations, 1937); M. S. Hessel, W. J. Murphy, and F. A. Hessel, *Strategic Materials* (New York: Hastings House, 1942); David G. Haglund, "The New Geopolitics of Minerals: An Inquiry into the Changing International Significance of Strategic Minerals," *Political Geography Quarterly*, 5,3 (July 1986): 221–240; Tor Egil Forland, "'Economic Warfare' and 'Strategic Goods': A Conceptual Framework for Analyzing COCOM," *Journal of Peace Research*, 28,2 (1991): 191–204; and Beverly Crawford, *Economic Vulnerability in International Relations: The Case of East-West Trade, Investment, and Finance* (New York: Columbia University Press, 1993).

9. The higher costs associated with vulnerability interdependence mean that it is likely to be more strategically significant than sensitivity. Waltz, "The Myth of Interdependence," p. 210. Hence, vulnerability should be a more powerful constraint on the risk-taking propensities of policymakers than sensitivity. For related points, see Keohane and Nye, *Power and Interdependence*, pp. 11–16.

10. Gordon A. Craig, "The Historian and the Study of International Relations," *American Historical Review*, 88,1 (February 1983): 1–11; and John Lewis Gaddis, "History, Science, and the Study of International Relations," in Ngaire Woods, ed. *Explaining International Relations Since 1945* (New York: Oxford University Press, 1996), pp. 32–48.

11. Norman J. G. Pounds, *Political Geography*, 2nd ed. (New York: McGraw-Hill, 1972), pp. 63, 157–160.
12. Harry Eckstein, "Case Study and Theory in Political Science," in Fred I. Greenstein and Nelson Polsby, eds. *Handbook of Political Science, VII* (Reading: Addison-Wesley, 1975), pp. 79–138.
13. On the importance of careful case selection, see Ronald Rogowski, "The Role of Theory and Anomaly in Social-Scientific Inference," *American Political Science Review*, 89, 2 (June 1996): 467–470.
14. For a similar point, see Gary King, Robert O. Keohane, and Sidney Verba, *Designing Social Inquiry: Scientific Inference in Qualitative Research* (Princeton: Princeton University Press, 1994), ch. 2.
15. For an historian's perspective, see, Gaddis, "History, Science, and the Study of International Relations."
16. An excellent discussion of the historical method can be found in Chevalier V. Langlois and Chevalier Seignobos, *Introduction to the Study of History*, trans. by G. G. Berry (New York: Holt, 1966). See also Marc Bloch, *The Historian's Craft*, trans. by Peter Putnam. (New York: Knopf, 1953).
17. See Alexander George and Timothy J. McKeown, "Case Studies and Theories of Organizational Decision Making," *Advances in Information Processes in Organizations*, 2 (1985): 21–58; Alexander George, "Knowledge for Statecraft: The Challenge for Political Science and History," *International Security*, 22,1 (Summer 1997): 44–52; and John Lewis Gaddis, "History, Theory, and Common Ground," *International Security*, 22,1 (Summer 1997): 75–85.
18. For a similar approach, see Norrin M. Ripsman, *Democratic Institutions and the Governance of Foreign Security Policy: Peacemaking after Two World Wars* (Ph.D. Dissertation, University of Pennsylvania, 1997).
19. Scholars studying closed societies (which do not freely disseminate documents or other reliable information on the policy process), issues on the negotiating table or still under dispute, or decision making of a fairly recent nature frequently do not have the luxury of using primary source materials. In these circumstances, the same rigor cannot be expected, but the researcher should still survey all available information to strengthen the judgments he or she makes. For a recent work on East Asian border issues that uses such an approach, see Jean-Marc F. Blanchard, *Borders and Borderlands: An Institutional Approach to Territorial Disputes* (Ph.D. Dissertation, University of Pennsylvania, 1998).
20. In this regard, we were heavily influenced by Bruce N. Russett, "International Behavior Research: Case Studies and Cumulation," in Michael

Haas and Henry S. Kariel, eds. *Approaches to the Study of Political Science* (San Francisco: Chandler, 1970), pp. 425–443; and Sidney Tarrow, "Bridging the Quantitative-Qualitative Divide in Political Science," *American Political Science Review*, 89,2 (June 1996): 471–474.

21. Rosecrance et al., "Whither Interdependence?" pp. 426–427.
22. Ibid. and Gasiorowski, "Economic Interdependence and International Conflict." Mary Ann Tetreault has expressed doubts about the accuracy of such bilateral indices in measuring systemic interdependence. "Measuring Interdependence," *International Organization*, 34, 3 (Summer 1980): 429–443.
23. See, for example, Deutsch and Eckstein, "National Industrialization and the Declining Share of the International Economic Sector" pp. 267–299; Waltz, "The Myth of Interdependence"; Richard Rosecrance and Arthur Stein, "Interdependence: Myth or Reality," *World Politics*, 24,1 (October 1973): 1–27; Polachek, "Dyadic Disputes;" Polachek, "Conflict and Trade;" Mark Gasiorowski and Solomon Polachek, "Conflict and Interdependence: East-West Trade and Linkages in the Era of Détente," *International Studies Quarterly*, 30 (1986): 709–729; William Domke, *War and the Changing World System* (New Haven: Yale University Press, 1988); and Michael S. de Vries, "Interdependence, Cooperation and Conflict: An Empirical Analysis," *Journal of Peace Research*, 27,4 (1990): 429–444.
24. Albert O. Hirschman, *National Power and the Structure of Foreign Trade, Expanded Edition* (Berkeley: University of California Press, 1980).
25. Rosecrance and Stein, "Interdependence."
26. Gasiorowski employs both of these indices of vulnerability to test the proposition that more costly forms of interdependence produce rather than restrain conflict. "Economic Interdependence and International Conflict."
27. Arthur A. Stein, "Governments, Economic Interdependence, and International Cooperation," in Philip E. Tetlock et al., eds. *Behavior, Society, and International Conflict, III* (New York: Oxford University Press, 1993), pp. 241–324.
28. A recent study which examines the strategic context of trade is Edward D. Mansfield and Rachel Bronson, "Alliances, Preferential Trading Arrangements, and International Trade," *American Political Science Review*, 91,1 (March 1997): 94–107.
29. Blanchard and Ripsman, "Measuring Economic Interdependence."
30. Staley, *Raw Materials*, p. 3; Yuan-li Wu, *Economic Warfare* (New York: Prentice-Hall, 1952), pp. 12–13; Yuan-li Wu, *Raw Material Supply in a Multipolar World* (New York: Crane, Russak, & Company, 1973), p. 2; and Haglund, "The New Geopolitics of Minerals," pp. 225–233.

31. Emeny, *Strategy of Raw Materials*; Harry N. Holmes, *Strategic Materials and National Strength* (New York: Macmillan, 1942); Pound, *Political Geography*, pp. 157–186, particularly, pp. 176–180; and Wu, *Raw Material Supply in a Multipolar World*, especially chs. 2, 4.
32. Pound, *Political Geography*, pp. 159, 169–171.
33. For instance, it takes almost two years to build a tin-processing plant. Hessel, Murphy, and Hessel, *Strategic Minerals*, pp. 20–28.
34. William Yandell Elliott et al., *International Control in the Non-Ferrous Metals* (New York: Macmillan, 1937), pp. 210–276.
35. Edward. S. Mason, "American Security and Access to Raw Materials," *World Politics*, 1,1 (1949): 147–160, especially p. 153.
36. Staley, *Raw Materials*, p. 24.
37. For a general discussion of the efficiency costs of recycling, see Talbot Page, *Conservation and Economic Efficiency* (Baltimore: Johns Hopkins University Press, 1977).
38. C. K. Leith, *Raw Materials in Peace and War* (West Point: U.S. Military Academy Printing Office, 1947), pp. 162–163.
39. G. A. Roush, *Strategic Mineral Supplies*, 1st ed. (New York: McGraw-Hill, 1939); Bruce Carlton Netschert, "Point Four and Mineral Raw Materials," *Annals of the Association of American Geographers*, 41 (1951): 133–145; H. R. Warman, "The Future of Oil," *The Geographical Journal*, 138,3 (September 1973): 287–297; Peter R. Odell, "The Future of Oil: A Rejoinder," *The Geographical Journal*, 139,3 (October 1973): 436–454; Peter Beaumont, "Water and Development in Saudi Arabia," *The Geographical Journal*, 143,1 (March 1977): 42–60; and Stephen B. Jones, "The Power Inventory and National Strategy," in W. A. Douglas Jackson and Marwyn S. Samuels, eds. *Politics and Geographic Relationships*, 2nd ed. (Englewood Cliffs, NJ: Prentice-Hall, 1971), pp. 164–186.
40. de Vries, "Interdependence, Cooperation and Conflict."
41. The research in this section has been reported elsewhere. For more detailed discussions of our reasoning and choices, see Blanchard and Ripsman, "Measuring Economic Interdependence" and Ripsman and Blanchard, "Commercial Liberalism Under Fire."
42. Carlo M. Cipolla, ed. *The Fontana Economic History of Europe, 5, The Twentieth Century, Part 2* (New York: Barnes and Noble, 1977), pp. 409–415; Culbertson, *Raw Materials and Foodstuffs*, p. 183; Leo Grebler and William Winkler, *The Cost of the World War to Germany and to Austria-Hungary* (New Haven: Yale University Press, 1940), p. 9; League of Nations, *Report on the Problem of Raw Materials and Foodstuffs* (Geneva: League of Nations, 1921), pp. 82–102; League of Nations, *Memorandum on Balance of Payments and Foreign Trade*

Balances, 1910–1923, 2 (Geneva: League of Nations, 1924), pp.
113–128; League of Nations, *Memorandum on Balance of Payments
and Foreign Trade Balances, 1910–1924,* 2 (Geneva: League of
Nations, 1925), pp. 131–133; and B. R. Mitchell, *European Historical
Statistics, 1750–1975,* 2nd ed. rev. (New York: Facts on File, 1980),
pp. 264–281.

43. Sweden was not an option since it produced only small quantities of
agricultural goods. Mitchell, *European Historical Statistics,* pp.
277–281. Regarding Austro-Hungarian production of foodstuffs, see
League of Nations, *Report on the Problem of Raw Materials,* pp.
82–102.

44. We are indebted to Captain Lynn Wong for this observation.

45. Cipolla, *The Fontana Economic History of Europe,* p. 447; and Grebler and Winkler, *The Cost of the World War to Germany and Austria-
Hungary,* p. 80.

46. Killough and Killough, *Raw Materials of Industrialism,* pp. 271–289;
League of Nations, *Report on the Problem of Raw Materials,* pp.
175–196; and Mitchell, *European Historical Statistics, 1750–1975,*
pp. 392–393.

47. Grebler and Winkler, *The Cost of the World War to Germany and Austria-Hungary,* pp. 24–72.

48. Edson S. Bastin, "Minor Metals," in George Otis Smith, ed. *The Strategy of Minerals* (New York: D. Appleton, 1919), p. 189; Gustav Cas-
sel, *Germany's Economic Power of Resistance* (New York: The
Jackson Press, 1916), p. 16; Elliott et al., *International Control in the
Non-Ferrous Metals,* pp. 109–209; Grebler and Winkler, *The Costs of
the World War to Germany and Austria-Hungary,* pp. 103–107; Frank
F. Grout, "A Case of National Dependence: Germany," in George Otis
Smith, ed. *The Strategy of Minerals* (New York: D. Appleton, 1919),
pp. 307–313; Hessel, Murphy, and Hessel, *Strategic Materials,* p. 49;
United States Department of the Interior, *Mineral Resources of the
United States—1914, Part I* (Washington, D.C.: Government Printing
Office, 1916), pp. 161–181; and W. S. Woytinsky and E. S. Woytinsky,
World Population and Production (New York: Twentieth Century
Fund, 1953), pp. 776–838.

49. Culbertson, *Raw Materials and Foodstuffs,* pp. 149–153; and Holmes,
Strategic Materials and National Strength, pp. 12–27.

50. Grebler and Winkler, *The Cost of the World War to Germany and Austria-Hungary,* p. 45. See also Cassel, *Germany's Economic Power of
Resistance,* p. 20.

51. League of Nations, *Report on the Problem of Raw Materials and
Foodstuffs,* pp. 82–102; and Royal Commission on the National

Resources, Trade, and Legislation of Certain Portions of His Majesty's Dominions, *Memorandum and Tables Relating to the Food and Raw Material Requirements of the United Kingdom* (London: H. M. Stationary Office, 1915), pp. 1–7.

52. Ronnie Lipschutz, *When Nations Clash: Raw Materials, Ideology, and Foreign Policy* (New York: Ballinger, 1989), p. 50; League of Nations, *Report on the Problem of Raw Materials and Foodstuffs*, pp. 175–195; and Royal Commission, *Memorandum and Tables Relating to the Food and Raw Material Requirements of the United Kingdom*, pp. 87–90.

53. Smith, *The Strategy of Minerals*, pp. 186–211.

54. Culbertson, *Raw Materials and Foodstuffs*, pp. 149–153; Holmes, *Strategic Materials and National Strength*, pp. 12–27; and Woytinsky and Woytinsky, *World Population and Production*, pp. 615–622.

55. Culbertson, *Raw Materials in the Commercial Policies of Nations*, pp. 149–153.

56. Derek H. Aldcroft, *The British Economy Between the Wars* (Oxford: Philip Allan, 1983), p. 72; Deutsch and Eckstein, "National Industrialization," pp. 274–275; and League of Nations, *International Trade Statistics, 1935* (Geneva: League of Nations, 1936), pp. 119–121, 244–248.

57. Derek H. Aldcroft, *The Inter-War Economy: Britain, 1919–1939* (New York: Columbia University Press, 1970), pp. 263–266; and Royal Institute of International Affairs, *The Problem of International Investment* (London: Oxford University Press, 1937).

58. Neil Forbes, "London Banks, the German Standstill Agreements, and 'Economic Appeasement' in the 1930s," *Economic History Review*, 2nd ser. XL, 4 (1987): 571–587; and David E. Kaiser, *Economic Diplomacy and the Origins of the Second World War: Germany, Britain, France, and Eastern Europe, 1930–1939* (Princeton: Princeton University Press, 1980), pp. 96–97.

59. Royal Institute, *The Problem of International Investment*, chs. 2, 9, 12–13.

60. Jean Bouvier, "The French Banks, Inflation and the Economic Crisis, 1919–1939," in Francois Crouzet, ed. *The Economic Development of France Since 1870, 2* (Hants: Edward Elgar Publishing, 1993), pp. 387–438; Julian Jackson, *The Politics of Depression in France, 1931–1936* (Cambridge: Cambridge University Press, 1985); and Stephen Schuker, "France and the Remilitarization of the Rhineland, 1936," *French Historical Studies*, 14 (1986): 299–338, especially pp. 330–335.

61. During the Rhineland crisis, the French experienced significant outflows of gold and heavy withdrawals from savings banks. Schuker, "France and the Remilitarization of the Rhineland," p. 334.

62. James T. Emmerson, *The Rhineland Crisis* (London: Maurice Temple Smith, 1977), pp. 111–112; Jackson, *The Politics of Depression*, especially chs. 5, 8, Epilogue; and Schuker, "France and the Remilitarization," p. 330.

63. We could also have analyzed the British decision to go to war in 1914, but this would have been less interesting from the point of view of theory testing. On the other hand, the German decision to go to war in the face of German vulnerability presents a hard test case for the commercial liberal argument if it can be shown that German decision makers were aware of their vulnerability. Similarly, the British and French decisions not to go to war in 1936 present hard test cases for the contrary position that trade does not restrain conflict, especially if they were dependent to a lesser extent—that is, sensitive rather than vulnerable—and if that dependence was the reason for their caution. Since the British in 1914 were sensitive rather than vulnerable, even if we could have determined that British decision makers were aware of that dependence, it would not be conclusive evidence against the commercial liberal argument, since it would remain hypothetically possible that the constraints of vulnerability would have prevented them from joining the war.

64. Avner Offer, *The First World War: An Agrarian Interpretation* (New York: Oxford University Press, 1989), pp. 321–353.

65. This is an important point, although it contradicts the conventional wisdom. For a complete explanation and justification of the conclusion that the Germans believed a long war was possible, see Ripsman and Blanchard, "Commercial Liberalism Under Fire," pp. 22–23.

66. Particularly instructive in this regard were three documents. First, Undersecretary of State's Zimmermann's memorandum to Chancellor von Bethmann-Hollweg, reporting the existence of a military alliance between Great Britain, France, and Russia made it clear early on to the political elite that a war with Russia over the Serbian incident would entail a war with Britain. Zimmermann to Bethmann-Hollweg, June 27, 1914, Karl Kautsky, ed. *Outbreak of the World War: German Documents Collected by Karl Kautsky* (New York: Oxford University Press) (hereafter *KD*), p. 59. Later in July, Prince Lichnowsky, the German Ambassador to London, warned the German Foreign Office that a refusal to accept the British proposal for mediations and negotiations to settle the conflict would necessarily draw England into a war against the Germans. Lichnowsky to Foreign Office, July 25, 1914, and July 27, 1914, *KD*, pp. 199, 247. Finally, Kaiser Wilhelm's comments on a (July 29, 1914) telegram from Lichnowsky reporting British Foreign Secretary Grey's measured threat of British intervention—"This means

they will attack us"—leaves no doubt that before Germany was irrevocably committed to war they were aware that Great Britain would stand against them in battle (*KD*, pp. 321–322).

67. *KD*, and Imanuel Geiss, ed. *July 1914: The Outbreak of the First World War, Selected Documents* (London: Batsford, 1967).

68. In the months leading up to the crisis, Eden's reports to the Cabinet stressed that British military unreadiness made a German attempt to remilitarize the Rhineland inevitable and unstoppable. Therefore, he advocated allowing a German presence on the Rhine in exchange for an Anglo-German air pact. *Documents on British Foreign Policy 1919–1939* (London: HMSO, 1977), 2nd ser., 15, 521 and 16, 48 and 60.

69. R. A. C. Parker, *Chamberlain and Appeasement: British Policy and the Coming of the Second World War* (New York: St. Martin's Press, 1993), pp. 60–61; Robert G. Kaufman, "'To Balance or Bandwagon?' Alignment Decisions in 1930s Europe," *Security Studies*, 1,3 (Spring 1992): 417–447, especially, pp. 430–431; Emmerson, *The Rhineland Crisis*, pp. 142–143; and Harold Macmillan, *Winds of Change* (New York: Harper & Row, 1966), pp. 460–465.

70. See, in particular, *Documents Diplomatiques Français 1932–1939* (Paris: Imprimerie Nationale, 1963), 2e ser., t. 1, nus. 196, 203, 334.

71. Pierre-Etienne Flandin, *Politique française 1919–1940* (Paris: Les Editions Nouvelles, 1947), pp. 198–199; Schuker, "France and the Remilitarization," pp. 317–330; and Réné Albrecht-Carrié, *Diplomatic History of Europe* (New York: Harper & Row, 1973), pp. 491–496.

72. Anthony Eden, *Facing the Dictators* (Boston: Houghton Mifflin, 1962); and Flandin, *Politique française*.

73. See also Jean-Marc F. Blanchard and Norrin M. Ripsman, "Asking the Right Question: *When* Do Economic Sanctions Work?" in Jean-Marc F. Blanchard, Edward D. Mansfield, and Norrin M. Ripsman, eds. *Purchasing Power and Peace: The Political Economy of National Security,* Special Issue of *Security Studies* 9, 1 (Autumn, 1999).

4

CONSTRUCTING
CONCEPTS OF IDENTITY

Prospects and Pitfalls of a
Sociological Approach to World Politics

ANNE L. CLUNAN

Over the past decade, an increasing number of scholars in the field of international relations have turned to sociology for approaches that illuminate the complexity of international life. These scholars generally agree that the reality we see is socially constructed and that social forces, in addition to individual rationality or material structures, are necessary to explain international politics. Many international relations scholars who draw on sociology refer to themselves as constructivists, and constructivism is being put forward as a new approach to international relations. The borrowing from sociology has a long pedigree in international relations theory. Despite this pedigree, constructivists have not systematically imported sociological approaches in ways that make the development of a new research program in international relations theory easy or certain.[1] This essay marks an effort to assist in the development of such a research tradition while simultaneously exploring the analytic boundary between international and national processes of identity formation.

Those who call themselves constructivists reject both ontological positivism and relativism, while accepting that reality is socially constructed. They share a substantive interest in the development of aspects of international society—in how norms, cultures, and debates about identity influence the development of collectively accepted international rules and practices, and how these international rules and practices affect domestic politics. Constructivists agree that the spread of collective ideas, in the form of collective learning, adaptation, or socialization, is a key mechanism in the transformation of and reproduction of international political structures. I discuss these elements of commonality among constructivists throughout this essay.

The essay is structured as follows: In the two sections immediately following, I briefly discuss the understanding of reality underlying constructivism as well as the roots of the sociological turn in international relations theory. In the third part of the essay I analyze how two constructivists, Alexander Wendt and Ernst Haas, employ the concept of identity. Where Wendt emphasizes the international aspects of states' identity formation, Haas privileges domestic struggles over national identity. In the fourth section I offer a guide to identity conceptualization that brings together some of the sociological insights about the effects of social interaction at *both* the interstate and domestic levels. In the fifth section I focus on how constructivist agreement on the importance of the spread of collective knowledge in transforming international relations may serve as the basis for a constructivist theory of social change, while noting the barriers to agreement on such a theory. I argue that given consensus that the spread and institutionalization of collective ideas and knowledge are crucial mechanisms of change in social structures, constructivists may be able to agree on *collective learning and adaptation* as the primary mechanisms of change in international society. I again ground the discussion of a theory of international change by comparing the work of Alexander Wendt and Ernst Haas. In the conclusion, I pick up the issue of whether constructivism can become a coherent research program that is both non-positivist and non-relativist, and what stakes rest on this development. Before turning to these issues, in the remainder of this section I discuss a constructivist ontology drawn from sociological understandings of the social construction of reality, and what this has meant for the study of international relations.

Constructivists and the Social Construction of Reality

Scholars who call themselves constructivists agree that the bulk of what is considered "reality" is the product of shared human perceptions and social action. Reality is socially constructed, as was argued by sociologists in the 1960s.[2] Our collective understandings of state, nation, utility, war, peace, power, marriage, and capitalism make these concepts "real" in the sense that it is only by virtue of our common understanding and acting as if these concepts are real that they have any meaning. What is a state in reality may not accurately be reflected by our shared conceptions of it, but one of the goals of social science is to more accurately capture reality through the progressive evolution of concepts. A social constructivist ontology rests between the positivist emphasis on the material forces in world politics and the relativist position that all reality is the effect of discourse.[3] I return to the issue of constructivist ontology and epistemology in the conclusion.

Constructivists agree that "ideas matter," not just as intervening variables between a material cause (such as power or material gain) and its effect, but in making most of these "material causes" real to us in the first place.[4] Material things are real, but we create their meanings. Our collective ideas about bits of paper and a soldier's medals determine the value of money and the power of rank. In this sense, reality is based on intersubjective concepts and meanings, or shared ideas. Actors make reality by endowing certain actions and things with meaning. These meanings can then become firmly entrenched, becoming "structures" that enable actors to act and understand one another, but that also can constrain the realm of possible action.

The acceptance of a social constructivist ontology opens up an array of substantive topics to constructivists that have been pushed aside by rationalist international relations theory. It has drawn attention away from the behavior, "revealed preferences," and assumptions of rational, unitary actors toward the web of social institutions and social discourse that surround actors, and to their ideas, identities, and interests. Constructivists have turned to study concepts widely employed in sociology: ideas, norms, cultures, and identities. In doing so, they address an important gap in rationalist theory by focusing on questions of how national interests are formed, how constitutive principles of international politics such as sovereignty are developed, and how national identity affects the future of the nation-state, to name but a few.[5] Unlike rationalist structural theorists, who can only study change in "preferences over actions or policies" within their models, constructivists can analyze what "preferences over outcomes" are, and where they come from.[6] In other words, constructivists can analyze how and why the "game" was set up in the first place. The search for the sources of actors' interests leads to an investigation of norms, culture, and identity, which in turn offers a fuller account of actors' goals than the parsimonious assumptions of rational choice theory.

Constructivists also study how ideas, cultures, norms, and identities may shape how actors link their interests with the means to achieve them. Actors' conceptions of what methods or technologies are available or appropriate may be shaped by such social structures as national identity, human rights norms, or scientific knowledge.[7] Ideas, identities, and norms may lead to changes in other social structures. Wendt argues that changes in state identity will lead to changes in the culture of anarchy.[8] In explaining the shift to the territorial system of states, John Ruggie describes how

> The demise of the medieval system of rule and the rise of the modern resulted in part from a transformation in social epistemology. Put simply, the mental equipment that people drew upon in imagining and symbolizing forms of political community itself underwent a fundamental change.[9]

How actors conceive of appropriate orders of rule and exchange, of their own identity will shape the creation of social orders and societal interests. Actor identities will affect how actors interpret social rules, and these social rules will affect which behaviors are possible. Constructivism encourages the scientific exploration of the construction of international social life, instead of assuming that it is unimportant or unscientific.

If reality is constructed by our shared understandings of it, then constructivists believe we should focus on the shared understandings which are social reality, how they develop, and how they affect actors' understanding of and behavior in the external world. The social construction of reality naturally focuses attention on the content of collective ideas, or social structures (and the related concepts of norms, identities, cultures, and institutions), and on how these ideas diffuse and become institutionalized as social structures. This in turn focuses attention on an empirical question: How much influence do ideas and social structures have in "bringing about physical changes in the physical world."[10] Constructivists agree that the process of sharing new ideas and building social structures can lead to changes in, for example, physical power (the idea of arms control)[11] and the nature of anarchy.[12] The acceptance of the social construction of reality allows constructivists to specify the interests of actors, the sources of those interests, and how those interests change. It also allows them to account for persistent differences that actors display in their interpretations of external political structures.[13] Moreover adherence to the social construction of reality promotes investigation of how international social structures, such as sovereignty, diplomacy, and anarchy, are formed, maintained, and changed.

While an emphasis on the sociology of international society has opened up international relations to subjects such as identity and interest formation, constructivists disagree on the implications of sociological approaches for the concrete analysis of international affairs, as well as on how they conceive of social relations. This disagreement yields different approaches to the conceptualization of identity in international politics. These approaches do, however, share a common heritage of borrowing from sociology. It is to this heritage that I now turn.

Origins of the Sociological Turn in International Relations Theory

The renewed emphasis on the sociological concepts of identity, culture, norms, and ideas has old roots within international relations theory. Scholarly interest in international integration, the nature of international order, and the growth of international regimes brought together theorists who focused on national and transnational actors and the evolving processes of cooperation they engaged in. These pluralist theorists all rejected the sparse view of international reality that structural realists and neoliberals accept.[14] Challenging the utilitarian roots of neorealists and neoliberals, theorists like Hedley Bull, Karl Deutsch, and Ernst Haas drew on the insights of sociology to argue for a richer view of international life. These theorists focused analysis on sociological questions—on the development and integration of international and supranational society. Karl Deutsch is famous both for his study of the development of security communities in Western Europe, held together by a sense of "we-feeling," and for his study of the role of social communication in the integration of nation-states. Ernst Haas' well-known analysis of the development of supranational institutions in the European Community emphasized the importance of affect and loyalty in making integration possible. Hedley Bull focused explicitly on the development of international society in the absence of global government.[15]

For these theorists, international politics was a complex web of social relationships crossing the boundaries between domestic and international politics, and its trends were better captured through analysis of process than of material structures such as the distribution of power. We see in Ernst Haas' understanding of international relations a precursor of contemporary constructivism:

> What matters is process. The actors' perceptions of reality result in policies that shape events; these effects create a new reality whose impact will then be perceived all over again, ad infinitum. . . .[16]

Haas' attention to process and interaction, to interest definition and redefinition, and the spread of collective knowledge are essential elements of a constructivist research program.

These theorists were centrally concerned with the development of elements of supranational and international society. They suggested that social communication (Deutsch), the spread of new collective loyalties (Haas) and the creation of ordering rules (Bull) were essential to the development of a more integrated international society. These theorists recognized that the process of social interaction is the essence of international politics, and that human agents can alter the process of international life. This emphasis has continued in research on international regimes. Today's constructivists draw on these early insights, and focus on similar aspects of the development of international society. Unlike their forebears, they draw more explicitly on developments in sociological theory, particularly on a social constructivist ontology, sociological institutionalism and structuration theory in their analyses of international social processes. They study the rise of human rights norms, the development of security communities, liberal economic orders, and changes in the structure of international society itself.[17] All share the belief that the spread of collective ideas is critical to the development of the social practices and institutions that constitute international society.

Constructivists do not assume that international society is harmonious. They accept that it is anarchic and that no natural harmony of interests makes this society cohere. But constructivists stress that there is order in anarchy, as Hedley Bull pointed out two decades ago. It is the development of international institutions, practices, identities, and norms that have brought order into anarchy and which create international society. The overarching substantive interest of constructivism, its dependent variable, is the development of international society:

> A society of states (or international society) exists when a group of states, conscious of certain common interests and common values, form a society in the sense that they conceive of themselves to be bound by a common set of rules in their relations with one another, and share in the working of common institutions . . . such as the forms of procedures of international law, the machinery of diplomacy and general international organisation, and the customs and conventions of war.[18]

The flourishing of the "new institutionalisms" in sociology and political science also spurred the sociological turn in international relations theory.[19] The rise of the new sociological institutionalism and the new historical institutionalism in political science both arose out of the apparent failure of and distaste for deterministic grand theory, be it Parsonian systems theory, Marxist world systems theory, or modernization theory. At the same time, behavioralism's emphasis on the behavior and belief of actors had downgraded the attention given to the institutional context of behavior.[20] Sociologists and political scientists sought to create midlevel theories that avoided the teleological aspects of determinism, and also emphasized how institutional context shapes political behavior and interests. Sociological and historical institutionalists take the interests of actors as problematic, and argue that social and political institutions not only shape the strategies but also the goals of actors.[21] The emphasis on the institutional context of political and social life led scholars to study what international institutional contexts exist, how they are created and how they affect international politics.

Constructivists accept the sociological institutionalist argument that social and political institutions shape and define interests. But they also draw heavily on developments in the sociology of knowledge, particularly work on the social construction of reality and structuration theory.[22] In subscribing to the social construction of reality, constructivists reject claims that interests are given, and that social and political structures alone are solely responsible for political outcomes. They argue that the process of creating social institutions is where scholars should look for explanation of particular political events and for the creation of particular political interests. In this view, agents interact with each other in an environment laden with both social and material structures. These structures are not objective facts that constrain human behavior. They were originally authored by human agents, and when institutionalized they become resources for human action, not only constraints on behavior. Through their reason, communication and actions human agents reproduce and change the social structures around them.[23]

Armed with these sociological insights, theorists have been focusing on the *social* structure of international relations—the social institutions, norms, values, rules, and ideas that constitute international life. These theorists, like historical institutionalists, should view themselves as engaged in "midlevel" theorizing about the institutionalization of international practices and the development of international society.[24] Emanuel Adler, David Dessler, Martha Finnemore, Ernst Haas, Peter Katzenstein, Elizabeth Kier, Audie Klotz, Friedrich Kratochwil, Thomas Risse, John Ruggie, and Alexander Wendt, to name only some constructivists, have all drawn on sociology for their work. The wide variety of disciplinary roots and substantive interests of these authors indicates that "constructivism" as a school of thought is not well delineated or defined. One of the goals of this chapter is to set out some of the conceptual issues that unite and divide those who call themselves constructivists. For this reason I focus on two very different theorists, Alexander Wendt and Ernst Haas, to highlight some of the important issues I believe unite and divide constructivists. In the section below I focus on how these scholars conceptualize identity formation, before returning to the broader discussion of constructivism.

Collective Identity and the Study of International Politics

Alexander Wendt has noted constructivism's early debt to integration theory.[25] He takes up the integration theorists' concern with collective identity formation at the international level.[26] Both Deutsch and Haas looked for changes in the locus and strength of actors' national loyalty and identification in their approach to international collective action and integration. As mentioned earlier, Deutsch discussed the development of "we-feeling" in NATO. Haas emphasized the need for a collective shift in loyalty away from the national center to a supranational organization as necessary for successful European integration.[27] This change in identification was agreed to be the necessary glue that holds a new society together.

Wendt has once again made the study of identity central to discussions of international relations. Wendt studies *how* the international system developed its current social structure, or what he calls the culture of anarchy. While different types of anarchy are possible, our current "self-help" or egoistic culture of anarchy arose out of the historical interaction of states—it was predetermined neither by human nature, nor the material structure of world politics:

> Self-help security systems evolve from cycles of interaction in which each party acts in ways that the other feels are threatening to the self, creating expectations that the other is not to be trusted.[28]

Without understanding how the current self-help culture of anarchy came into being, Wendt argues, we cannot properly explain egoistic state behavior and the possibility of transformation of the self-help culture that makes that behavior appropriate.[29] Wendt is interested in understanding how such an egoistic culture of anarchy may be changing in Western Europe. He argues that with regard to national security, state identities in Western Europe are evolving from individualist identities of "every state for itself," to a collectivist identity, where West European countries identify their security as bound up in a greater European whole, not merely in their nation-state. Wendt's substantive interests in this regard are similar to those of the integration theorists, who investigated the development of supranational communities in Western Europe.

Wendt's conceptualization of identity formation is however quite different from that of Deutsch and Haas. Wendt argues that states form their security identity through a process of reiterated interaction with other states. Security identities take the form of roles that states play. The experience and content of social interaction at the state-to-state level defines a state's security identity, its security role. Russia develops its security identity based on how another state, such as the United States, acts toward and speaks to it. An iterated process of friendly behavior and rhetoric from the U.S. would lead to the development of Russia's identification of the U.S. as a friend and Russia's adoption of the role of ally. Hostile behavior would lead to identification of the U.S. as a foe and Russia's taking on the role of enemy. This process is what Wendt, drawing on the sociology of Herbert Mead, calls the logic of reflected appraisals. In Wendt's view, a long process of friendly interaction may lead states to not only identify each other as allies and friends, but to view their security interests as intertwined and consequently to identify *with* each other as belonging to the same community.

In his published work, Wendt has emphasized states' relations at the *systemic,* or state-state level. It is the logic of reflected appraisals, or the roles that states assign to one another, that determine the type of international structure we inhabit. This approach deemphasizes national collective identity. While like Deutsch and Haas, Wendt is interested in what makes an international community cohere, he overlooks the integration theorists' concomitant interest in *national* collective identities. Karl Deutsch in *Nationalism and Social Communication* (1953) and Ernst Haas in *Beyond the Nation State* (1964) analyzed nationalism's role and effects on regional or global integration. Their interest in nationalism, and the creation of collective identities more generally, reflects their concern for the domestic factors that facilitate and inhibit the process of integration and the formation of international society. Deutsch and Haas saw national collective identity as one of the greatest obstacles to supranational integration. While Wendt shares their interest in the development of international society and its integration, he is primarily concerned with the international factors that determine collective identity formation. Wendt and Haas do not refer to each others' work on the processes of integration and identity change. While they may share agreement about the importance of the social construction of reality and the substantive interest in the integration of international society, they have to date operated in fairly separate realms.

This separation of international and domestic elements of identity formation has the potential to keep constructivists divided. Such division in my view hinders the development of a coherent research tradition that can further the analysis of the development of international society that both theorists make their main concern, and prevents the cumulation of constructivist insights about world politics. The end result is that the rationalist research tradition proceeds without coherent and progressive criticism and adjustment by a well-developed alternative research program. I return to this theme in my conclusion. Below I sketch the conceptual minefield of identity and develop the differences in Wendt's and Haas' understandings of identity formation. I put forward my own conceptualization of identity that comprises both international and domestic factors and lay out a framework of questions to guide such conceptualization. While international roles are clearly important in understanding a state's identity, a true constructivist approach should reject any empirical distinction between the analytic categories of systemic and domestic politics, and recognize that the two analytic categories *both* contribute to the process of state identity formation.

Wendt is correct that a state's identity is indeed comprised in important part by how it has been and is treated by other states. But a state's identity is also critically made up of the ideas about their national self-image that political elites advocate to their citizens and use to justify their foreign claims and obligations to both domestic and foreign constituencies. The "Other" or "Others" play a vital role in the definition of identity but the current "Other" is viewed through the lens of the historical traditions and contemporary political discourses of the state in question. These traditions and discourses do not relate solely to the country's past dealings with other countries but also to elites' ideas about their state's political-economic structure, historical mission, and international position and status.

Part of the division sketched above stems from the different disciplinary and subdisciplinary roots of constructivists. Constructivist explanations may be based on Weberian or structurationist sociology, role theory, and/or cognitive psychology, and this naturally affects whether their arguments can be conceived of as a coherent research school or program. Constructivists use the term identity widely and loosely. The concept of identity is used in conjunction with "ideas," "norms," and "cultures."[30] A sample of the definitions offered in Peter Katzenstein's edited volume *The Culture of National Security* (1996b) makes the point. "The essays refer to *identity* as a shorthand label for varying constructions of nation- and statehood . . . [T]he authors . . . invoke the term *culture* as a broad label that denotes collective models of nation-state authority or identity."[31] "[I]dentities come in two basic forms—those that are intrinsic to an actor (at least relative to a given social structure) and those that are relationally defined within a social structure . . . Intrinsic identities are constituted exogenously to a game . . . whereas relational identities ('role') are constituted by the game itself."[32]

In his contribution to the Katzenstein volume, Robert Herman conceptualizes identity as a set of ideas about cause and effect and values *and* as a constitutive norm,[33] but he defines norms "as collective beliefs that *regulate* the behavior and identity of actors."[34] Thomas Berger treats certain institutionalized beliefs and values as integral parts of national identity, *and* as constituting political-military cultures.[35] Thomas Risse-Kappen also sees identity as based on

> *norms* firmly embedded in the political *culture* of . . . states and
> [these] *norms* shape the *identity* of political actors through

processes of socialization, communication, and enactment. . . .
Collectively held identities not only define who "we" are, but
they also delineate the boundaries against "them," the "other."
Identities then prescribe *norms* of appropriate behavior.[36]

Michael Barnett adopts a relational definition of identity; it is a "relational construct that emerges out of the international and domestic discourse and interactions."[37] Paul Kowert and Jeffrey Legro distinguish between norms and identities, but emphasize their common prescriptive aspect. "We . . . divide social prescriptions into these two categories: prescriptive accounts of actors themselves (identities) and behavioral prescriptions for the proper enactment of these identities (behavioral norms)."[38] They stress that "even our treatment of identity focuses explicitly on the regulative (rather than merely) constitutive effects of norms."[39]

As mentioned above, Wendt's conception of identity is based fundamentally on role-taking, or on *relations* between "Self" and "Other." Of the formulations above, Barnett's is closest to Wendt's. Wendt draws heavily on symbolic interactionism and role theory, which hold that

> Conceptions of self and interest tend to "mirror" the practices
> of significant others over time. This principle of identity-formation is captured by the symbolic interactionist notion of the
> "looking glass self," which asserts that the self is a reflection of
> an actor's socialization.[40]

In other words, an actor's identity and interests are formed based on how a significant other acts, both behaviorally and discursively, toward it. State identity formation is based on role-taking, where how others view one shapes one's beliefs about one's self. How states act and talk to each other determines whether they will take on the role identities of friend or foe, ally or enemy. Implicit in the conception of role identity is the concept of power. Who "Self" takes a role in contrast to is a function of the power of the various "Others."

Wendt states that state identities are a function of both the roles that states adopt vis-à-vis other states on particular issues, and their "intrinsic" characteristics. Intrinsic identities of states "are their constituent individuals, physical resources, and the shared beliefs and institutions in virtue of which individuals function as a 'we.'"[41] Wendt argues that intrinsic identities generate something akin to biological needs of an individual. Like individuals, states need to have assurance of their physical security including their difference from other actors, their ontological security (predictable relationships to the outside world), recognition of their status as actors, and their aspiration for a better life.[42] But in constructing his theory of identity formation, Wendt tends to leave identity to be generated by roles alone. While corporate identities (or the internal, "subjective" identities) of states are the source of eventual transformation of structures, it is only the role identities that constitute the "culture of anarchy," or system *structure*.[43] In my view, this results from Wendt's treatment of states as unitary actors.

Wendt treats states theoretically as if they are structures or "social kinds," but then in turn confers agency upon them, especially in the crucial area of identity formation.[44] Yet states themselves are in large part a collective identity made concrete in organizations and policies. From this perspective it is crucial to look at the internal elements of identity and the domestic actors who create it. Wendt's reification of the state turns our attention toward the interaction of states, and away from the domestic sphere and the historical experiences that the leadership of the state collectively remember and reinterpret in shaping the state's current identity. Concretely, this means that Wendt's conception of state identity misses out on the influence that, for example, nationalism and religion have in shaping a leadership's view of its state's international role. Russian leaders may derive an adversarial identity vis-à-vis the United States from collective beliefs about the role of Slavic Russia in the former Yugoslavia, for example.

The state cannot be treated analytically as an individual by constructivists concerned with identity formation. Constructivists correctly attempt to delimit which elements of identity are relevant for their particular substantive interests. To this end, some have roughly divided the elements of identity into those that "intrinsic" and those that are "social."[45] This division unfortunately parallels the personal identity of an individual and the social role identities that person occupies—as teacher, parent, employee, friend, Republican, Asian-American, and so on. The division tends to reinforce the notion that the internal identity of a state—the "personal" side of identity—is fixed, and is not affected by the state's external social interactions. But states are the product of ongoing internal social struggles that are intertwined with their external interactions.

Where Wendt stacks the deck in favor of international social relations and roles, Ernst Haas privileges domestic social roles and politics over international ones. Haas, along with other theorists who adopt the label of constructivist, such as Risse-Kappen and Ruggie, argues that the *internal* characteristics of a state, often in conjunction with desires for particular world roles or domestic political power, produce a state's identity.[46] These theorists, like Wendt, admit that external and internal conceptions of identity are important for the creation of a state identity. However, these theorists tend to emphasize internal over external characteristics.

Haas draws heavily on the sociology of Max Weber for his understanding of the ideational sources of interests. Like Weber in his study of world religions, Haas studies whether national identities create coherent social institutions: nation-states. In contrast to Wendt, for Haas identity-creation is a task that political leaders set themselves in trying to make their society cohere.[47] When a society has developed a "national myth," it is an indication that the society is becoming more integrated. Haas defines a national myth as

> a core of ideas and claims about selfhood commonly accepted by all the socially mobilized. Put differently, the national myth represents those ideas, values, and symbols that most citizens accept despite their being divided into competing ideological groups.[48]

For Haas, national identity is based on symbols and ideas of distinction and uniqueness that differentiate a set of people from outsiders.[49] Chief among these are status, religion, race and language and "abstract ideas about law, cosmology, origins, futures, and science."[50] Haas stresses that "[n]ational identities are chosen, not genetically implanted, and they are subject to change. Yet none of this denies that nationalist convictions are sometimes held tenaciously, that they provide the socially constructed realities of human actors."[51] Haas emphasizes human agency in the process of identity formation much more than Wendt does.

Only when national symbols and ideas cease to differentiate the group from outsiders does Haas argue that it is possible for collective identity to change in the direction of a supranational identity. Haas argues that such identity change usually occurs through collective learning and adaptation. Collective learning takes place when changes in beliefs about cause and effect lead to value change, as well as behavioral change. Robert Herman's conception of identity cited above is closest to Haas'. Collective learning "implies that the organization's members are induced to question earlier beliefs about the appropriateness of ends of action and to think about the selection of new ones, to 'revalue' themselves."[52] Such value change among a political elite is usually triggered by instrumental power relations or policy failure and does not inevitably lead to supranational identification.[53]

Thus for Haas, collective identity change is brought about either by interaction of political elites within a country or the failure of a political program, not just through a process of reflective role-taking as in Wendt's conceptualization. Haas takes up the issue of identity formation as a *task* for political elites, who consciously seek to create or maintain an collective identity in order to build stable and coherent states. While Haas agrees with Wendt that distinctions between "us" and "them" are a critical part of identity, he focuses less on how "they" treat "us" and vice versa (the basis of Wendt's identification process), than on ideas about political, economic and legal governance "for us" which may often make "us" believe we are better than "them."[54] He emphasizes the internal or domestic aspects of a state's identity, while Wendt focuses on a state's external, or role identity.

The two conceptions of identity formation are not mutually exclusive. Part of the disagreement stems purely from the fact that Haas focuses on the domestic elements of *national* identities while Wendt focuses the external role-based *state* identities. Haas allows that the process of creating new national identities is in large part a function of the development of collective knowledge that stems from social interaction. Wendt accepts that states may initiate a process of learning for instrumental reasons.[55] Without agreement on whether identification takes place primarily internally or externally to a state, however, constructivists will develop different theories of how actors' identities are constituted, what interests will develop, and how the actual process of structural transformation and reproduction works. Below I suggest a conception of identity that tries to bridge the gap between internal and external conceptions.

A Framework of Questions for Identity Conceptualization

I believe it is a mistake to focus on the externally defined identity of state actors to the exclusion of internally defined identities and vice versa.[56] An exclusive focus on role identity, the "we-they" identity employed by Wendt, obscures what I argue are important elements of a political elite's collective identity, and crucially, what it is that may lead to long-term transformation of the state's role in international relations. Likewise an emphasis on the purely domestic and instrumental aspects of identity formation misses the significant influence that the process of international comparison has on the formation of a state's identity.

Let me be more specific. As Wendt and many others argue, an individual's identity is in large part shaped by how others treat that person. In oversimplified but concrete terms, if the United States government treats the Russian government as an adversary, Russian leaders will define themselves as adversaries of the United States government. An individual, in Wendt's case, a state, will step into the shoes of the "other" and assume some of the perspective of that "other's" views of itself. This view is certainly a mainstay of theories of identity, and is not inaccurate in and of itself. What I quarrel with is the heavy emphasis given to *external* role relationships in Wendt's definition of a state's collective identity. The process of social interaction is not only between states and state leaders, but also between state leaders and their publics. A state's role identity is fundamentally influenced by a state's domestic politics as well as by state-state inter-actions. The times and places that one matters relatively more than the other in the definition of identity cannot be specified a priori by the observer, but will depend on what particular issue is being studied. In general both national and international interactions are important for the definition of identity.

I argue that ideas about appropriate domestic political and economic structures, traditions of the role and status of the state in world affairs and its historical mission fundamentally influence the state's collective identity. These factors are often influenced by external actors and international norms. International comparison of one's society with others is a critical element of identity formation. Haas understates this influence in his conceptualization of identity formation.[57] But it is important to note that internal aspects of identity formation cannot be easily separated from external aspects. External elements of state identity, such as who is the "Other" and which "Other" are "we" like, are inherently bound up in what Jepperson, Wendt, Katzenstein, and others have inappropriately labeled "intrinsic" elements of identity. These elements are not intrinsic, or "constituted exogenously to a game"[58] and therefore immutable, rather they are the product of political struggles over the creation of social institutions. As stated above, Jepperson, Wendt, and Katzenstein define intrinsic identity as the set of ideas and institutions which differentiate a *society* from others. This is a collective identity not an individual one.

For constructivists to truly understand how state identities shape and are shaped by international society, the divide between international and national societies has to be bridged. At the state level, I argue that the definitions of "social" identities encountered in the constructivists literature are inadequate, because theorists have tended to emphasize only one of *two* societies: either domestic society, or international society. In doing so they have missed the obvious but important realization that states are social institutions whose characteristics are determined in the main by the domestic societies which they govern. Constructivists need to combine elements of both sets of social relations in their studies of identity formation.

Some analysts may reply that this makes the study of identity formation impossible, as there are too many inputs to consider. Quite right. I believe that the formation of a state's collective identity is not a seamless process that encompasses all aspects of a state's international affairs. Rather, a state's collective identity is issue specific, with general elements of identity becoming salient with the particular exigencies of a given issue. Concretely this means that in order to find out what a state's identity is and how it is formed, we study the national self-images of political elites who are involved in the particular issue area of concern to the researcher. These national self-images of political elites are *not* their individual senses of identity. National self-images are the collective ideas of appropriateness that political elites hold about the political-economic structure, role, status, and mission of their country in international affairs. These ideas combine both internal and external elements of identity. In other words, both domestic and international societies are the sources of these ideas.

The political elite of the state will often consciously seek to mold the state's identity as a particular type of state with a particular character and a corresponding set of interests. President Yeltsin launched such a project in Russia.[59] Elites forge a state's identity not merely with an eye on their foreign audience but in large measure on their domestic public. Identity formation develops out of both action and communication. Since elites make pronouncements for their domestic audience that are also heard by their foreign audience, we cannot separate the domestic and international processes of identity formation.

Wendt recognizes that both international and domestic society are important to state identity formation, but he errs in arguing that "intrinsic" identity in the case of states can be separated either from domestic social identity or external role identity. He proceeds to assume away the issue of how domestic and international social practices interact to create state identities by an act of reification: "[Intrinsic] identities have histories, but these do not concern me here; a theory of the states system need no more explain the existence of states than one of society need explain that of people."[60] But states, as Wendt argues elsewhere,[61] are not people—they are not biological but *social* facts, and a theory of collective identity formation at the international level does need to take account of how and why states exist. This is precisely the problem that led the integration theorists to study nationalism.

Wendt's work has stressed international social interaction. However, in his latest book he argues that domestic level "homogenization" of domestic institutions and values is one of three necessary mechanisms (the other two being a shared sense of common fate and the activity of self-restraint) for the transformation of the international system.[62] In doing so, he goes an important part of the way to resolving many of the problems I have highlighted above, and makes the unification of constructivist approaches to identity formation conceivable. He also indicates that the mechanisms of change in identity are collective learning and adaptation. This increases the potential for a constructivist theory of change. I will return to these issues below.

In order to unify internal and external conceptions to identity formation, I offer a series of questions as a guide to the conceptualization of state identity. The units of analysis depend on the researcher's interests. They may be a political elite, a state, a nation, a citizenry, or an organization. In what follows, I use the state as the unit of analysis.

The first question the theorist needs to ask is What is the content of identity? The answer comes in the form of further questions, each one of which entails corollaries. *Who should "we" be?* This question asks both what the physical and membership boundaries of the unit of analysis are and what form of domestic political and economic governance structures are appropriate. This question leads to two corollaries that focus on what boundaries now exist and compare their appropriateness with the past: *Who have "we" been?* and *Should "we" be that "we" now?* The second main question is *What should "we" do?* What historical mission or aim do the state leadership and citizenry believe they are or should be embarked on. Candidate answers might include a "civilizing mission," "survival," "modernization," and "messianism." Again this question has two corollaries: *What have "we" done?* and *Should "we" do it now?* A follow-on to this last set of questions is *How should "we" do it?*, with potential answers being militarily, economically, culturally, ideologically, through imitation or pursuit of the status quo. A third main question is *How should "we" be regarded?* This question asks what international role and status the society believes it should be accorded. Are *"we" to be considered "big brother," or "bully," or "global cop," or "victim"? Is "our" status that of a "great," "super," or a "small" power?*

The next series of questions capture beliefs of a society about *other* societies that enter into the formation of a state's identity. *Who are "they"?* I expect the answer to be determined by the particular substantive issue under study. *What do "they" do?* This question refers to the state's understanding of other societies' past and present historic missions and international roles. A corollary question is *What do "they" do to "us"?* This question gets at the society's perception of past and present interaction with other societies in question. A second question related to how a society views other societies' historical missions is *How do "they" do it?* The question probes the issue of threat definition and role definition as Wendt understands it. If a foreign society has pursued its historical missions militarily against a third society but not against "us," "we" may still assign this society the identity of aggressor. If the foreign society is militaristic toward "us" we will define them as an enemy. The final question is *How do "we" regard "them"?* This is the society's assignment of role and status to other societies based on its answers to the previous questions.

All the answers to these questions are interrelated and combine external and internal identity elements. The historical mission of the state is both a function of founding myths and historical interactions with other states. The sources of these missions are not determined only by, for example, Russia's historical treatment by other states, but also by the founding myths and contemporary discourse about the goals of the state. Russia's definition of its role in international affairs is influenced both by how it has been treated by other states and its leaders' beliefs about how it should have been treated. Russian leaders may believe Russia is a great power, even though it feels it is not treated as such by the Western great powers. In fact such perceived treatment of the Soviet Union by the West, rather than leading to Soviet identification of itself as a lesser power as we would expect from a role-identity perspective, led Soviet leaders throughout the Cold War to demand treatment as a great power. Russia's perception of its status is both a function of its historical missions as civilizing state and a big brother of all Slavs, and its feeling of inferiority toward the West. Which aspects of this status become salient at particular times is dependent on domestic politics (such as the political elite's quest for domestic legitimacy) and current international interactions (such as the Serbs' claim to Moscow's allegiance as the patron of its Slavic brothers), as well as on which issue area we analyze. Which domestic economic and political structure is considered appropriate by a state's elite is primarily an internal characteristic of national self-image, though its constitution as such may have been influenced by adaptation or learning from external actors.

The theorist then needs to ask, Which domestic and international aspects of identity are important for the purposes of my research interest? I argue that both internal and external aspects of identity are important to almost every study of identity, be it at the international system or domestic level, but the degree of importance will likely depend on the issue being studied. Finally, the analyst needs to ask, Where is collective identity located? Is collective identity located primarily in actors' heads or in social institutions and practices such as the state? Answering these latter two questions will enable the theorist to place themselves relative to Haas' and Wendt's conceptualizations of identity. Is collective identity located primarily in elites or publics? The answer to this question is largely determined by the analyst's substantive interest. If one studies the effect of collective identity on domestic politics, then publics must be taken into account. If one studies foreign policy, then a case can be made for emphasizing elite notions of collective identity.

As the questions above make clear, identity is both a constitutive and prescriptive concept. Without the prescriptive element, identity is a static concept, as it does not motivate us to become anything. Without the constitutive element, identity is ideology that is easily manipulable by actors. Let me make clear that the prescriptive element of identity is also inherently relational. Prescriptions are bases of comparison. An "ought" is defined by comparison with some other characteristic, action, or idea. When a society answers questions of what it ought to be and do, it is comparing itself with what others are and do. All the characteristics of identity above are based on *actors'* perceptions of what their state's identity is, what other states think it is, and what it ought to be. Social interaction shapes those perceptions, but identity neither floats above individuals prescribing their behavior, nor does it only come into being during interaction. Since identities are constitutive of state action, they shape the definition of a state's interests, which in turn may lead to a change in identity further down the road. Because identities entail prescriptions for state actions, they are regularly contested by domestic and foreign actors who question these prescriptions or state actions that result from them. In this way actors can change identities from within and from without.

I make this move to include actors' perceptions in the definition of identity because a role-taking conception of identity tends to be based almost entirely on structures of state interaction and power. This obscures the role of human creativity in developing those structures, and implies that state identities are fairly well specified, or easy to determine. Since I study Russia, I first have to determine whether we can speak of a Russian *state* identity, since even Russia's territorial sovereignty, one of the fundamental constitutive and regulative structures that define a state, is being violently and nonviolently contested from within. It is also hard to determine what kind of state-society relations exist in Russia, and what types of role identities it has with the West, the East and with the former Soviet republics. Therefore, in some places at some times, it is best to leave the existence of identity as an empirical question, and best not to assume that one exists.

If a constructivist research program is to be built, constructivists will need to sort out their analytic concepts, arrive at shared definitions, and specify the relationships between these concepts and other concepts familiar to international relations theory, such as interdependence, and power. Here I have taken a stab at the concept of identity, but much more work needs to be done on this, as well as on the concepts of culture, norms, rules, and ideas. Crisp conceptualization is important to the creation of a coherent research program. It is also important for the possibility of comparing constructivist arguments to other theories, and the development of scientific knowledge. Concepts and their relationships to one another constitute the fundamental assumptions of a research program. As constructivists are only now coalescing into something approaching a school of thought, conceptual confusion is not surprising. This is where much productive work by constructivists can be done. This discussion of conceptualization of identity formation also highlights the importance of agreement among constructivists about the mechanisms of how identities, and other social institutions, change. In the section below I take up this issue, suggesting that a theory of evolutionary learning may provide the basis for a unified constructivist theory of change.

Evolutionary Logic: Learning and Adaptation as Mechanisms of Structuration?

Emanuel Adler quite rightly argues that constructivists require a theory of institutional selection that accounts for why some social identities and institutions "stick" while others do not. He advocates a theory of cognitive evolution. His understanding of cognitive evolution bears quoting at some length:

> Cognitive evolution is a theory of international learning, if by learning we understand the adoption by policymakers of new interpretations of reality, as they are created and introduced into the political system by individuals and social actors. The capacity of institutions in different countries to learn and to generate similar interests will depend not only on the acquisition of new information, but also on the political selection of similar epistemic and normative premises. The political importance of these premises lies not in their being "true," but in their being intersubjectively shared across institutions and nation states.[63]

Currently, few constructivists place "learning" at the heart of their explanations. However, all constructivists are concerned with *the spread of collective ideas or knowledge*, either as the mechanism for change in identities, norms, cultures, and institutions, or as the mechanism by which current identities and institutions have come into being. Constructivists have described these mechanisms as learning, adaptation, or socialization. A necessary complement as Adler points out is a theory of selection. I believe that a constructivist theory of learning, built on the consensus of the centrality of the diffusion of collective ideas, can serve as the basis of a constructivist theory of change.[64] Below I discuss Haas and Wendt's work on learning before returning to cognitive evolution as a candidate theory of social change.

Ernst Haas makes collective knowledge the centerpiece of his study of nationalism. Whether particular types of collective knowledge spread among an elite and a public significantly influence the integration or disintegration of national communities. The nature of this collective knowledge is critical to the possibility of international integration, or moving beyond the nation-state.[65] Haas distinguishes between adaptation, or change in the beliefs about which methods to employ based on new information, and collective learning, which is consistent with complex learning, as actors come to question their implicit theories of cause and effect and question their values and goals in addition to the means to achieve them. Haas views new information as one of the key triggers of collective learning. Collective learning is a rare event, and adaptation is more common.[66]

Alexander Wendt, in his latest work on collective identity formation, focuses on learning as a mechanism of what he calls cultural selection. Cultural selection is "the transmission of the determinants of behavior from individual to individual, and thus from generation to generation, by social learning, imitation, or some other similar process."[67] Wendt sees social learning as more important than what he calls the imitation of successful others for collective identity formation (a conception similar to Haas' understanding of adaptation).[68] Wendt views social learning as social interaction that changes the identities and interests of actors, a definition that is compatible though not identical with Haas' and Adler's conceptualization.[69] Through the process of social interaction, and presumably the acquisition of new knowledge, actors transform their understandings of each other, and of the world around them. States that regard themselves as enemies may alter that identification to one of allies through repeated amicable interaction, if these states come to share a sense of common fate and exercise restraint in their reciprocal actions. For Wendt, then, it seems that social learning is potentially more pervasive.

Haas bases the process of learning in the human capacity to reason, whereas Wendt locates the process of learning in social interactions. The two theories of learning are not mutually exclusive, as the consensual knowledge that usually triggers Haas' learning is partly a result of social interaction, and Wendt allows that states may initiate a process of learning for instrumental reasons.[70] Without agreement on the frequency of learning and developing a consensual definition, constructivists will develop different theories of how actors' identities and interests are constituted, and how the actual process of structural change and reproduction works. Given the common elements shared by Wendt and Haas, the prospects for agreement on a theory of learning appear to be good, and this agreement may very well provide the basis for a deeper engagement among constructivists and a more unified constructivist theory of change.

The recognition that human beings can and do learn is an important addition to the study of international politics. The focus on the spread of collective knowledge by Haas, Wendt, and others distinguishes constructivist approaches from rationalist ones. Rationalists can explain simple learning, or adaptation to changes in price. By bringing human reason back into intentionality, constructivists enrich our intuitive understanding that humans can and do learn to overcome many of the social and physical structures that constrain them. Constructivists also remind us that the process of learning usually means the creation of new structures, such as identities. The recognition of learning adds an important element of agency to constructivist approaches. And it may serve as the bridge between the more individualist constructivists, like Haas, and the structural constructivists, like Wendt. The constructivist project needs a better account of how agency brings about change in structures,[71] and learning may serve the purpose. I agree with Adler when he says,

> A cognitive evolutionary theory [of learning] is structurationist to the extent that individual and social actors successfully introduce innovations that transform or even constitute new collective understandings, which, in turn, shape the identities and interests, and consequently the expectations, of social actors. Collective understandings, such as norms, are not sufficient cause for actions; individual agents must act, according to their identities and as their interests dictate. Domestic and international politics, however, may sometimes keep them from acting this way. . . . In any case, a cognitive evolutionary approach requires that new or changed ideas be communicated and diffused and that political stakes be created, which political groups may then help maintain through the use of power.[72]

Constructivists may be able to be agree on the role that such collective learning plays in producing both the social structures and the interests of actors in international affairs. The nature of learning, whether it is simple or complex, may be the key to developing a constructivist theory of change. Simple learning, or change in the beliefs about which means to employ based on new information (Wendt's imitation of successful others, and Haas's adaptation) may characterize or in some cases define the process of *reproduction* of extant social institutions. Complex learning, or recognition of a conflict among values, and a subsequent modification in goals as well as means, may capture the process of *change or alteration* of social structures, or may signal the onset of such a change.[73] Thus, learning may be the key to explaining social structural change, while adaptation may explain structural reproduction. Both however must include an explanation of timing and an account of the *political* process through which new collective identities are selected and institutionalized in order to create a constructivist theory of structural change.

Conclusion

Agreement on the social construction of reality, the potential for transforming international relations through the spread and institutionalization of collective ideas, and the interest in the development of elements of international society joins constructivists in a common project of demonstrating that theories based on rationalistic intentionality miss the effects that the interaction of agents with their social context have on international outcomes. In addition to the points of consensus that have been developed throughout this essay, however, constructivists are also joined by a common rejection of both positivism and relativism. Despite the variety of approaches taken by different constructivists, it is this epistemological convergence that can make the development of a coherent constructivist research program possible if conscious efforts in that direction are taken.

Constructivists reject the positivist claim that scientific knowledge can only be obtained with "the abstract, rigorous exercise of logical proof."[74] Primary among the reasons for this rejection is that positivist science encourages the development of theories whose assumptions may be completely unrealistic as long as they can generate powerful predictions. This puts positivist epistemology and formal methodology ahead of accurate explanation.[75] What separates constructivist scholarship from deductive rationalist approaches is its emphasis on laying out the specific, not logically determined, causal *mechanisms* which make an event necessary. Constructivists rely on induction or abductive inference and explanation and description instead of establishing a logical premise for an event through deduction.[76] These methods are the constructivist means of acquiring a better approximate knowledge of reality.

Constructivists generally agree that all observation is theory-laden. This does not prevent them from believing that the unobservable objects of theory may in fact be real, and that there is some basis for establishing our knowledge of them. Haas and Adler agree with Wendt and Dessler that there is an external, independent reality to be studied, and this further separates them from relativists and postmodernists. Social scientists "must accept a belief in the existence of an external world."[77] In this constructivists differ from those critical theorists, feminist theorists, poststructuralists, and postmodernists who accept a relativist philosophy of science and interpretivist epistemology.[78] Constructivists also reject the relativist position that "there is no consensual or true knowledge based on science,"[79] and the postmodern position that reality *is* discourse.[80] They agree that scientific reasoning can increase our knowledge of external reality. They tend to disagree on the extent to which scientific knowledge is permanent.[81] However, because scientific reasoning is designed to be self-critical and self-correcting, constructivists agree that we can develop scientific methods for generating and evaluating scientific knowledge of the social world.[82] For these reasons, constructivist research can be compared to rationalist work.

In many respects constructivist scholarship complements as well as challenges rationalist approaches, by unpacking the assumptions that rationalists make about what interests actors have and how world politics is structured. Moreover, the rationalist and constructivist approaches can fruitfully build off each other, recognizing the limitations of one-sided analyses and incorporating each others' insights in the process of building theories that better capture and explain world politics.

The sociological turn in international relations is able to generate new insight and understanding of how international relations operate, what the elements of international order are and how they develop, what national interests are, and how national and state identities constitute those interests. It also generates new hypotheses about the sources and processes of change. It may create a coherent research program if differences over levels of analysis, the relative importance of agents and structures, conceptualizations of change, and learning can be overcome. Whether this happens or not, in this chapter, I have sought to lay the basis for building a constructivist conception of identity formation. I have attempted to demonstrate the possibility of creating a constructivist theory of change based on a distinctive ontology and epistemology, and I have emphasized the importance of the substantive focus driving the constructivist research program—the development of international society. These are small steps toward the consolidation of a constructivist research tradition and the crossing of the boundary between sociology and IR, but the prospects and payoffs of the subsequent cumulation of constructivist knowledge about world politics are likely to be positive.

These prospects of the sociological turn in international relations theory come at the cost of parsimony and the hope of objective, transhistorical knowledge. Constructivists focus on historically and geographically contingent processes, and appreciate that where the theorist cuts into the process of international relations will shape what she sees. However, the gains to science are the cumulation of knowledge already produced by constructivist research, and the progressive refinement of such knowledge through comparison and critique with work in the rationalist tradition. Whether these gains justify the costs depends on the reader's ontological and epistemological commitments, not on "science."

Notes

1. I have more fully elaborated on the possibility of a constructivist research program and the issues that unite and divide constructivists elsewhere. See Anne L. Clunan, "Prospects and Pitfalls of a Social Constructivist Approach to International Relations" (paper presented at

the International Studies Association Annual Meeting, Toronto, Canada, March 18–22, 1997). Given space limitations, I cannot develop here what the requirements for a successful research tradition are, and the full extent to which constructivists meet and fail to meet these requirements. Very briefly, the requirements are: (1) ontological and epistemological agreement; (2) agreement on appropriate methods of analyzing politics; (3) consensus on the major mechanisms of change; and (4) an overarching substantive interest that joins researchers.

2. Peter Berger and Thomas Luckmann, *The Social Construction of Reality* (New York: Anchor Books, 1966).

3. See Clunan (1997) for a fuller development of these issues.

4. See Alexander Wendt, *Social Theory of International Politics* (Cambridge: Cambridge University Press, 1999) chapter 3.

5. For examples see the contributions to Peter J. Katzenstein, ed., *The Culture of National Security: Norms and Identity in World Politics* (New York: Columbia University Press, 1996), John Gerard Ruggie, "Territoriality and Beyond: Problematizing Modernity in International Relations," *International Organization* 47, 1 (1993a): 139–174, and his "Multilateralism: Anatomy of an Institution," in *Multilateralism Matters*, ed. John Gerard Ruggie (New York: Columbia University Press, 1993b), Audie Klotz, *Norms in International Relations: The Struggle Against Apartheid* (Ithaca: Cornell University Press, 1995a), and Ernst B. Haas, *Nationalism, Liberalism, and Progress* (Ithaca: Cornell University Press, 1997). For an analysis of sociology's contribution to international relations theory, see Martha Finnemore, "Norms, Culture, and World Politics: Insights from Sociology's Institutionalism," *International Organization* 50, 2 (1996): 325–347.

6. Robert Powell, "Anarchy in International Relations Theory: The Neorealist-Neoliberal Debate," *International Organization* 48, 2 (1994): 318.

7. Paul Kowert and Jeffrey Legro, "Norms, Identity, and Their Limits: A Theoretical Reprise," in Katzenstein (1996): 463, and Ernst B. Haas, "Reason and Change in International Life," *Journal of International Affairs* 44 (1990a): 32.

8. Alexander Wendt, "Collective Identity Formation and the International State," *American Political Science Review* 88 (1994): 384–396, and Wendt (1999).

9. Ruggie (1993a): 157.

10. Emanuel Adler, "Cognitive Evolution," in *Progress in Postwar International Relations*, ed. Emanuel Adler and Beverly Crawford (New York: Columbia University Press, 1991): 48, and Wendt (1999): chapter 2.

11. Emanuel Adler, "The Emergence of Cooperation: National Epistemic Communities and the International Evolution of the Idea of Nuclear Arms Control," *International Organization* 46 (1992): 101–145.

12. Wendt (1994, 1999).

13. Kowert and Legro in Katzenstein (1996): 468.

14. For a sampling of neorealist works, see Kenneth Waltz, *Theory of International Politics* (Reading, Mass: Addison-Wellsley, 1979), Stephen D. Krasner, "State Power and the Structure of International Trade," *World Politics* 28 (1976): 317–347, and his "Westphalia and All That," in *Ideas and Foreign Policy*, ed. Judith Goldstein and Robert O. Keohane (Ithaca: Cornell Unliversity Press, 1993), as well as Robert Gilpin, *War and Change in World Politics* (Cambridge: Cambridge University Press, 1981). For the neoliberal institutionalist position, see Robert O. Keohane, *International Institutions and State Power* (Boulder: Westview Press, 1989) and his *After Hegemony* (Princeton: Princeton University Press, 1984).

15. See Ernst Haas' and Karl Deutsch's work on integration and changes in identification, and Hedley Bull's work on international order and society. Hedley Bull, *The Anarchical Society* (New York: Columbia University Press, 1977), Karl W. Deutsch, *Nationalism and Social Communication* (Cambridge: MIT Press, 1953), *The Nerves of Government* (London: Free Press of Glencoe, 1963), Karl W. Deutsch et al., *Political Community in the North Atlantic Area* (Princeton: Princeton University Press, 1957), Ernst B. Haas, "Words Can Hurt You: Or Who Said What to Whom about International Regimes," *International Organization* 36, 2 (1982): 207–244, *Beyond the Nation State* (Stanford: Stanford University Press, 1964), and *The Uniting of Europe* (Stanford: Stanford University Press, 1958).

16. Haas (1982): 241.

17. On human rights, see Klotz (1995a), and her "Norms Reconstituting Interests: Global Racial Equality and U.S. Sanctions Against South Africa," *International Organization* 49, (1995b): 451–478. On security communities, see Thomas Risse-Kappen, *Cooperation among Democracies* (Princeton: Princeton University Press, 1995). Ruggie studies the creation of the postwar liberal economic order in John Gerard Ruggie, "International Regimes, Transactions, and Change: Embedded Liberalism in the Postwar Economic Order," *International Organization* 36, 2 (1982): 374-415. See Wendt (1994, 1999) for studies of international societal change.

18. Bull (1977), 13. Bull's usage of institutions is a sociological one. In the constructivist literature, the term "institutions" have been used interchangeably with "rules," "norms," "structures," or "practices." "Insti-

tutions" are generally understood to mean social practices that have become taken-for-granted and which structure meaning and action. There is obvious difficulty in using these terms interchangeably, since norms, rules, and practices may or may not be taken for granted, and institutions may be either social or concrete organizations. This is an issue which I cannot fully develop in this chapter.

19. For overviews of the new institutionalisms in sociology and politics, see Walter W. Powell and Paul J. DiMaggio, eds., *The New Institutionalism in Organizational Analysis*, 1st ed. (Chicago: University of Chicago Press, 1991), and Sven Steinmo, Kathleen Thelen, and Frank Longstreth, eds., *Structuring Politics* (Cambridge: Cambridge University Press, 1992).

20. Kathleen Thelen and Sven Steinmo, "Historical Institutionalism in Comparative Politics," in Steinmo, Thelen, and Longstreth (1992): 4–5.

21. Thelen and Steinmo (1992): 9.

22. See Berger and Luckmann (1966) and John Searle, *The Construction of Social Reality* (New York: Free Press, 1995) for explanations of the social construction of reality. Note that Anthony Giddens in *Central Problems in Social Theory* (Berkeley: University of California Press, 1979) and *The Constitution of Society* (Berkeley: University of California Press, 1984) offers a different conception of structuration theory than Roy Baskhar's, *The Possibility of Naturalism* (Atlantic Heights, N.J.: Humanities Press, 1979).

23. Roger Friedland and Robert R. Alford, "Bringing Society Back In: Symbols, Practices, and Institutional Contradictions," in Powell and DiMaggio (1991).

24. Thelen and Steinmo in Steinmo, Thelen, and Longstreth (1992) and Emanuel Adler, "Seizing the Middle Ground: Constructivism in World Politics" (paper presented at the International Studies Association Annual Meeting, Toronto, Canada, March 18–22, 1997). The latter was later published under the same title in *European Journal of International Relations*, 3 (1997): 319–363.

25. Wendt (1994): 384.

26. I define collective identity as a set of ideas that are generally accepted by a group of individuals as defining their society. These ideas are not necessarily endorsed by all members of society at all times. One can accept that the United States is a capitalist society without endorsing capitalism. I use the term with this definition in mind. This definition differs from Wendt's usage. Wendt uses collective identity to mean a specific type of identity in which a state sees itself as like other states—as part of a "we" of several states. I prefer to think of this as a *collectivist* state identity to keep it distinct from the more generic concept of collective identity.

27. Deutsch (1957) and Haas (1958).
28. Alexander Wendt, "Anarchy Is What States Make of It," *International Organization* 46, 2 (1992): 406.
29. See Wendt (1994, 1999) for his discussion of the process of identity formation, and the formation of a collectivist state identity in Western Europe.
30. See the contributions by Robert Herman, Thomas Berger, Thomas Risse-Kappen, and Michael Barnett to Katzenstein, ed., *The Culture of National Security* (1996), and Wendt (1999). All references in this section are to this Katzenstein volume.
31. Peter J. Katzenstein, "Introduction: Alternative Perspectives on National Security," Katzenstein (1996): 6.
32. Ronald L. Jepperson, Alexander Wendt, and Peter J. Katzenstein, "Norms, Identity, and Culture in National Security," in Katzenstein (1996): 59, fn. 85.
33. Robert Herman, "Identity, Norms and National Security," in Katzenstein (1996): 275, 283, 285.
34. Herman in Katzenstein (1996): 274, fn. 6. My emphasis.
35. Berger in Katzenstein (1996): 318.
36. Thomas Risse-Kappen, "Collective Identity in a Democratic Community," in Katzenstein (1996): 366–367. My emphases.
37. Michael Barnett, "Identity and Alliances in the Middle East," in Katzenstein (1996): 403.
38. Kowert and Legro in Katzenstein (1996): 453.
39. Kowert and Legro in Katzenstein (1996): 452, fn. 1.
40. Wendt (1992): 404 and (1999): chapter 7. Wendt draws on Mead's and Stryker's work on symbolic interactionism and role formation. See George Herbert Mead, *Mind, Self, and Society* (Chicago: University of Chicago Press, 1934) and Sheldon Stryker, *Symbolic Interactionism: A Social Structural Version* (Menlo Park: Benjamin/Cummings, 1980).
41. Wendt (1994): 385.
42. Wendt (1994): 385.
43. Wendt (1999): chapter 8.
44. Alexander Wendt, "The Agent-Structure Problem in International Relations Theory," *International Organization* 41, 3 (1987): 365–369.
45. Wendt (1994): 385, and Jepperson, Wendt and Katzenstein in Katzenstein (1996).
46. Haas (1997), Risse-Kappen in Katzenstein (1996) and Ruggie (1982).
47. Haas (1997): 24–25, 29.
48. Haas (1997): 43.
49. Haas (1997): 23 and 324.
50. Haas (1997): 23, 38–40.

51. Haas (1997): 2.
52. Haas, *When Knowledge Is Power* (Berkeley: University of California Press, 1990b): 23–24.
53. Haas (1990b): 128–129.
54. Haas (1997): 23.
55. Wendt (1999): chapter 7.
56. I would like to thank the members of the Working Group on the Role of Norms and Identity in Cooperation in the Former Soviet Union and Western Europe, sponsored by the Institute of International Studies at the University of California, Berkeley and the MacArthur Foundation Program on Multilateral Governance, for considerably sharpening my thinking about the conceptualization of identity.
57. While his conceptualization of identity formation does not emphasize external roles and actors, his empirical research gives more importance to these factors. See Haas (1997).
58. Jepperson, Wendt, and Katzenstein in Katzenstein (1996): 59, fn. 85.
59. Yeltsin called for the creation of a "national idea" in the winter of 1996.
60. Wendt (1994): 385.
61. Wendt (1987): 365–369.
62. Wendt (1999): chapter 7.
63. Adler (1997): 27.
64. Development of theories of change is one of the most significant contributions constructivists can make to the study of politics. Constructivists should draw on work in social psychology in generating and correcting such theories. As there is no universally accepted theory of learning in psychology, constructivist cannot adopt a model of learning wholesale. Instead we should employ candidate theories, and determine under what circumstances they appear to apply in political and international life.
65. Haas (1997), especially introduction and conclusion. See also his early work on international integration, *The Uniting of Europe* (1958) and *Beyond the Nation State* (1964).
66. Haas (1990b): 3 and (1997): 17.
67. Boyd and Richerson, (1980): 102, cited in Wendt (1999): chapter 7.
68. Wendt (1999): chapter 7.
69. Wendt (1999): chapter 7.
70. Wendt (1999): chapter 7.
71. Kowert and Legro in Katzenstein (1996): 470–492.
72. Adler (1997): 27.
73. For a comprehensive discussion of learning as it is applied to international affairs, Jack S. Levy, "Learning and Foreign Policy: Sweeping a Conceptual Minefield," *Intentational Organization* 48, 2 (1994): 279–312.

74. Bruce Bueno de Mesquita, David Newman, and Alvin Rabushka, *Forecasting Political Events: The Future of Hong Kong* (New Haven: Yale University Press, 1985): 129, cited in Wendt (1999): chapter 2.
75. Friedrich V. Kratochwil and John Gerard Ruggie, "Intemational Organization: A State of the Art on the Art of the State," *International Organization* 40, 4 (1986): 753–775.
76. Wendt (1987): 354–354. While I agree that abductive inference separates constructivists from logical empiricists, I disagree that constructivism entails the epistemology of scientific realism. Abduction is not the sole preserve of scientific realism, and even those who Wendt calls antiscientific realists (Larry Laudan is singled out) may rely on abduction.
77. Epistemological differences remain among constructivists. For an analysis of these differences see Clunan (1997). See David Dessler, "What's at stake in the agent-structure debate?," *International Organization* 43, 1 (1989): 441–473, and Wendt (1987, 1999) for two different explications of the scientific realist epistemology. For explanation of evolutionary epistemology, see Haas (1990a): 209–240, Adler (1991) and Donald T. Campbell, "Evolutionary Epistemology," in *The Philosophy of Karl Popper*, Vol. 14, 1, ed. P. A. Schilpp (LaSalle, IL: Open Court Publishing Co., 1974): 413–463. The quotation is from Haas (1990a): 221–222.
78. Adler (1997): 3 and Peter´J. Katzenstein, Robert O. Keohane, and Stephen D. Krasner, "*International Organization* and the Study of World Politics," *International Organization* 52, 4 (1998): 677.
79. Haas (1990b): 221.
80. Adler (1997), Wendt (1987) and Katzenstein, Keohane and Krasner (1998): 678.
81. See Clunan (1997), and Haas (1990b): 223.
82. Haas (1990b): 228–232, and Dessler (1989). See also Wendt (1999): chapter 2.

5

COLLECTIVE IDENTITY AS AN "EMOTIONAL INVESTMENT PORTFOLIO"

An Economic Analogy to a Psychological Process

TADASHI ANNO

Identity has become a "buzzword" in various branches of the social sciences and humanities. In international relations, too, there has been a veritable explosion of interest in the concept of identity, the sources of identities, and their implications.[1] But, as in the case of many fashionable concepts that have appeared, disappeared, and reappeared in the social sciences, the study of identity in international relations has become the object of yet another methodological battle that tends to yield more heat than light. On the one hand, theorists who emphasize the importance of identity invoke the concept often without a clear conception of what it is. On the other hand, others summarily dismiss the concept of identity as simply irrelevant to the study of the central issues that ought to constitute international relations.

Theorists of identity agree that identity concerns the question of who one is, that identity gives one a sense of security and continuity. Others add that identity is linked with one's sense of self-respect.[2] But often the concept of identity (or more particularly, collective identity) is left unclear in terms of its significance within a broader theory of social action. As a result, the discussion of identity in international relations, as in other social science disciplines, is often characterized by uncomfortable fuzziness. This makes the very notion of identity rather suspect in the eyes of the uninitiated.

Rational-choice theorists, for example, have either chosen to ignore the concept, or tried to interpret the phenomenon of identity within rational choice framework.[3] The result is a persistent and theoretically counterproductive division between economisic approaches emphasizing the centrality of interests in international life on the one hand, and more sociologically oriented approaches (as discussed in the chapter by Clunan) that emphasizes the importance of collective norms and shared identities without relating these to interest.

As one of the "foundational" concepts in social science, the notion of "identity" defies disciplinary boundaries and transcends methodological divides. It is necessary, therefore, to develop a broader framework for understanding the phenomenon of identity that represents a theoretical middle ground between rational-choice and sociological approaches while transcending standard boundaries between disciplines and subfields. In this essay, I search for such a theoretical middle ground by exploring the uses and limitations of an economic analogy in analyzing the psychological process of identity-formation. I argue that we should develop a more clear-cut concept of identity, and locate it within the framework of general theories of social action in such a way as to clarify the relationship between interests and identities. Without clarifying the relationship between interests and identities, we will likely be left with a fruitless and endless debate pitting rational choice theorists against identity theorists. Moreover, we should also make more effort at understanding the dynamics of the *formation* of identities. Without some understanding of the process of identity formation, the concept of identity will become another explanatory *deus ex machina* that in fact explains nothing.

In this essay, I specifically address four related points. First, I attempt to clarify the position of collective identity in relation to a general theory (or model) of social action. Second, I discuss the implication of the phenomenon of collective identity for the behavior of groups, and to clarify the relationship between identity-based and interest-based explanations of group behavior. Third, I advance a novel hypothesis on the mechanism of the formation of collective identities. I call my approach an "emotional investment portfolio" approach, for it seeks to understand the process of identity formation and the politics of identity by an analogy with the investment decisions of the investors and their impact on the "fund managers." As is evident from the metaphor of the financial market, my approach suggests the utility of an analogy—if not the theory—of rational choice in accounting for the dynamics of the formation of identities. Yet, the analogy also clarifies the limitations of rational-choice arguments by pointing to the possible role of the "subversion of rationality" in the process of identity-formation.[4] Finally, I illustrate the utility of the "emotional investment portfolio" approach to collective identity-formation by applying it to the case of Japanese national identity, with some comparative references to Russia.

The approach presented here has emerged out of my research into a concrete historical problem: the evolution of national identity and its effects on relatively backward countries, specifically Japan and Russia (1860–1945).[5] A central issue in the modern history of relatively backward countries is the impact of the West and the problem of national identity: namely, how to reconcile the pursuit of continuity in distinctive national traditions with the pursuit of status, security, and welfare in the modern world. It is in the course of drawing general lessons from this comparison that I have come to appreciate the significance of national identity in the analysis of international life. This in turn led me to a more theoretical investigation of the phenomenon of collective identity presented here. I have found the approach developed below useful in my empirical research, but discussion of this research is limited to a bare minimum in this chapter, for my purpose here is to introduce an interdisciplinary analytical tool and to illustrate its utility rather than to prove a historical point. The approach presented below does not represent an alternative "paradigm" or a full-blown model of social action, but it does offer a useful, synthetic framework for a more comprehensive understanding of the phenomenon of identity without being restricted to any one discipline, subfield or paradigm.

Social Theory and the Concept of Collective Identity

Any discussion of "collective identity" presupposes a general theoretical framework or model of human action that goes beyond the individualistic theory of rational choice commonly found in economics and in some other branches of the social sciences. To oversimplify for the sake of clarity, "orthodox" versions of rational-choice theory assume that individuals are self-regarding and rational. That is to say, it is assumed that individual actors are interested in their own individual welfare,[6] and that they pursue their interests by calculating the best course of action, based on best available information.[7] The implication of this model for group behavior is that individual actors form groups only when it is in their individual interest to do so. Group behavior, according to this model, is nothing more than a "bundle" of coordinated individual behavior. Similarly, organizations are understood to be products of rational calculus for minimizing transaction costs.[8] In this manner, groups and collectivities are consistently "reduced" to the ultimate unit of social explanation: the rational, self-contained individual. From this perspective, the phenomenon of collective identity remains incomprehensible.

Although there is a great deal of discussion at present regarding the prospects for a new, unifying rational-choice "paradigm,"[9] the core theoretical assumptions and propositions that supposedly define this paradigm are hardly new to the social sciences. In explaining group action by reference to the self-interests of rational individuals, contemporary theorists of rational choice are simply carrying on the core tradition of modern social/political thought, which takes autonomous, self-regarding individuals as its starting point, and attempts to interpret social groups through the prism of voluntary associations.[10] But the critique of modernity is as old as modernity itself. The notion of autonomous, self-contained individual has been subjected to criticisms from various quarters from the very inception of modernity. This is not a place to discuss, let alone resolve the diverse and far-flung philosophical debates on modernity or on individualism. Yet some telling criticisms that have been raised against the modern individualistic conception of human beings are quite relevant for our purposes. According to these critics, individuals belong to groups not only because they calculate that it is in their individual interest to do so. They also derive from group membership diverse *emotional* benefits—benefits that are not to be obtained through conscious, goal-oriented action. We may generally divide these "emotional benefits" into two major categories: (1) concern for *continuity and security*; and (2) concern for *recognition and prestige* of one's own group.

These two types of emotional benefit jointly constitute the core of the phenomenon of identity. The first category of benefits is the more fundamental of the two. If "identity" is indeed an answer to the question of who one is, this answer cannot be given without reference to the past and the future. If our lives consisted of a bundle of random, unconnected events, we would not have a sense of personhood.[11] Individuals are individuals only because the past, the present, and the future are constantly connected and reconnected in our psyche.[12] From this derives the need for maintaining *continuity* in our life. In the model of rational choice, this element of personal continuity is "boiled down" to the assumption of continuity of preferences. Yet, our sense of personal continuity is dependent not only on what is within ourselves, but to some extent, what surrounds us. Individuals often develop emotional attachment to people and things that they are familiar with. These people and things become part of their "way of life" that give them a sense of *security*. Membership in a group, especially communities (groups that are bound together by more than rational calculation of interests) can be an important guarantor of the individual's sense of security.[13] These groups provide the individual with a sense of continuity that is essential for individuals to maintain sanity and to function efficiently.

The second type of emotional benefit is closely linked to the first. Individuals, in trying to make sense out of their lives, strive for *recognition* by others.[14] Having a recognized place in society may be part of what gives individuals a sense of security in society. Yet, the striving for recognition goes beyond the simple desire to be recognized and understood. Individuals also attempt to gain a sense of *self-respect*. They want their lives not only to be coherent, but also to be meaningful and worth living. Moreover, while individuals search for recognition and self-respect primarily at the personal level, they also extend the search to those groups with which they are identified. To the extent that individuals are emotionally attached to the groups that they belong to, individuals want their groups to be recognized and respected in the wider world. The emotional benefit of recognition and respect as a member of a group, in turn, may provide individuals with an additional incentive for group identification.

The phenomenon of collective identity (including national identity) is closely related with these emotional benefits of group membership. Identity is one's answer to the question of who one is. For individuals to function effectively, this question must be answered in such a way so as to address both the concern for continuity/security and the concern for recognition/respect. Since membership in communities provide individuals with such important "psychological goods" as the sense of security and meaning, individuals usually "identify" with certain collectivities; that is to say, these groups are felt to be the *extension of the individual self*.[15] In so far as individuals identify with their collectivities, the "management" of the latter becomes a matter of concern for individual members. Individuals identified with groups want the groups to be "managed" in such a way as to address their concern for continuity/security and for recognition/respect. The "management" of the collectivity consists not only in allocation of material resources. Most of all, successful management of the collective identity involves articulating a "vision" for the collectivity that satisfies the emotional needs of the individual members.[16]

The theory of public choice tells us that collective goals of social groups are ultimately reducible to the individual interests of the members. But the perspective on motivations for group membership outlined above suggests that the collective goals of societies such as polities are not necessarily limited to the pursuit of aggregated individual interests. It can also involve the *management of collective identity* of the group that serves as a guarantor of individuals' sense of continuity and security, and as a depository of their sense of self-respect. To the extent that this is true, our analysis of the behavior of groups must take into account the dimension of collective identity.

Identities, Interests, and Public Policy

Aspiration for belonging to and identifying with some collectivities may be universal to human psyche, but the central objects of identification have changed over time. For reasons that I am not prepared to address in this chapter, "nations" have come to occupy a central position as a locus of individual loyalty in the modern era.[17] Modernization theorists have argued that such concern for collective identity is characteristic of traditional status societies, and it would either disappear or at least become negligible as societies modernize.[18] I do not address the question of whether rational calculation of individual interests alone can provide a sufficient basis for a viable society. Here, I limit myself to the observation that collective identity continues to play a significant role in international relations, including those countries where nationhood is defined in civic rather than in ethnic or cultural terms.

Rational-individualistic theorists attempt to reduce the phenomenon of nationalism into individual interests as far as possible by emphasizing the instrumental use of nationalist propaganda by political "entrepreneurs." In doing so, they provide a much-needed antidote to the reification of the collectivity that is characteristic of nationalists. Also, as I argue below, the analogy between politicians and "entrepreneurs" is quite useful. Yet, a strictly instrumental approach to nationalism (and more generally to role of ideas in history) is ultimately ineffective, because political entrepreneurs can use ideas instrumentally for their political purposes only when there are at least some "true believers." Why such "true believers" in nationalist myths exist in the first place cannot be explained unless we consider the fact that individuals have collective identities, and to that extent, they need to believe in those myths that answer their psychic needs for continuity, recognition, and self-respect. One might also add that there is little justification for the implicit, dualistic assumption that cool-headed, power-seeking politicians are a different brand of people than the general masses, who are foolish enough to be duped by the politicians' machinations. If there are "true believers" among the people, it is reasonable to assume that some politicians are true believers, too.

Public policy, then, is not just about arbitration and organization of individual interests. It also concerns the management of the "collective identities." This means that major strategic choices made by polities in the sphere of foreign policy, long-term economic policy, and social and educational policy often imply certain choices in the identity of the collectivity. In making strategic choices, political elites in modern nation-states have not simply searched for the best way to satisfy their nations' (or their own) economic, security, and political interests; they have also searched for ways of satisfying the demands of managing the collective (national) identity.

Many acknowledge that both identities and interests matter. But, how are these two related? There are at least three logically possible ways of conceptualizing the relationships between identities and interests (see Figure 5.1). The first group of theorists (including some recent theorists of identity in international relations) prioritizes identities over interests by arguing that interests can be defined only in the context of given identities.[19] The second group (rational choice theorists) argues that identities may be reduced to interests, one way or another.[20] The third group looks at identities and interests as two separate factors that operate independent of each other.

My own position is closer to this last view. I regard the pursuit of interests and expression of identities as two distinct modes of behavior through which human beings strive to satisfy their physiological and psychic *needs*.[21] In both modes of behavior, ideas (perceptions, causal beliefs, worldviews) play an important mediating role by informing our conceptions of interests and identities. But while identity-oriented behavior is *expressive* in its pure form,[22] interest-oriented behavior is *purposive* by definition. Thus, in effect, interests and identities are distinct from each other, and the two concerns coexist as separate factors affecting behavior.

Obviously, some types of behavior can be explained by interests alone, without reference to identities. Other types of behavior are almost purely expressive and have no purposive content. But the two concerns may become intertwined in complex ways. Sometimes, our need to act out our identities create certain conceptions of interests as a derivative effect.

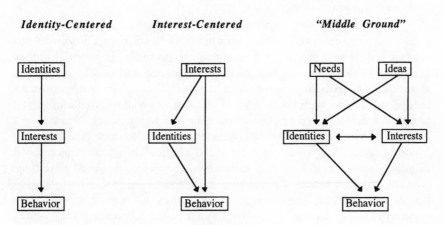

Figure 5.1
Alternative Conceptions of the Relationship
among Interests, Identities, and Behavior

Contrariwise, some actors may feign certain types of identity (e.g., a civilized, democratic country") in pursuit of material interests.[23] Alternatively,
certain actions can be purposive and expressive at the same time. Indeed,
this last possibility is an important one for students of public policy, for in
making important strategic decisions, political leaders can hardly ignore
their vital interests in security and welfare, and at the same time, such
momentous choices must of necessity affect conceptions of collective identity. Thus, as far as strategic policy choices are concerned, we may safely
assume that the choices matter from the point of view of both interests and
identities.

The Dynamics of National Identity Formation

So far I have argued that strategic choices made by political elites can be
affected both by interests and identities. But how do the two factors interact in concrete historical contexts? Below, I will explore this issue, focusing
on the cases of relatively backward countries faced with the impact of
Western civilization. A common problem faced by these countries was how
to reconcile the desire for the continuity of "national traditions" with the
pursuit of status, security, and welfare in the modern world. On the one
hand, relatively backward countries had to borrow the technologies, institutions, and practices developed in the West if they were to secure survival
and prosperity. To some extent, the search for recognition and respect for
the nation simply tended to reinforce the pursuit of security and welfare—
for "respect" in the international society often came with the achievement
of wealth and power.[24]

   On the other hand, successful management of national identity also
required maintaining the sense of continuity of "national traditions." Citizens wish their nation to be recognized and respected in the world, but they
wish their nation to be respected for *what they are,* rather than for having
abandoned cherished "national traditions." This desire for continuity
tended to interfere with the pursuit of security and welfare. In addition, the
search for national self-respect could also become a major hindrance to
conformity to prevailing international standards and norms. "Slavish" imitation of foreign ways was often regarded as humiliating, and was resisted
for this reason. This was especially true when elites believed that their
country had no chance of improving its international status by following
the Western path of development. In such cases, elites in relatively backward countries often resorted to theories of "transvaluation," which
claimed that the success of the West was essentially a sour grape, and that
the discredited native traditions of their own country in fact provided a
superior model.[25] Thus, for relatively backward countries of the "non-

West," the choice of strategic alternatives was shaped by a complex inter-action between interests and identities, between the need to be recognized and respected in the world as well as the need to maintain the continuity of "national traditions."

This process of formation and evolution of national identities is in many ways analogous to financial investments. National identities (and collective identities in general) may be usefully understood as "emotional investment portfolios." The analogy yields a useful set of hypotheses about the formation of collective identities. As we shall see, this analogy is far from perfect, but it is useful as a metaphorical and heuristic device to illu-minate the complex dynamics of identity-formation.

First of all, the content of personal or collective identity is similar to financial portfolio in that at any given point, identity consists of a collec-tion of "emotional investments" in various symbols, things, and groups. Each of these symbols is assigned by public opinion (by world public opin-ion in the case of national identities) certain "values" in the market for "respect." The total "value" of a nation's emotional investment portfolio is the sum of the "market value" of these symbols, each multiplied by the weight of the nation's emotional investment in it.[26] We are flattered by favorable comments on the symbols that we are attached to, and we tend to react negatively to any attacks or threats to these symbols, as we would to a fall in the price of stocks that we own.

Second, like investors in the stock market, individuals with emotional investments in symbols strive to maximize the value of their portfolio by "buying" (identifying) or "selling" (disowning) those "stocks" (or sym-bols) so as to secure the highest possible "returns" (respect).[27] When the respect value of certain symbolic assets (such as constitutions, colonial pos-sessions, or the gold standard) increases, nations rush to acquire those "assets" in the hope of increasing the value of their emotional investment portfolio.[28] Conversely, a decline in the respect value of a symbolic asset induces its "sell-off." Obviously, the investment strategy is subject to severe "budget constraints." In the case of national identity, native or assimilated cultural elements in the nation's history serve as the "endowments" that can be used in the investment. These "endowments" impose elastic yet real constraints in what sort of cultural symbols one can invest in. For instance, in the nineteenth century, "European civilization" was a very prestigious symbol that many elites in the non-European world wished to identify with. But such an option was obviously not available to every nation.

Third, the role of political leaders may be compared to the role of fund managers at investment banks. Even though national identity exists nowhere except in the heads of *individual* members of the nation, the power of each individual to influence the affairs of the collectivity is quite limited, just as average individual investors are powerless to influence today's giant corporations. Thus, political leaders are entrusted (explicitly or implicitly) by the members of the nation to manage the public affairs in such a way as to maximize the value of the "emotional investment portfolio" of the nation. By adopting major public policy decisions, political leaders not only address the questions of interests; in so doing, they also channel the "emotional investment" of the nation in certain directions. The concept of "political entrepreneurs" takes on a deeper meaning when placed in this context. The concept is intended to capture the process of political competition in which power-seeking politicians propose alternative programs to capture popular support. While the concept of political entrepreneurship is usually nested in a rationalistic understanding of the political process, the metaphor of "emotional investment portfolio" shows that the concept sheds some light to the politics of identity as well.

Yet, the analogy with the stock market also clarifies important differences between financial and emotional "investments." First, emotional "investment" is characterized by a high level of inertia. As I pointed out earlier, identity concern involves not only craving for respect, but also for continuity and security. This tends to magnify the obstacle for changes in the investment portfolio. Purchasing and selling off of emotional assets is rarely a clear-cut, one-time deal as in the financial market. Assimilation of new elements into the portfolio may face tenacious resistance from those committed to the old ways. To use Albert Hirschman's terminology, the market for emotional investment is characterized by a high degree of customer "loyalty." For this reason, "entry" and "exit" are often quite difficult.[29]

Second, in the market for symbolic assets, values are essentially subjective. The market for respect does not have a single currency that serves as a unified measure of values.[30] Rather, it is a market where a number of mutually incommensurable currencies vie for influence. While world public opinion provides some guideline, different people have different value assessments of the same symbol, and hence of the same investment portfolio. For instance, Russia's commitment to Europe was a positive emotional asset for "Westernizers" of the nineteenth century, but for Russophiles, this was not the case. The anarchy of currencies mean that there is no single "optimal" portfolio mix that satisfies every "customer." The subjectivity of values also means that "the bottom line" can be improved not only by wise investment strategy, but also by skillful manipulation of the measure of valuation. By manipulating the value standard according to which nations were measured (transvaluation), elites in relatively backward societies could psychologically compensate for the debilitating sense of inferiority vis-à-vis the West.

Third, the valuation of "respect" a nation enjoys is subjective in another sense—and here the investment analogy really begins to break down. In the market for respect, "when everybody's somebody, then no one's anybody." That is to say, the satisfaction to be gained from any given portfolio mix of a nation is relative to the nation's own past performance, and to the performance of other nations that serve as the "reference point" for that nation.[31] For the relatively backward societies of the modern era, the West was the reference point of paramount importance. But as we shall see in our empirical illustrations, other points of reference (Asia in the case of Japan) could play a significant role in the process of formation of national identities. Satisfaction with the respect value of a nation's emotional investment portfolio depended on the baseline against which the nation was being measured. Hence, manipulation of reference groups provided another way in which elites in relatively backward countries could compensate for their sense of inferiority vis-à-vis the West.

The final and most fundamental difference, however, is the mode of "decision making" in the two markets. In contrast to financial markets, investment decisions in the market of symbolic assets are usually not the results of rational calculations of benefits and costs. Take, for instance, our identification with favorite sports teams.[32] The emotional benefits to be gained from this "investment" are clear: vicarious experience of the drama of struggle and victory, and the sense of solidarity with other fans. However, few people would choose their favorite sports teams based on a careful calculation of the team's past performance, the degree of excitement involved, and the number of fans of the team around us. A gambler bets on sports teams (or horses) because he thinks they have the best chance of winning. By contrast, a fan emotionally invests in "his" or "her" team because it happens to be his or her favorite team. The emotional benefits of psychological investment is often dependent on the "non-utilitarian" nature of our relationship with the objects of identification.[33] While our choice of objects of identification may be guided by some sort of calculus, the emotional benefits of identification can be obtained only if this calculus is "repressed" and hidden from our consciousness. For this reason, the formation of identities must be an emotional rather than a rational process.

An Empirical Illustration: Japan and Russia between East and West

How does the "investment" analogy developed above illuminate concrete historical cases? Here, I will illustrate the utility of our model by using the case of Japanese national identity as an example. In the process, I will also make some comparative references to the Russian case.[34]

The fact that the Japanese civilization had developed on the periphery of the Chinese world order[35] before it encountered the Western impact in the mid-nineteenth century is central to any discussion of modern Japanese national identity. By virtue of its size, and by virtue of having provided the basic framework of civilization for the area, China was for two millennia the undisputed center of the East Asian world. Like other "peripheral" countries in East Asia, Japan was profoundly influenced by Chinese civilization. Japanese elites, like elites in other peripheral civilizations of East Asia, traditionally suffered from inferiority complex vis-à-vis China. For a small minority of elites who were aware of Japan's position in East Asia, the problem of how to maintain and enhance self-respect of the country in the face of overwhelming evidences of Chinese superiority was a matter of acute concern.

Since Chinese civilization carried much prestige in East Asia, an obvious strategy of emotional investment was to define Japan's "protonational" identity in terms of similarity to China. While this strategy was constantly attempted, it was not quite effective, because the Japanese could not match up with China in terms of sheer size and in the historical achievement of having founded a great civilization. Even though many Japanese elites wished to shore up the image of their land by identifying it with China, the "budget constraints" (real differences between the two countries) precluded the long-term success of this strategy.

Attempts to define Japanese identity in terms of proximity to China was particularly ineffective because of Japan's "relative distance" from China in comparison with Japan's immediate neighbor, Korea. By virtue of geographical proximity to China, Korea was, throughout much of history, a better student of Chinese civilization than Japan was, and often acted as a "creative transmitter" of advanced civilization to Japan. Korean elites often took pride in their country's position as a "small brother" of China. Obviously, Korean elites suffered from the same inferiority complex toward China which the Japanese had to grapple with. But since Korea was "relatively proximate" to China (compared with Japan and other peripheral countries), Korean elites could take solace in the notion that their country is the most civilized among "barbarian" countries. A similar strategy of manipulation of reference groups was not available to Japanese elites, because Japan was literally on the edge of the Chinese world.

The strategy adopted by the Japanese elites in gaining a sense of self-respect vis-à-vis China was twofold. First, they invested heavily in the few "bright spots" in their emotional investment portfolio.[36] Second, they invented a variety of theories of transvaluation, designed to overturn the criterion according to which the "value" of emotional investments were measured. Ideology of transvaluation was hoisted to the level of fine art by scholars of the "National Learning" school during the Tokugawa period (1603–1868). Their writing is a testimony to the vainglory and creativity of human beings faced with the problem of regaining self-respect.[37]

The impact of the West changed this traditional picture entirely. China's defeat in the Opium War (1840–1842) was a major shock to the Japanese elites. Within a few decades, the Japanese switched their "model civilization" from China to the West. Japanese intellectuals' effort to combine Japanese traditions with Chinese importation was summarized in the slogan, "Japanese spirit, Chinese Learning" (*wakon kansai*). With the advent of the Western impact, a new slogan was developed to suit the new era: "Japanese spirit, Western learning" (*wakon yosai*). The easy substitution of the West for China in these two slogans (which was accomplished by substituting one Chinese character for another) is symptomatic of the relative ease with which the Japanese elites shifted their model from China to the West. Because Japan had suffered from inferiority complex vis-à-vis China, and thus had not invested too heavily in the Chinese civilization, the collapse of the Chinese world order was not so painful for the Japanese elites. This was in striking contrast to the case of the Chinese and the Koreans, who had invested heavily in the tradition of Chinese civilization.

Not only was it relatively easy for the Japanese to shift their "model civilization" from China to the West. What is more, the context for the definition of national identity had changed from a dyadic one, involving China and Japan, to a "triadic" situation, involving the West, Japan, and the rest of Asia. In this new triad, Japan emerged as the most "advanced" or "Westernized" country in Asia. Taking advantage of Japan's "relative proximity" to the West (compared with the rest of Asia), many among the Japanese elites adopted a "small brother" doctrine vis-à-vis the West, and assumed a condescending attitude toward her "stagnant" neighbors in Asia. It was as if an asset that had been kept idle in the sluggish stock of "Japanese nativism" could suddenly be reinvested in the growth stock of Western civilization. Small wonder that the slogan of "exit from Asia, entry into Europe" became the keynote of modern Japanese history.

To the extent that Japan remained backward vis-à-vis the West, Japanese intellectuals continued to suffer from a sense of inferiority. The absolute cultural distance between Japan and the West was much larger than the distance between Japan and China had been. But while the need for psychological compensation for inferiority complex remained, the strategy of compensation now adopted was markedly different from the previous ages. The strategy of transvaluation was conspicuously absent from Japanese nationalist ideologies of the modern era. Except for the 1931–1945 period, Japanese nationalists defined Japan's national identity in terms of Japan's relative proximity to the West, somehow trying to combine this with the notion of Japan's "uniqueness." Japan's "national mission" was defined not in terms of spreading a uniquely Japanese (or Asian) principles, but in terms of building a bridge between the East and the West, or even spreading Western civilization to the East.[38] Even as the nationalists deplored the loss of traditional culture, they approved of the improved international standing of Japan, which was a result of the Westernization of the country. In this instance, international recognition and respect gained from Westernization more than compensated for the moderate costs of gradual changes. The real cost of this strategy was that it fostered among the Japanese a condescending attitude toward their Asian neighbors—an attitude that became appallingly manifest during Japan's expansion into Asia.

As Japanese intellectuals shifted their model of civilization from China to the West, two intellectuals living in another "peripheral" country observed this process with acute interest, and recommended that their country do something similar. The country was Russia, and the writers were N. V. Shelgunov and M. L. Mikhailov—two representatives of nativist, agrarian socialism known as Populism in Russia. They were criticizing the slavish imitation of Western Europe by their compatriots, and their recommendation was to look elsewhere: America.[39] But their strategy of manipulation of reference groups, unlike Japan's shift from China to the West, could not quite succeed.

Like Japan, Russia started her historical development on the periphery of a great civilization—Byzantium.[40] Because of the sheer size of the country, its natural environment, and geographical distance from Constantinople, Russia, like Japan, developed a distinctive national culture early on. From the sixteenth century onward, Russia was increasingly exposed to the impact of the rising, Western civilization. An important difference between the Russian and Japanese case was the fall of the Byzantine empire at the hands of the Ottoman Turks in 1453. Unlike Japan, which had remained a "peripheral" country within the Chinese world order, Russia since the mid-fifteenth century emerged as the center of the Orthodox civilization.[41] Russia did not develop a secure consciousness of centrality, because Russia was soon faced with the challenge of the rising, Western civilization. But since Russia had become the "center" of the Orthodox world before she encountered modern Western civilization, Russia's position vis-à-vis the West was different from Japan's. In terms of absolute cultural distance, Russia was obviously closer to Europe than Japan was. Yet, Russia was *relatively distant* from Europe, because she did not possess a valid point of reference in contrast to which she could define herself as proximate to Europe.

Beginning from the eighteenth century, Russian elites emphasized Russia's belonging to the European family of nations. But this strategy was self-defeating in the long term, given Russia's "relatively distant" position in relation to the Western civilization. The sense of belonging to Europe led the Russian elites to judge Russian achievements against the European standard.[42] But measured against the leading countries of Europe, Russia was found wanting in many respects. Theoretically, of course, Russian elites had the option of emphasizing Russia's proximity to Europe in contrast to East Asia or to the Muslim world. However, since Russia never belonged to the East Asian or Muslim world, Russians could not derive much comfort from the notion of superiority over Asian peoples.[43] Another possible strategy of manipulation of reference groups was the one recommended by Shelgunov and Mikhailov—the strategy of building a coalition of young, continental states (Russia and America) against stale, old, smaller countries of Western Europe.[44] Yet in the love triangle involving Russia, Europe, and America, the tie between Europe and America has generally proved to be the more stable one, and it has more often been the fate of Russia to be left alone in search of an ally.

Deprived of the strategies of identification with Europe and of manipulation of reference groups, Russian nationalists often turned to the strategy of transvaluation.[45] In most relatively backward countries, ideologies of transvaluation boiled down to contrasting the sour grapes of the materialistic, egoistic civilization of Europe with the spiritual, organic tradition of the country. While this path most often led non-Western nationalists to turn away from the West completely, the case of Russia had a particular twist, because Russia's sense of self-respect could be fully satisfied only when her place was recognized by European states. Thus, from Slavophilism of the 1830s and 1840s to the Populism of the late-nineteenth century to the revolutionary theory of Leninism, Russian ideologies of transvaluation were characterized by an ideological one-upmanship in which Russia claimed to represent the "truer" version of European principles. In this connection, the prediction that the French conservative thinker Joseph de Maistre made in 1848 proved remarkably prescient: 'Yesterday Russia claimed, 'I am Christianity.' Tomorrow, she might say, 'I am socialism.'"[46]

Conclusion

This chapter has argued that the phenomenon of collective identity should be taken seriously, and that our theoretical "toolbox" for analyzing this phenomenon in the broader framework of social action should be enriched by linking economistic understandings of interests to psychological dimensions of emotional gratification in the identity-formation process. Collective identities constitute an important part of the identity of individuals.

They occupy an important place in our conception of who we are, where we come from, and where we are going. They also tells us why our collective national life is "meaningful," and what kind of behavior is needed to keep or make it meaningful. By doing so, collective identities perform the important function of providing individual members with the sense of security, continuity, recognition, and self-respect. To the extent that we make emotional investments in groups, the strategic choices for groups can become a matter of expression of collective identity as much as an issue of rational pursuit of individual interests.

I have not offered a new unifying "paradigm" or developed a new grand "general theory." Instead, I have laid out a set of concepts and hypotheses based on an analogy between emotional and financial investments for the sole purpose of understanding the complexity of collective identity-formation. The illustrations provided above are no substitutes for rigorous "testing" of any of the hypotheses. But they are sufficient to show that at least in some cases, the analogy serves as a useful metaphorical-heuristic device that can generate some hypotheses on the processes of identity-formation. The content of identities tends to be defined in such a way as to maximize the value of the nation's emotional investment portfolio, within the constraints imposed by the concern for continuity and security. This process, however, is complicated by the availability of essentially psychological strategies for gaining self-respect, namely, the manipulation of reference groups and ideologies of transvaluation.

The importance of collective identities for the study of international relations should be obvious. In the wake of the Cold War, the contradiction between liberal individualism and collectivist nationalisms have become all too evident. Historically, the development of liberalism in Western Europe was closely linked with the consolidation of a strong national state. But from the very beginning, this alliance of nation-states and liberalism concealed within itself a fundamental contradiction. As Friedrich List pointed out already in 1841,[47] liberalism is an individualist *and therefore cosmopolitan* doctrine which provides no justification for the division of the world into separate states, except for expediency-based reasons, such as the technical efficiency of governance, and the difficulty of communicating across languages.[48] In the eighteenth and nineteenth centuries, there may have been good technical reasons for nation-states, on the basis of which nationalists and liberals could form an alliance. But that is now a thing of the past.

It is important to note that I do *not* treat the problem of collective identity as something limited to those areas of the world where ethnic nationalisms are creating violent conflicts and ugly ethnic cleansing. Whether civic or ethnic, nation-states treat individuals differently on the basis of citizenship, and this differential treatment is now increasingly being challenged by the trend toward globalization. Why do average children born in Japan, Germany, or the United States deserve a better opportunity to achieve higher standards of living than their peers in Malaysia, Turkey, or Mexico? (Or Bangladesh, Cameroon, or Bolivia for that matter?) Orthodox liberalism provides no answer to this question. If "inheritance" of national wealth is considered legitimate, it is only because we treat nations somewhat like families, as exclusive communities bound together by the ties of collective identity.

I am not proposing to use the notion of collective identity to provide justifications for the perpetuation of international income inequality. I am rather making a theoretical point that the logical consequence of purely individualistic liberalism can only be cosmopolitan, and that the Grotian-Wilsonian solution of "liberal internationalism" cannot be sustained theoretically, unless we find a way to incorporate the phenomenon of collective identity into our theoretical toolbox for the analysis of social action, and thereby start a more informed discussion about the place that culture and identity should occupy in international life.[49] It is for this reason that the question of collective identity constitutes a central issue in contemporary theories of international relations.

Acknowledgements

I thank Pierre Ostiguy, George Breslauer, and the volume's editors for helpful comments.

Notes

1. Yosef Lapid and Friedrich Kratochwil, eds., *The Return of Culture and Identity in IR Theory* (Boulder: Lynne Rienner Publishers, 1996); Peter J. Katzenstein, ed., *The Culture of National Security: Norms and Identity in World Politics* (New York: Columbia University Press, 1996); and Alexander Wendt, "Collective Identity Formation and the International State," *American Political Science Review* 88, 2 (June 1994): 384–396.
2 Among many works on the general question of identities, I have found the following works useful: Michael A. Hogg and Dominic Abrams, eds., *Social Identifications: A Social Psychology of Intergroup Relations and Group Processes* (London: Routledge, 1988); Craig Calhoun, "The Problem of Identity in Collective Action," in Joan Huber, ed., *Macro-Micro Linkages in Sociology* (Beverly Hills: Sage, 1991).
3. A recent, sophisticated discussion of identity from the point of view of rational choice theory is Russell Hardin, *One for All: The Logic of Group Conflict* (Princeton: Princeton University Press, 1995).

4. Jon Elster, *Sour Grapes: Studies in the Subversion of Rationality* (New York: Cambridge University Press, 1983).

5. Tadashi Anno, *The Liberal World Order and Its Critics: Nationalism, State Interests, and the Rise of Anti-Systemic Movements in Russia and Japan, 1860–1945* (Ph.D. Dissertation in progress, University of California, Berkeley).

6. Sophisticated theorists of rational choice make allowance for the phenomenon of "utility interdependence," that is, the possibility that the utility of one individual depends on that of others. "Sympathetic" individuals' utility covary positively with those of others, while malicious individuals derive happiness from other people's misfortunes.

7. The model of rational choice is summarized succinctly in Jon Elster, ed., *Rational Choice* (Oxford, UK: Basil Blackwell, 1986), chapter 1. See also idem., *Sour Grapes*, chapter 1. Of course, many theorists who are basically "rational choice" in orientation allow for the possibility of incomplete information, cognitive short-cuts, and other limitations of rationality.

8. Mancur Olson, *The Logic of Collective Action* (Cambridge: Harvard University Press, 1971); Oliver Williamson, "The Economics of Organization: The Transaction Cost Approach," *American Journal of Sociology*, 1981.

9. This is perhaps most explicit in the field of comparative politics as evident in the recent debates between rational-choice theorists and defenders of area-studies and cultural theory. See Robert Bates, "Rational Choice and Culture"; David Laitin, "Game Theory and Culture"; and Ian Lustick, "Culture and the Wager of Rational Choice," in *APSA-CP: Newsletter of the APSA Organized Section in Comparative Politics*, 8, 2 (Summer 1997): 5–23.

10. George H. Sabine, *A History of Political Theory*, 4th ed. (Hinsdale, IL: Dryden Press, 1973), p. 401.

11. Bertrand Russell once argued that just as there is no such thing as "France" over and above its various parts, so there is no "Mr. Smith" apart from the various observable "occurrences" associated with this proper noun (such as the pattern of colors we see, the series of sounds we hear, etc.). "Mr. Smith," then, is simply a collective name, a "mere imaginary hook" from which the various "occurrences" are supposed to hang. See Bertrand Russell, *A History of Western Philosophy* (London: George Allen & Unwin, 1979), pp. 211f. This may be good philosophy, but certainly not a formula for sanity—for most people at least.

12. Cognitive psychology has consistently emphasized the individuals' need to maintain "cognitive consistency," and how that need some-

times "distorts" our perception of reality. See Donald R. Kinder and Janet A. Weiss, "In Lieu of Rationality: Psychological Perspectives on Foreign Policy Decision Making," *Journal of Conflict Resolution* 22, 4 (December 1978), pp. 707–733.

13. Durkheim's famous study of suicide becomes comprehensible in this context. What he found was that rate of suicide is consistently higher among those social categories that are "cut off" from communities that provide individuals with a sense of security. See Emile Durkheim, *Suicide: A Study in Sociology* (Glencoe: The Free Press, 1951).

14. On the "recognition" aspect of identity, see Charles Taylor, "The Politics of Recognition," in Amy Gutman, ed., *Multiculturalism: Examining the Politics of Recognition* (Princeton: Princeton University Press, 1994), pp. 25–73.

15. This phenomenon of collective identity cannot be captured by the notion of "utility interdependence." For instance, during the Olympic games, we root for athletes from our own country not necessarily because we can empathize with them more deeply than with athletes from other countries; rather, we root for "our own" team because we feel our own country to be an extension of our "selves." Ability to sympathize with the athletes *as individuals* (i.e., utility interdependence) is not required in this process.

16. The role of these "visions" are especially important for satisfying the cravings for self-respect. The creation of mythologies for the collectivity (e.g., nationalist ideologies) is an important part of the management of collective identity.

17. For some interesting hypotheses, see Ernest Gellner, *Nations and Nationalism* (Ithaca: Cornell University Press, 1983); Benedict Anderson, *Imagined Communities: Reflections on the Origin and Spread of Nationalism*, 2nd ed. (London: Verso, 1988).

18. For a short, representative statement of the thesis, see Talcott Parsons, *Societies: Evolutionary and Comparative Perspectives* (Englewood Cliffs, NJ: Prentice-Hall, 1966), pp. 22–23.

19. See Ronald L. Jepperson, Alexander Wendt, and Peter J. Katzenstein, "Norms, Identity, and Culture in National Security," in Katzenstein, ed., *The Culture of National Security*, pp. 33–75, esp. pp. 52f.

20. Russel Hardin (fn. 3) comes close to this position.

21. I emphasize the distinction between needs and interests. The former are "raw" and rather amorphous human desires or "drives" that motivate us from "behind" the realm of our consciousness. Interests, by contrast, belong in the realm of our consciousness, and as such, are informed by our understanding of the world (ideas). Since it is informed by our understanding of the world, interests have more spe-

cific directions than do pure physiological or psychic needs. My main disagreement with rationalistic explanations of identities (e.g., Hardin, fn. 3) hinges on this distinction. Whereas Hardin emphasizes the role of "interests" in the formation of identities, I argue that identity-formation is a largely unconscious or semiconscious process that is driven by needs rather than a conscious process driven by calculation of interests.

22. In identity-oriented behavior, actors behave in such a way as to express their identification with certain objects such as groups, symbols, or norms. If the actors' identification with the objects is sincere, their behavior is driven by the need to prove to themselves and to others who they are. The point of identity-driven action is the *process* of expression of the identity, rather than *ultimate outcome* which is expected to result from our action.

23. In such cases, the "acting out" of the constitutive norms of an identity may assume a ritualistic, rather than a genuinely expressive character. For many Americans, holding (and participating in) free elections may be genuinely expressive of their sense of "what America is about." For leaders of authoritarian regimes trying to secure financial support from the West, elections may have little more than ritualistic value.

24. Gerrit W. Gong, *The Standard of 'Civilization' in International Society* (Oxford, UK: Clarendon Press, 1984).

25. For an illustration of the concept of transvaluation with reference to the problem of relative backwardness, see Joseph Levenson, Confucian China and Its Modern Fate (Berkeley: University of California Press, 1968).

26. For instance, for a German nationalist of the late-nineteenth century, his "national identity investment portfolio" may have included heavy investment in a sense of belonging to "European civilization" (as opposed to Asiatic and African barbarism), substantial commitment to German distinctiveness focusing on its peculiar history (*Sonderweg*), and much emphasis on the achievements of German scholarship (Kant, Hegel), music (Beethoven, Brahms, Wagner), and literature (Goethe, Sciller), plus pride in Bismarck's political achievements since 1862, and in the growing economic and military power of the *Reich*. To the extent that these symbols (from Kant to Beethoven to victory in the Franco-Prussian War) evoke the respect of non-Germans, his investment portfolio has high "respect value."

27. Albert Einstein is reported have said: "If my theory of relativity is proved successful, Germany will claim me as a German and France will say I am a citizen of the world. Should my theory prove untrue, France will say that I am a German and Germany will declare that I am a

Jew"; quoted in Ernst B. Haas, *Nationalism, Liberalism, and Progress: The Rise and Decline of Nationalism, Volume 1* (Ithaca: Cornell University Press, 1997), pp. 1–2. This is an example of expediency-driven labeling by others. Something similar takes place in our own self-definition. For instance, since 1991, politicians and intellectuals in the three Baltic republics (and more generally, in the former Soviet-bloc states outside of Russia) have been busy trying to "sell off" the "symbolic asset" of communism, which was an imposed gift in the first place and which has long since become an emotional liability.

28. This is exactly what happened in Eastern Europe in the late-nineteenth century. In Romania, for instance, the constitution was accepted in part because the elite had what one scholar, Joseph Rotshchild, called "fetishistic fascination . . . with foreign politico-legal models"; quoted in Kenneth Jowitt, *The Leninist Response to National Dependency* (Berkeley: Institute of International Studies, 1978). In Hungary, a finance minister called for the adoption of the gold standard because Hungary cannot tolerate "the stigma of a paper economy unworthy of a civilized nation"; Koloman Szell, quoted in Leland B. Yeager, "The Image of the Gold Standard," in Michael D. Bordo and Anna J. Schwartz, eds. *A Retrospective on the Classical Gold Standard, 1821–1931* (Chicago: University of Chicago Press, 1984), p. 657

29. Albert O. Hirschman, *Exit, Voice, and Loyalty: Responses to Decline in Firms, Organizations, and States* (Cambridge: Harvard University Press, 1970).

30. Respect is inherently relative, and the "supply" of respect within a given society is limited. In this sense, respect is a type of what economists call "positional goods"—or, goods that are sought after not so much because of any intrinsic quality they possess as because they compare favorably with others in their own class (a "good" school, most sought-after jobs, mates, etc.). The "market" for respect is a peculiar type of market where relative gain counts. Mercifully, measurements of respect (at least self-respect) is essentially subjective, and this relativity of value tends to alleviate the potentially fierce competition for positional goods. On positional goods, see Robert H. Frank, *Choosing the Right Pond: Human Behavior and the Quest for Status* (New York: Oxford University Press, 1985), pp. 3–16.

31. The sociological theory of reference groups is relevant in this context. See, for instance, Robert K. Merton, *Social Theory and Social Structure*, enlarged ed. (New York: The Free Press, 1968), pp. 279–440; and R. Frank, op. cit.

32. My argument here is inspired by a stimulating discussion of the topic in Hardin, pp. 46–71.

33. If a rich country decides that it wants more gold medals in Olympic games, the easiest way to achieve this goal would be to lure the top athletes from other countries by offering monetary incentives, perhaps handsome retirement plans. "Muscle drain" of athletes from poor to rich countries does, in fact, take place, but the whole point of the Olympic games will be lost if it becomes too evident that the tie binding the athlete to a country is only financial.

34. The discussion draws on the following works, as well as on my original research: Sadao Nishijima, *Nihon rekishi no kokusai kankyo* [The International Context of Japanese History], (Tokyo: Tokyo University Press, 1985); Seizaburo Sato, "Bakumatsu Meiji shoki ni okeru taigai ishiki no sho-ruikei" [Conceptions of International Relations in Japan during the Late-Tokugawa to Early-Meiji Era] in Seizaburo Sato and Roger Dingman, eds., *Kindai Nihon no taigai taido* [Modern Japan's Attitudes toward the Outside World] (Tokyo: Tokyo University Press, 1974), pp. 1–34; and Marius Jansen, "On Foreign Borrowing," in Albert M. Craig, ed., *Japan: A Comparative View* (Princeton: Princeton University Press, 1979), pp. 18–44.

35. For a general discussion of Chinese world order, see John K. Fairbank, ed., *The Chinese World Order: Traditional China's Foreign Relations* (Cambridge: Harvard University Press, 1968).

36. It is well-known that the name of the country Japan (*nihon* in Japanese) means "the land of the rising sun," but the psychological function that the name has performed is less well understood. The exact origin of this name is shrouded in mystery, but experts agree that a letter sent by the Japanese emperor to the Chinese emperor in 618 was one of the first instances of usage of this term. In the letter, the Japanese emperor referred to himself the "emperor of the land of the rising sun," and addressed the Chinese emperor as "the emperor of the land of the setting sun." The point of the letter was to contrast rising Japan with declining China. While there is no way of proving the point definitively, it seems clear that the name of the country reflected the fact that Japan's geographical position and its association with sunrise was one of the very few things that Japanese elites could be proud of in the face of overwhelming sense of inferiority vis-à-vis China.

37. For instance, Norinaga Motoori (1730–1801), the greatest of the National Learning scholars, made the paradoxical argument that the cultural backwardness of Japan is itself an evidence of her superiority: "It is wrong to assume that China is better than Japan simply because civilization developed there earlier. In fact, Chinese civilization developed early because everything changes rapidly in China, due to the false and superficial character of the Chinese ways. . . . By contrast, our

Imperial country changes more slowly, because of the honest and serious ways of our country. . . . Speaking of the pace of change, animals such as cows, horses, roosters, and dogs grow quite fast, while humans grow more slowly. By analogy, we might say that great things change slowly." Quoted in Sato, *"Bakumatsu . . ."* p. 9.

38. Japanese ideologists of imperial expansion wrote with enthusiasm about Japan's mission to "civilize" Asia. One prominent ideologue of expansion, Soho Tokutomi, even wrote an essay on "the Yellow Man's Burden." For Japanese ideologies, see Marius B. Jansen, "Japanese Imperialism: Late Meiji Perspectives," in Ramon H. Myers and Mark R. Peattie, eds, *The Japanese Colonial Empire, 1895–1945* (Princeton: Princeton University Press, 1984), pp. 61–79.

39. Appealing to Russia's younger generation in 1861, they wrote: "Recently, we see more and more precociously old men. . . . They want to make Russia look like England. But is there anything common between the two countries? We are already aping the French and the Germans. Do we still have to become the apes of the Britons?" Turning their eyes to Asia, they went on to say: "China's neighbors do not know of countries more civilized than China. . . . Now the Roschers and Molies [referring to German economists of the historical school] of China would tell them that the law according to which the Chinese civilization developed is precisely the law according to which all nations have to develop. The neighbors believe this and try slavishly to become like China with all their might. But all of a sudden, there appear other civilizations with different aspirations unknown to the Chinese. . . . Those who look to Europe do not realize that things are very different in America." Shelgunov and Mikhailov were attempting to transform the "dyadic" situation of Russia versus Europe (in which Russia must be defeated by comparison) into a "triadic" situation where the rising, new states of Russia and America may look favorably in comparison with old, stale Europe. See N. V. Shelgunov and M. L. Mikhailov "K molodomu pokoleniiu [To the Younger Generation]," in N. K. Karataev, ed., *Narodnicheskaia ekonomicheskaia literatura: Izbrannye proizvedeniia* [Populist Economic Literature: Selected Works], (Moscow: Izdatel'stvo sotsial'no-ekonomicheskoi literatury, 1958), pp. 83–98.

40. On the position of Russia in the Byzantine world, see Dmitry Obolensky, *The Byzantine Commonwealth* (New York: Praeger, 1971).

41. From the middle of the fifteenth century, Russian rulers began to refer to themselves as *tsar'*, a title which derived from the Roman title Caesar, and which had previously been reserved for Byzantine (and later Mongol) rulers. Tsar Ivan III (ruled 1462–1505) married Sophia Pale-

ologus, the niece of the last emperor of Byzantium, and appropriated the Byzantine double-headed eagle to his family coat of arms. In this way, he dramatized the "transfer of empire" from Byzantium to Moscow. It was around this time that some Russian monks developed the notion of Moscow as the "Third Rome" (after Rome and Constantinople), the seat of true Christianity.

42. The Populist V. P. Vorontsov explained this quite clearly: "Russia belongs to the family of civilized nations. . . . This means that her needs and the forms of their fulfillment are measured not against her own backward culture, but with those forms which Western Europe developed and put into practice." See his *Sud'ba kapitalisticheskoi Rossii* (The Fate of Capitalist Russia), St. Petersburg: M. M. Stasiulevich, 1907, p. 194.

43. In contrast to the Japanese case, "mission" in Asia did not arouse much excitement in the Russian public opinion. See Dietrich Geyer, *Russian Imperialism: The Interaction of Domestic and Foreign Policy, 1860–1914* (New Haven: Yale University Press, 1987), conclusion.

44. After World War II, when the United States emerged as the center of the West, some Soviet theoreticians resorted to another strategy of manipulation of reference groups—Euro-Soviet coalition against the United States. Gorbachev, for instance, emphasized the ties between Russia and Europe, and ominously referred to the danger of an onslaught of "mass culture" from across the Atlantic that is encroaching upon the "high culture" of Europe (including the USSR). See Mikhail S. Gorbachev, *Perestroika: New Thinking for Our Country and the World,* 2nd. ed. (New York: Harper and Row, 1988), p. 194. See also Frederick C. Barghoorn, *The Soviet Cultural Offensive: The Role of Cultural Diplomacy in Soviet Foreign Policy* (Princeton: Princeton University Press, 1960), pp. 226–267.

45. V. V. Bervi-Flerovskii explained this mechanism with unusual candor when he wrote in 1869: "If we continue to go along the path we have taken so far, we will be forced to remain at the tail of the civilized world forever. . . . Such a situation cannot but disturb the national pride of every Russian." He then went on to attack contemporary European civilization, and to argue that Russia should follow a new, better way to civilization. See his *Izbrannye ekonomicheskie proizvedeniia.* Moscow, 1958–1959, Vol. 1; pp. 561ff.

46. See Hans Kohn, *Pan-Slavism: Its History and Ideology* (University of Notre Dame Press, 1953), p. 103.

47. In his landmark book, List pointed out that the classical "political economy" of Adam Smith and David Ricardo was in fact a "cosmopolitical economy," and contrasted it with his national system of

political economy. Friedrich List, *The National System of Political Economy*, trans. Sampson Lloyd (London: Longmans, Green & Co., 1928).

48. Some liberal European thinkers (Hume, Montesquieu, and Kant) did come up with a more positive rationale for the division of Europe into states—the argument that the competition among different parts contributed to the general progress of Europe. On this point, see F. H. Hinsley, *Power and the Pursuit of Peace: Theory and Practice in the History of Relations Between States* (New York: Cambridge University Press, 1963), pp. 153–185. This argument does not answer the question why competition among *individuals* of an all-European state is not enough to stimulate progress. In making the argument for division of Europe into states, these thinkers were accepting an essentially culturalist (and thus collectivist) understanding of states.

49. Recent attempts to develop a theory of "liberal nationalism" represents a much needed step in this direction. See, for example, Yael Tamir, *Liberal Nationalism* (Princeton: Princeton University Press, 1993); Michael Lind, *The Next American Nation; The New Nationalism and the Fourth American Revolution* (New York: Free Press, 1995); and Yasusuke Murakami, *An Anti-Classical Political-Economic Analysis: A Vision for the Next Century* (Stanford: Stanford University Press, 1996).

PART TWO

REORIENTING
THE FOUNDATIONS?

6

AGAINST EPISTEMOLOGICAL ABSOLUTISM

Toward a "Pragmatic" Center?

RUDRA SIL

The philosophical foundations for a systematic science of social and international life have long been the subject of highly contentious debates that transcend disciplinary and methodological boundaries. Over the past two decades these debates have become more intensified. As social scientists have themselves failed to reach consensus on questions of method and evaluation, the very foundations of positive social science have come under fire from postmodern skeptics who argue that "questions of fact, truth, correctness, validity, and clarity can neither be posed nor answered."[1] Committed positivists have responded by simply dismissing relativistic approaches and doggedly pursuing a unified science of social and international life based on replicable methods of empirical investigation and uniform standards for evaluating theories. Although most postmodernists or interpretive scholars offer quite sophisticated and valuable insights on the basis of their context-specific interpretations and their deconstruction of texts, these insights are simply dismissed out of hand by positivists insisting on an adherence to strict and uniform standards and methods for scientific inquiry. For their part, the postmodern skeptics show no appreciation for the methods and research products of positivist science as they apply to particular contexts or situations. The result is the fragmentation of the community of scholars studying international life even where they share a common interest in a particular set of phenomena or a particular historical episode.

This chapter represents a modest effort to help bridge the vast chasm between these epistemological "absolutists" and, in the process, to improve the level of communication among a wider community of scholars embracing a variety of epistemological positions. Below, I proceed by first identifying a wide range of nuanced, intermediate positions between logical positivists and postmodern relativists, positions that have explicitly or implicitly informed many of the great works of social science. These positions are evident in philosophical assumptions made in regard to such questions as the objective/subjective nature of social reality; the role of empiricist and deductive logic in forming trans-contextual generalizations; the purpose of social analysis and the significance of the investigator's biases and normative commitments; and the question of how interpretations and theories might be evaluated in the absence of uniform methods of verification or falsification.[2] This chapter identifies not a dichotomy but a "spectrum" of distinct perspectives on these questions, and seeks to define a "pragmatic" epistemological middle-ground from which to proceed. Such a middle-ground is not offered as a superior or definitive alternative to logical positivism or postmodern relativism. Rather, given the low likelihood of a lasting consensus on the philosophical foundations of the social sciences, it is seen as a more flexible and practical approach that allows for greater communication among a larger number of scholars despite the diversity of their epistemological orientations.

The Problem of Social Reality:
A Weberian "Intersubjective" Ontology

The postmodern skeptic and the committed "hard" positivist at least implicitly espouse diametrically opposed perspectives on a number of quite familiar issues concerning the possibility of identifying and analyzing "social reality." At one extreme, the postmodern skeptic calls into question the very possibility of "representation" in social life, thereby summarily rejecting the theoretical endeavors of social scientists along with their epistemological assumptions, their application of scientific methods, as well as their "objective" empirical findings. At the other extreme, the "hard" positivist continues to posit an external social reality that is distinct from the subjective consciousness of actors and is governed by objective "laws" of human behavior. The sole objective in the social sciences, then, is to develop generally applicable theories about social phenomena based on the identification of "lawlike regularities" and discrete cause-and-effect relationships by trained scholars whose personal values are rendered unproblematic by adherence to uniform rules of observation and inference. There are, however, interesting differences *among* different kinds of "positivists" and "relativists," and these differences suggest the possibility of more differentiated and nuanced set of entirely reasonable intermediate positions.

Even to nineteenth-century positivists, Comte's vision of a unified positive science of social and natural reality went too far. Kant, for example, argued that social reality was fundamentally different from natural reality, and that social phenomena had to be understood within the realm of "practical reason," and not simply through the "pure reason" employed to analyze natural phenomena. But there were still universal categories (time, space, etc.) that existed *prior* to the individual subjects' categorization of experiences; it was through these universal categories that all human beings perceived their subjective experiences, thereby allowing social scientists to make sense of a common social reality.[3] In challenging Comte, Kant sought to rescue and refine positivism, and it is this Kantian version of positivism that either explicitly or implicitly informs many theories in the contemporary study of international life.

Other positivists tend to draw on the philosophical empiricism apparent in the ontologies of Hume, Mill, and Durkheim. Hume and Mill questioned not only the Comtean notion of objective social and natural laws but also Kant's universal categories given the complexity of social reality. However neither viewed the subjectivity of individual human experiences as a logical challenge to the possibility of objective observations of social phenomena. Thus, rather than dismissing the idea of a positively founded social science altogether, Hume opted for an empiricist approach oriented toward a systematic, objective knowledge of sequences that lead to actions and events.[4] Mill, too, had reservations about applying inductive methods of comparative analysis to social phenomena, but he also insisted that the only thing that separated the social sciences from the natural sciences was the *degree* of confidence the scientist could possess in his or her explanations and predictions.[5] Durkheim rejected both Kant's separation of universal categories from subjective experience and Hume's emphasis on non-causal inferences drawn from lawlike regularities. Instead, Durkheim held that the only social reality that mattered was one that could actually be observed in the interactions and relationships between people within collective settings; these regular interactions were related to aspects of individual consciousness, and represented "social facts" with observable and measurable aspects.[6] Kant, Hume, Mill, and Durkheim did not question the existence of an objective social reality, but their refinements to Comte's logical positivism undermined the notion of a monolithic positive philosophy and unintentionally pointed to the possibility of a more nuanced ontology of social reality.

At the other end, the idea that the subjectivism of human experience prohibits a science of society can be found among the first advocates of phenomenology and hermeneutics, although their position was not as starkly relativistic as the antirepresentational stand of contemporary postmodernists. To phenomenologists like Edmund Husserl, for example, social reality was manifested only in highly subjective experiences and only in strictly defined contexts, and if this reality was to be explored by human observers, it was to be through unique methods invoked by gifted philosophers attempting to identify a transcendent reality through the "bracketing" of subjective experiences in the mundane world. Husserl himself may have viewed phenomenology as a "scientific" endeavor, but the method of bracketing, far from being a replicable means for uncovering objective laws, placed a tremendous burden on the individual philosopher's self-discipline, insight, intuition, and even imagination.[7] Subsequent advocates of phenomenology such as Alfred Schutz and Robert Nisbet defined phenomenology as a much more limited enterprise, designed to aide our understanding of sequences of events, actions, and experiences within concrete historical contexts, but explicitly rejecting the notion of a transcendent social reality that can be "objectively" grasped by the skilled philosopher.[8]

In a similar vein, scholars in the hermeneutic tradition argue that subjective experience may be rendered meaningful through "translation," but there are no general "lessons" or "laws" to be divined from this process since each act of translation remains uniquely bound to particular contexts.[9] For Hans-Gorg Gadamer, perhaps the best-known representative of this tradition in postwar theory, hermeneutics represents "the corrective through which thinking reason escapes the spell of language."[10] But, unlike Habermas, who embraces this definition but nevertheless seeks to build an evolutionary theory of universal "communicative action," Gadamer sees an emphasis on uniform, replicable methods as counterproductive to understanding social reality given that this reality consists of action and communication that are only rendered meaningful within highly specific contexts. That is, method is inherently opposed to "truth" in the analysis of context-bound subjective experiences since "method" presupposes a transcendent reality apart from subjective experience.[11] Thus, Gadamer, along with such interpretivists as Peter Winch, Charles Taylor and Paul Ricoeur, all explicitly or implicitly focus on the model or metaphor of translation, but they reject the possibility for systematically exploring general patterns behind intersubjective meanings since all meaningful action is strictly intertwined with specific social practices within specific social contexts.[12] Only postmodern skeptics would go further, attacking hermeneutic "translation" as merely another form of "representation."

The differences among the ontologies of various positivists at one end, and the different degrees of subjectivism among various interpretive theorists at the other end, both suggest that moving a little further away from each extreme might get us closer to a "middle ground" on the issue of an objective/subjective ontology of social reality. This "middle ground" may be best exemplified in Max Weber's position on the problem of subjectivity. Although there are contending perspectives on where the "real" Weber came down on this question,[13] Weber is clear that his empirical analysis is not intended to support analytic laws or even provide exhaustive causal explanations of all aspects of a social phenomenon. In his famous essay, "'Objectivity' in Social Science and Social Policy," in addition to placing quotation marks around the word "objectivity," he states that "as far back as we may go into the gray mist of the far-off past, the reality to which the laws apply always remains equally *individual,* equally undeducible from laws." Weber goes on to note that his method of classification through "ideal-types" are designed not to objectively capture general laws, but only to generate a better understanding of an "infinitely complex" reality through the "analytic accentuation" of certain aspects on the basis of the investigator's own interests.[14] In another essay on "Basic Sociological Terms," Weber argues that subjectivity does *not* rule out the possibility of a systematic investigation into certain aspects of a phenomena because "'recapturing an experience' is . . . not an absolute precondition for its interpretation."[15]

It is easy to interpret these statements as indicative that Weber was ambivalent in addressing the problem of subjectivity, and yet the ambivalence itself might be indicative of a pragmatic intermediate position that is no less compelling than the more definitive positions staked out by positivists and relativists. Clearly, Weber is hardly being a radical subjectivist or relativist when he argues that interpretation does not presuppose "recapturing" an experience or when he constructs "ideal types" to categorize social phenomena; at the same time, he is cautious about inferring too much from social patterns or regularities given that these regularities are abstracted from a complex reality by individual social scientists primarily on the basis of what is of interest to them. Taking the lead from this interpretation of Weber's ontology, we can identify an approximate "center" on the problem of objective/subjective reality in social analysis reflected in the following proposition: *While social reality is subjectively experienced and socially constructed, it is sufficiently "intersubjective" to permit the investigator opportunities to extract a generalizable "interpretive understanding" of the meanings that individuals attach to actions and subjective experiences in different historical and cultural contexts.* Such an "intersubjective" ontology, while hardly unique to Weberians, leaves the door open to a wider variety of social analysis and enables all but the most extreme objectivists and subjectivists to communicate with one another in attempting to better grasp aspects of social reality.

Intersubjectivity and General Propositions:
Empiricism, Inductivism, Deductivism

The ontological problem of social reality bears directly on the epistemological problem of the logics through which one attempts to grasp that social reality. Kant, while rejecting the application of "pure reason" in the study of social phenomena, posited the existence of objective categories of understanding that were universal and indispensable for making sense of empirical observations. Durkheim, although he was firmly committed to substantiating his categories and theories on the basis of observable "social facts," emphasized logical conceptual schemes of functional and monocausal relationships based on axiomatic assumptions about the psychological needs of individuals, the function of cultural beliefs, and the consequences of a complex division of labor for forms of "solidarity," law, and morality. In contrast to both Kant and Durkheim, Hume emphasized the problems of establishing causality without empirically observing the process of causation, and he questioned whether causes could ever be distinguished from sequences of events given the difficulties of judging the effects of causes located in the distant past. Mill sought to emphasize an empiricist tradition of causality based on the inductive logic of controlled comparison, but unlike Hume, he was willing to view the presence of various factors in various cases as a reasonable basis for cautious causal inferences. However, unlike Durkheim, Mill was interested not in single, permanent causes, but multiple causes, and he was acutely aware of the difficulties of inductive analysis in social science even as he devised methods of controlled comparison.[16] These nineteenth-century theorists anticipated long ago the importance of methodological issues that plague contemporary social scientists: Are logical propositions deduced from existing analytic laws any more or less compelling than inferences drawn from empirical observations?

The most relevant distinctions here are between deductivism (Kant/Durkheim), empiricism (Hume), and inductivism (Mill). Deductivists are able to discuss *unobserved* causal mechanisms as long as the *effects* are observable. But rather than begin with the study of possible causal factors in case after case, they emphasize the primacy of internal logical consistency in a causal explanatory model. Axiomatic principles are made the basis for a theoretical explanation that can be systematically tested against empirical reality, but the empirical analysis is meaningful only *after* the explanation is shown to be logically consistent. The process of theory-construction itself is viewed as distinct from and, more significantly, *logically and temporally prior* to the actual observation and categorization of empirical processes.[17]

In contrast, empiricists and inductivists share a common belief in the primacy of the empirical and discourage *a priori* exercises in formal logic or abstract theorizing, but they differ in terms of the extent to which general, causally significant propositions can be inferred from the empirical. For radical empiricists, the purpose of empirical observation is not to lend substance to deductively derived logical constructs or produce causal inferences, but to employ statistical analysis in order to demonstrate lawlike regularities and to offer some descriptive inferences based on those regularities.[18] Inductivists, working in the tradition of Mill's controlled comparisons, vary in their degree of ambition, but they do rely on carefully selected matrices of variables and cases in order to draw inferences ranging from descriptive inferences to full-blown causal explanation. In contrast to the empiricists' emphasis on quantitative indicators and statistically proven correlations that appear with lawlike regularity, these inductivists typically rely on more thorough investigations of historical cases, attempting to generalize from their penetrating accounts of processes, actions, and sequences leading up to a particular outcome or a class of events.[19]

In both cases, however, the goal is to provide the best possible descriptive inferences on the basis of careful empirical observations of a few or many cases. And, both empiricists and inductivists view the very axioms on which deductive theories are formed as simply one set of possible explanations to be tested against alternative hypotheses, and the temporal and logical priority is assigned to the study of empirical processes and concrete social "facts." To the extent that structures or causal mechanisms are identified, they *emerge* from the study of actual historical events, empirical processes, and the beliefs and behavior of real individuals, groups, or institutions.[20]

In dealing with the debate between deductivists on the one hand, and empiricists/inductivists on the other, two points are worth bearing in mind. First, there are important differences among deductivists as well as among inductivists or empiricists. For example, the agent-structure problem in comparative and international studies involves very different understandings of "patterns" in social life, and these understandings divide both deductivists and empiricists/inductivists. Many deductivists (rational-choice theorists) and empiricists (cognitivists or ethnographers) share a common belief that only individuals are "real," thereby reducing broader regularities or patterns to the decisions and actions of individuals. Other deductivists (systems theorists such as Waltz or Parsons) and inductivists (historical-structuralists such as Wallerstein or Skocpol) converge on the point that observable regularities and patterns in social and international life are commonly shaped by dynamics of interactions that could never be reduced to the individuals themselves. However, these differences over the appropriate focus of empirical analysis and theoretical explanation do not alter the more fundamental epistemological distinction between deductivists partial to general theorizing and empiricists/inductivists partial to empirically grounded study.[21]

Second, the distinction between the two positions is hardly absolute. As Bueno de Mesquita, himself a deductivist, points out: "[T]heory construction always follows on from our previous experience and observation. Which axioms we choose . . . is largely a function of our unscientific personal *judgment* . . . [and our] individual experiences and observations." However, while the choice of axioms may be shaped by individual experiences, the logic behind the axioms themselves are not. Thus, for deductivists, "internal logical consistency is a fundamental requirement of all hypotheses . . . [and] *formal, explicit theorizing takes intellectual, if not temporal, precedence over empiricism.*"[22] In other words, even if there is no purely deductive model and even if prior observations and experiences influence the selection of an axiom, a "deductive" approach can be distinguished on the basis of this crucial point: the role of empirical research is to demonstrate the validity of formal theoretical models, and explicit analysis of empirical processes is performed *after* a model is offered as a set of testable hypotheses. It is not a matter of choosing between logic and observation since both are necessary to social science research, but there is a claim here that formal logic takes *precedence* over empirical study.[23]

Is there a "pragmatic" approach to dealing with the contentious debates between deductivists and the empiricists/inductivists? Are these entirely irreconcilable perspectives offering incompatible modes of analysis? Not as long as we dismiss the strong claims in regard to the primacy of internal logical consistency in deductive theorizing. It is possible to accept the possibility that *some* universally valid causal mechanisms are not empirically observable, but in this case, the causes cannot simply be deduced solely from abstract "laws" through logical procedures as might be the case in mathematics or theoretical physics. In the social sciences, the very notion of "internal logical consistency" becomes problematic in the absence of empirical referents. In the case of rational-choice models, for example, how can we know for certain that one person's "rational" preference will inevitably correspond to another's in a given choice situation? Why are variations in the choice situations for different actors not given the same intellectual priority as individual preferences? Since the circumstances that shape the choice situation itself precede the actual calculation of costs and benefits, it seems that the first step would be to analyze the actual situations, material conditions, norms, and power structures that result in a person confronting a particular choice and having to determine the balance of "risks," "costs," and "benefits." In light of this point alone, it is difficult to justify the decision to assign primacy to the process of deducing human behaviors from universally "rational" preference-structures rather than to the empirical study of the social context that governs the range of available choices and the values attached to them.[24]

Thus, deductively generated models, no matter how parsimonious or elegant, cannot stand on their own. Inductively generated inferences do not have to be dependent on deductively driven general models in order to be insightful or useful. It is only when strong causal inferences are drawn that inductivists enter the realm of general theory, and only then do issues of logical consistency become important; short of general causal theorizing, modest causal or descriptive inferences can be generated with only minimal attention to the construction of prior categories without imputing causes. In contrast, at some point, deductive models, in order to be rendered meaningful or useful, *must* be translated into substantive propositions that can be "tested" in one form or another on the basis of empirical observations. And while the problem of *why* X might cause Y can be addressed through deductive logic, insofar as the issue is *whether* X and Y can be established empirically as components linked within a single process, empirical observation must provide the starting point. We can debate the elegance of models that suggest answers to the "why," but the debate would be moot in the absence of the "whether." My point is not that general deductive theory is irrelevant or insignificant; I only wish to contest the aforementioned claim that deductive theorizing has "intellectual, if not temporal precedence over empiricism."

At the same time, deductivists are right to note that empiricists and inductivists, when they are themselves not cautious about the concepts they employ and the inferences they draw as a result, often end up committing "the inductivist fallacy" and are unable to fall back on the logical consistency of a theoretical model. Neither statistical correlations between a few variables, nor generalizations from a few cases, can establish causality without risking spurious inferences from observed regularities. Moreover, it is true that historical or empirical research is never conducted on a *tabula rasa,* and that every theorist is guided by some preconceptions or theoretical agenda. Often, some of the "assumptions" made by empiricists prove to be central to their organization of empirical facts and to their subsequent theoretical inferences. Thus, often what they are offering is not hypotheses generated solely on the basis of inductive logic applied to empirical research, but rather empirical claims shaped by prior intellectual constructs smuggled in as assumptions. Assumptions that take on the function of representing unfalsifiable principles asserted by the investigator are not much different from the axiomatic principles that drive deductive theories. In both cases, hypotheses appear compelling only on the condition that the assumptions are accepted.

Nevertheless, it is important to recognize the difference between a history interpreted entirely through the lens of full-blown theoretical models and a history mediated only by concepts serving heuristic purposes.[25] In this context, it is interesting to note that Weberian "ideal-types" are supposed to be derived by each investigator to help sort out empirical information and interpret the causal significance among variables; but a Weberian epistemology neither posits *universal* ideal-types, nor treats the formulation of ideal-types as an exercise in building *a priori* conceptual schemes. Weber emphasizes the "analytical accentuation" of certain elements of complex social phenomena, and he explicitly recognizes concept-construction as not the end of theory, but only one possible means to understanding the significance of events.[26] Approaching inferences in this way requires accepting some form of empirical or historical analysis as at least temporally, if not logically, prior to the transformation of concepts and frameworks from heuristic devices into explanatory models.

Such an argument, however, does not in the least suggest that deductive theorizing is unimportant unless one is committed to an extremely relativistic epistemological perspective. A more reasonable option might be to adopt a more flexible, even agnostic, perspective on the question of inductive-versus-deductive logics in social theorizing. Scholars can leave open to the possibility of causal inferences, with deductive logic playing a valuable role in deriving testable propositions from existing theories, in axiomatically limiting the range of possible explanations, and in providing some heuristic devices to guide the investigation and categorization of empirical objects. It is possible to simultaneously embrace an empirically or historically grounded approach to theory building and recognize the potential value of deductively driven general theory as long as we refrain from making indefensible claims about the temporal and logical primacy of the latter.

The Purpose of Theory and the Role of Values

For the absolute positivist and stark relativist, one's ontology of social reality also corresponds directly to one's views concerning the role of values and the purpose of social theory. The positivist, assuming the existence of an objective social reality, endeavors to generate "value-free" causal explanations of social phenomena through strict adherence to uniform methods, and regards the relationship between theory and practice as purely technical (i.e., theory is to be invoked only in the selection of means, not the discussion of ends). For the postmodern skeptic, facts and values are indistinguishable, and the social theorist can do nothing more than try to evocatively narrate the subjective experiences of actors while attempting to uncover hidden intentions and contradictions in the existing corpus of "scientific" knowledge. In between these two poles, however, there is no obvious correspondence between the relationship between one's ontology and one's view of the purpose of social theory. A view of social reality as a realm of intersubjectively shared meanings may be consistent with an explanatory theory based on modest causal claims, a more limited quest for interpretive understanding *(verstehen)*, or a normatively oriented theory to be united with practice.

The position of interpretive or relativistic scholars is seen in their rejection of methods and standards of verification borrowed from the natural sciences. As Charles Taylor has argued: "We need to go beyond the bounds of a science based on verification," because, as investigators, we are caught in a "web of signification we ourselves have spun."[27] In fact, as far back as the turn of the century, Wilhelm Dilthey argued the case that the "mental sciences" *(geisteswissenschaften)* ought to be sharply distingusished from the natural sciences: "Nature we explain; psychic life we understand."[28] Causality and explanation, for interpretive or relativistic scholars, are no longer reasonable endeavors; this is not only due to the absence of consensus on standard methods of causal analysis, but due to the fact that the social reality being explained is a product of social construction that the theorist also participates in. Thus, an interpretive view of the social sciences begins from "the postulate that the web of meaning constitutes human existence to such an extent that it cannot ever be meaningfully reduced to . . . any predefined elements."[29] Thus, not explanation, but only *verstehen*, or "interpretive understanding," is the only reasonable and valid objective for a social theorist.

Weber himself, although he would probably agree with many of these points, is often ambiguous on the issue of whether explanation or interpretation is the goal of the theorist. When he writes of "explanatory understanding," it is not clear whether he would emphasize the "explanatory" aspects or the "understanding" itself.[30] Dallmayr and McCarthy's argument on this point might make sense here: Weber's initial philosophical inclinations toward *verstehen* and his empirical studies of religion, economy, and society brought him gradually to a middle ground in between explanatory causal analysis and cultural interpretation. In his writings on methodology, Weber viewed "ideal-types" as "indispensable for heuristic as well as expository purposes," but was also quite specific about the limits of this procedure: "It is possible, or rather, it must be accepted as certain that numerous, indeed a very great many, utopias of this sort can be worked out, of which none is like another and *none* of which can be observed in empirical reality."[31] Thus, rather than pursuing the "practically impossible" task of providing an exhaustive causal account of a phenomena, what we seek is a causal explanation of "only certain sides of the infinitely complex concrete phenomenon."[32] What we have here is a lucid statement on the limits and importance of *partial* explanations in the analysis of social phenomena across historical contexts.[33]

Even if this position on the purpose of theory is found to be ambiguous, I find this ambiguity to be unproblematic and perhaps even fortuitously pragmatic. Interpretation and understanding are not goals that are entirely at odds with explanatory social science. Explanatory approaches may be viewed as simply more ambitious and more abstract interpretations that transcend to a greater *degree* the particular context of any given action. Even though interpretations do not make the explicit causal claims made in explanatory theories, many "deep" interpretations do imply causally significant relationships among generalized actors and conceptions. Rather than treat interpretive and explanatory theory as two distinct types of social science, it is possible to see the difference as one of *degrees* of separation from purely descriptive narrative. In between *verstehen* and causal explanation, I find *partial* explanation to an entirely reasonable "middle ground" based on comparing deep interpretations of similar phenomena in different contexts.

Now, regardless of how ambitious an explanation or interpretation a theorist seeks, there remains the question of whether his or her values can and should be removed from the analysis. To positivists, values may affect the selection of problems, but they do not intrinsically negate the scientific objectivity of the analysis itself as long as there is strict adherence to formal methods.[34] Karl Popper sought to refine this position by, on the one hand, agreeing with skeptics that theorists often invoke "scientism" to hide their value-laden judgments, but on the other hand, insisting that intersubjective conventions and uniform standards for evidence offered means to separate the objective analysis of theorists from the values that may have influenced them.[35] Political Scientist Martin Landau, following the work of Israel Scheffler, similarly tried to preserve the objectivity of scientific theory by proposing "a network of highly redundant and visible public checks to protect against the inclusion of erroneous items in the corpus of knowledge." These "institutionalized control procedures" would guarantee that the subjective biases of human investigators did not taint the enterpirse of scientific inquiry.[36] So, while contemporary positivists recognize that individual scholars might fail to distinguish facts from values, there are objective procedures for extirpating value-laden judgments from theoretical knowledge.

At the other end, Karl Mannheim's sociology of knowledge may be regarded as one of the most significant early challenges to the very idea of an objective social science. Mannheim argued that all knowledge and all ideas could be reduced to the "subjective standpoint and social situation of the knower," suggesting that social analysis was intrinsically shaped by subjective interests and values no matter how objective the analyst.[37] While critical theorists in the postwar period have continued this line of attack on the products of dominant research traditions in the social sciences, Thomas Kuhn has launched a different kind of attack on the idea of a universally valid, cumulative social science as evident in his contention that theories and methods, far from being universal and cumulative, are entirely derived from a dominant paradigm that incorporated unprecedented systems of concepts, assumptions, and core propositions that were accepted as foundational by the adherents of the paradigm. Other scholars, responding to attempts by behavioralists and structural-functionalists to construct social science paradigms in the postwar era, have taken their cues from both Mannheim and Kuhn, and have sought to show that social theories are, in fact, founded on hidden, value-laden assumptions smuggled into the core of paradigms.[38]

For Weber, values not only influence the selection of questions, but they affect what facts are considered relevant or significant. The "analytical accentuation" of certain aspects of complex and chaotic social phenomena is not a value-free process, and thus "ideal-types" are in part products of the investigator's own subjective presuppositions. "Order is brought into this chaos only on the condition that in every case only a *part* of concrete reality is interesting and *significant* to us, because only *it* is related to the *cultural values* with which we approach reality."[39] However, for Weber, the modest explanations generated by studying the chosen "part of concrete reality" are nonetheless valuable propositions, and in the social sciences, this is the most we can hope for. Still, the investigator, for his or her part, can try to recognize the biases at work and can attempt to refrain from presenting a particular understanding of a situation as the total and objective knowledge about that situation.[40]

The problem of values does not end there, however, since the relationship between theory and *practice* is also the subject of debate. Three nonrelativistic positions stand out as the most significant in this regard. First, from the positivist perspective, social science theories can and should guide the selection of means to whatever ends one is pursuing, although the ends are themselves not selected on the basis of social theories. The relationship between theory and practice is purely technical, with choices governed on the basis of whatever theoretical knowledge is available. Second, there is Weber's position that science, morality, and art are three distinct and mutually exclusive spheres, and moreover, since social theories can never be purely objective, they cannot be expected to shed light on the most important moral choices confronting society.[41] Both of these positions have been challenged by a third position seen in the "critical theory" of Frankfurt School scholars who wed their dialectical philosophy to an overt critique of bourgeois ideology and political economy as well as to explicit calls for political action and social change—the "theory-praxis nexus."[42] Thus, critical theory rejects the technical rationality of positivists on the question of values, but also rejects Weber's separation of art, science, and morality into separate realms; in fact, the impossibility of a value-free science of society actually makes the science of society inextricably linked to normative choices and decisions.[43]

None of these positions are logically or empirically verifiable, but again a reasonable "middle-ground" is identifiable that takes into account all three positions. Values are clearly at work when a social scientist chooses a research question and identifies the "significant" or "relevant" social processes, agents, and structures. Some investigators will consciously recognize the influence of their biases, and others will overlook them, and there is something to be said for distinguishing the former from the latter. In either case, I agree with Weber that one should at least be cautious about equating possibly value-laden theoretical approaches with an objective method intended to yield a single truth and a comprehensive prescription for action. As for the issue of "praxis," I share Habermas's doubts about separating science from politics, and I suspect that at some level of consciousness, every social scientist has chosen a field of research for some reason, and this reason probably encompasses some normative commitment. However, it is worthwhile to distinguish *generalized commitments* to principles such as "greater equality" or "improved quality of life" or "peace and cooperation" from an *active commitment* to employing the social sciences to justify or advance a particular course of action or an explicit ideological program.[44] Where theoretical questions are located within a "problematique" dominated by social critique and a concern for political action, the possibility of reexamining one's biases and analyses is closed off *a priori*. In other words, although facts and values may not be easily distinguishable, it is important to distinguish a theorist committed to "praxis" from a theorist who entertains a degree of self-doubt or self-reflection and attempts to consciously seek out procedures for locating bias and minimizing its effects on even the most modest interpretation or partial explanation.[45] This leads to an even more fundamental problem: How do we decide which propositions to take seriously and which to reject?

Between "Proof" and "Anything Goes": A Flexible Evaluation of Theories

Many who previously subscribed to a positivist philosophy of science expected that it was simply a matter of time before social scientists developed uniform procedures for determining which theories to reject and which to regard as "laws." Initially, these procedures were based on "justificationism," the acceptance of theories only when they were "proven" to be "true" by external empirical facts.[46] From the point of view of later positivists, however, this approach reflected "the inductivist fallacy" since "any finite number of observations of an event, or relationship among variables, cannot be taken as *conclusive* evidence regarding the relationship among a potentially infinite number of instances of the event-category being explained."[47] Instead, as Popper argued, "not . . . the verifiability but the *falsifiability* of a system is to be taken as the criterion for demarcation."[48] Moreover, Popper warned against conflating the refutation of a theory with its disproof; if a "spatio-temporally singular" empirical statement were to appear inconsistent with a theory, this would only represent a single instance where the theory ought to be rejected. It was solely through "intersubjective convention" that social scientists could establish uniform criteria for evaluating theories.[49] This "conventionalist" reformulation does not seek to prove *or* disprove theories on the basis of empirical testing, but it does presume that standard, uniform principles can be established for objectively evaluating theories and subjecting them to the "systematic criticism of error" on the basis of specified empirically based observational statements.[50]

However, even with Popper's version of falsificationism, there is not only the risk of "falsely rejecting correct hypotheses," but also the problem of recognizing that "rejection alone does not facilitate scientific progress."[51] To deal with these problems, Imre Lakatos (in his later work) posited a more sophisticated version of falsificationism, one that allows for the continued consideration of theories and hypotheses even after they appear to be refuted by a single empirical observation. His now famous criterion for the falsification of theories is inherently linked to the devaluation of old theories and the acceptance of new ones:[52]

> A scientific theory T is *falsified* if and only if another theory T′ has been proposed with the following characteristics: (1) T′ has excess empirical content over T: that is, it predicts novel facts, that is, facts improbable in the light of, or even forbidden by, T; (2) T′ explains the previous success of T, that is, all the unrefuted content of T is included (within the limits of observational error) in the content of T′; and (3) some of the excess content of T′ is corroborated.

On the one hand, this "sophisticated falsificationism" offers hope for positivists since it allows for the cumulation of knowledge as each successive theory surpasses another, each time providing more comprehensive explanations and empirical corroboration. On the other hand, this formulation does call into question both, justificationists and most falsificationists, by suggesting that empirical evidence can neither verify, nor disprove, nor even refute a theory. It is only in relation to a second theory that a theory may be discarded. This leaves the door wide open for skeptics who regard the evaluation of theories as a *social* act, a product not only of conventions but also of "intertextuality," the reading of one text relative to another.[53]

Of course, Kuhn himself had begun to travel this path by questioning the validity of conventionalism for scientific knowledge. For Kuhn, not only did scientific communities ignore many socially important problems because these could not be incorporated into paradigms, but scientists' conventions for devising uniform criteria for evaluating theories were little more than arbitrary rules constructed by adherents to a paradigm.[54] Thus, although Kuhn treated "paradigm shifts" as revolutionary advances in scientific knowledge, he might also point out to Lakatos: T′ does not improve the quality of objective knowledge because the community that decides that T′ surpasses T does so, in the final analysis, by its own rules.

An even stronger case is made by Paul Feyerabend who attacks the very idea that a paradigm might provide some conceptual coherence to a body of theoretical literature; rather, the problem of incommensurable meanings in each and every theory, in each and every case, makes it impossible to generate shared paradigms. Thus, Feyerabend's relativistic epistemology provides no criteria whatsoever for the acceptance or refutation of theories, leaving social scientists with a growing body of inconsistent and incommensurable theories.[55] Feyerabend's position is implicitly accepted by many interpretive theorists as well as postmodernists. For relativists, it is not simply the "methodological immaturity" of the social sciences that produces debates over the relative merits of theories; the very nature of social inquiry makes it impossible to achieve a uniform set of methods or criteria for the evaluation of theory.[56] Postmodernists even make a virtue out of this criterionless social science where "anything goes." Some of the less skeptical postmodernists proceed to emphasize intuition and empathy as substitutes for positivist method, but the most extreme relativists can do no more than "deconstruct" texts to reveal hidden biases and challenge hidden assumptions. In both cases, there is no basis for determining when an insightful narrative or an act of deconstruction yields anything of significance to anyone other than author.

Is there a position between Feyerabend's relativism, on the one hand, and Popperian conventionalism or Lakatos's sophisticated falsificationism on the other? To most social scientists in their everyday work, the latter seems unfeasible and the former unthinkable. Instead, some have responded to the challenge of absolute relativism by calling for the use of compelling arguments and empirical findings not to test or falsify theories but to modestly engage in the "rational persuasion" of a given audience; thus, they posit a bounded notion of "rationality," stripped of its absolute universalism and consistent with socially constructed intersubjective realities.[57] Others suggest that theories may initially be incommensurable, but that they can be "translated" so as to enable at least a tentative comparison and evaluation on the basis of the same kind of empirical tests.[58] In these approaches, the result will not be definitive and theories will never become laws, but instead of criterionless narratives, scholars can at least make an effort to persuade audiences by appealing to their own common-sense version of "reason" by relating theories to compelling empirical observations.

In the end, there may be no alternative to relying on the judgment of other human beings, and this judgment is difficult to form in the absence of empirical findings. However, instead of clinging to the elusive idea of a uniform standard for the empirical validation of theories, it is possible to simply present a set of observational statements—whether we call it "data" or "narrative"—for the modest purpose of rendering an explanation or interpretation *more plausible* than the audience would allow at the outset. In practice, this is precisely what the most committed positivists and interpretivists have been doing anyway; the presentation of "logically consistent" hypotheses "supported by data" and the ordering of facts in a "thick" narrative are both ultimately designed to convince scholars that a particular proposition should be taken more seriously than others.

Social analysis is not about final truths or objective realities, but nor does it have to be a meaningless world of incommensurable theories where anything goes. Instead, it can be an ongoing collective endeavor to develop, evaluate, and refine *general* inferences—be they in the form of models, partial explanations, descriptive inferences, or interpretations—in order to render them more "sensible" or "plausible" to a particular audience. In the absence of a consensus on the possibility and desirability of a full-blown explanatory science of international and social life, it is important to keep as many doors open as possible. This does not require us to accept each and every claim without some sort of validation, but perhaps the community of scholars can be more tolerant about the kinds of empirical referents and logical propositions that are employed in validating propositions by scholars embracing all but the most extreme epistemological positions.

Conclusion: Toward a "Pragmatic" Middle Ground?

Let me now capture in full the range of positions on the above questions as a whole in terms of *eight* distinct ideal-typical positions along what I refer to as an "epistemological spectrum." It is the nuances that systematically distinguish these positions that enable me to conclude with the articulation of a "pragmatic" epistemological middle ground.

1. According to logical positivism, social reality is objective and independent of subjective experiences; it can be analyzed through methods modeled after those of the natural sciences, methods that involve the primacy of deductive logics and the replication of experimental control; the purpose of theory is to causally explain social phenomena in terms of a general theory; it is therefore imperative that scholars distinguish social facts from social values; theories are to be evaluated in terms of their internal logical consistency, and the hypotheses derived from these theories can be proven or disproven on the basis of objective criteria derived from empirical tests. (e.g., Comte, Ayer, Parsons).

2. The Kantian variant of positivism differs from the above in that it acknowledges subjectivity of human experience as problematic for the exercise of pure logic in the realm of social phenomena; methods borrowed from natural science are viewed as less useful, and "practical reason" or some other unique procedure must be employed in the social sciences; nevertheless, the existence of pregiven universal categories or ideas for comprehending collective experience make a science of society possible, with deductive theorizing having primacy given the existence of these universal categories; the purpose of theory is chiefly to causally explain phenomena, but the fact-value distinction is not always tenable, thereby requiring scientists to be self-consciously monitoring their own work (e.g., Kant, Hegel, Marx, early Parsons, neo-realism of Waltz, Habermas's work on communicative action).

3. In the empiricist version of positive social science, social reality can be objectively studied despite the subjectivity of experience, but the methods of analysis must be completely distinct from those in the natural sciences, with concepts and theories inseparable from empirical observation; as with logical positivism, the purpose of theory remains the causal explanation of phenomena, but the process first involves modest hypotheses formed on the basis inductive logics applied to sequences of events; the fact/value distinction remains possible and desirable, and empirical testing pro-

vides the basis for at least falsifying theories on the basis of some principles agreed on by intersubjective convention (e.g., Hume, Mill, Popper, postwar behavioralism, quantiative analysis, more ambitious variants of historical-structuralism).

4. Within a "soft" empiricist epistemology, social reality is constructed, but intersubjective realities do exist in the form of a set of shared meanings and a common-sense understanding of the social world; this reality can be analyzed through careful observation and the application of inductive logics; causality and the fact/value distinction are difficult to establish, but partial explanations, "explanatory understandings," and policy-relevant inferences are still possible; thus, empirical reality-checks, even if they do not verify or falsify a theory, make theoretical claims distinct from ideology or personal narratives because they allow for self-correcting procedures for employing empirical or historical observations to qualify or refine a general inference. (e.g., Weber, Toulmin, Haas, Katzenstein, and middle-range comparative-historical analysis).

5. A "comparative-interpretive" epistemology refers to a more ambitious version of interpretive theory than phenomenology and hermeneutics; social reality is subjective, but lends itself to interpretations that may be compared and contrasted across contexts on particular aspects of social or international life; this process is not inductive and does not yield causal inferences, but it does lead to a deeper appreciation of the meanings attached to similar social phenomena in different contexts; given the difficulty of separating facts from values, the purpose of social analysis must necessarily be confined to gaining an interpretive understanding *(verstehen)*; where values provide the motivation for social analysis, *praxis* may be the main purpose of theory (critical theory); external validation of theories cannot be achieved by using empirical facts, but juxtaposed interpretations of multiple contexts can play a role in persuading certain audiences of modest descriptive inferences (e.g., Berger, Geertz, later works of Bendix and Bellah).

6. The phenomenological and hermeneutic approaches are less ambitious and more context-specific; social reality is subjective, and whatever interpretations are possible are not only individual but also strictly bound within the context of prac-

tices; given the impossibility of trans-contextual social
knowledge, even inductive logics do not apply; the purpose
of theory can never be explanation or praxis, but simply
understanding of facts bound by time and space; also, facts
and values are inseparable, thereby rendering external
empirical validation pointless; the best the social sciences can
do is narrate actions and sequences, perhaps identify some
patterns without generally accounting for them, and gain
some insight into the contextual meaning by "translating"
the symbols and languages used in everyday practice (e.g.,
Heidegger, Schutz, Nisbet, Gadamer, Ricoeur).

7. The less skeptical, "contextualist" variant of postmodernism
suggests that the subjectivity of social reality can never be
overcome and that stocks of knowledge and beliefs themselves represent cultural objects of analysis; however, these
can be located in the context of social-historical processes
through archeological or genealogical methods that expose
heretofore hidden, multiple centers of power; the purpose of
such studies is not to explain or even understand existing
practices, but to note the contradictions and hidden assumptions behind "scientific" knowledge that is seen as indistinguishable from ideology; nevertheless, there is some attempt
to suggest an alternative narrative that challenges the dominant consensus on a given issue (e.g., Foucault).

8. The most extreme version of relativism is to be found in
postmodern deconstructionists who view social reality as
completely subjective; there is no point in even describing
sequences, tracing genealogies or recognizing the origins of
dominant ideas in society; deconstruction is the only alternative since it at least exposes the conscious and unconscious
intentions of authors and protects against the false claims
made by purveyors of scientific knowledge; the entire enterprise of academia is regarded as an aspect of "modernity" as
a whole, and modernists are regarded as arrogant oppressors
or naive believers in the myths of rationality and progress
through knowledge claims (e.g., Derrida, Lyotard).

These categories along the "epistemological spectrum" do not represent distinct points along a unidimensional axis, and the boundary separating each adjacent pair of categories is in each case quite fuzzy. This
fuzziness simply suggests that the various epistemological positions compared in this chapter, though idealized as categories, in reality, shade into

each other. Hence, the deliberate choice of the term "spectrum" to capture the wide range of nuanced distinctions that become evident when one gradually moves away from either the positivist or relativist extremes. And it is precisely these nuanced alternatives that mark the point of departure for the argument against epistemological absolutism. If various kinds of "positivists" and "relativists" cannot agree among themselves on a set of foundational propositions, perhaps it is best to shift our attention away from the debates between positivists and relativists and toward a reasonable epistemological "middle ground" that at least engenders or sustains communication among scholars studying similar kinds of substantive problems.

The first three categories are all variants of "positivism." While Comte's version of "logical positivism" may be uncommon in twentieth-century scholarship, the Kantian and empiricist traditions are very much alive and well, and indeed the contemporary debates over specific methodologies in social science are being framed by those who at least implicitly adhere to one of these two versions of positivism. The sixth category probably represents a more well-established and less stark version of relativism that can be traced to turn-of-the-century German phenomenologists and hermeneuticians who viewed the study of historical sequences or cultural interpretations as context-bound and thus rejected the idea of developing anything resembling general explanatory models. The last two categories include different kinds of "postmodernists" who have built on the skepticism of earlier relativists, but have gone further by adopting an "anti-representational" position.[59]

The epistemological "middle ground" I have been referring to is captured in the assumptions found in the *fourth* and *fifth* categories. These assumptions are either explicit or implicit in the works of many familiar scholars in postwar social theory who appear to converge on a Weberian "middle ground" despite differences in their substantive research interests and intellectual heritage. While not all are equally concerned with epistemological problems, they all recognize the social construction of reality, but nonetheless find an "intersubjective" realm based on common understandings and practices from which tentative inferences can be drawn through context-sensitive studies that are replicable at least in principle if not in fact.[60] On the basis of the foundational premises offered by scholars I place in these fourth and fifth categories, it is possible to identify an epistemological center consisting of the following unprovable but entirely "reasonable" and "pragmatic" philosophical propositions.

(1) Social reality is intersubjective and involves both complexity and regularity, leaving open the possibility of modest partial explanations and deep interpretations. (2) There is no reason to assume either the positivist position on the fact-value distinction or the skeptics' position that all

claims to knowledge are equally fraught by normative bias; rather, while facts and values may be difficult to separate, it is possible to recognize that they are in principle separable for the self-conscious investigator. (3) While research may not be intended to serve a particular ideological perspective, it is important to recognize that the questions to be investigated and the claims they generate have implications in the realms of policy-formation and ideology-critique. (4) Moreover, empirical reality-tests, while an insufficient basis for refuting or verifying a theory, are nonetheless one important aspect in the process of rendering an argument—whether a hypothesis or a narrative—more compelling to an audience.

In the final analysis, it may be best to regard the entire process of social research as an ongoing collective search for meanings by a community of scholars. This search may not result in any definitive answers to theoretical or practical questions given the diverse foundations informing the puzzles, texts, and models that preoccupy members of this community. Nevertheless, thanks to the mediating role played by those subscribing to a pragmatic epistemological middle-ground, the process can still yield valuable insights, partial explanations, and even modest "lessons" and that can be judged as *more* or *less* convincing in the eyes of one's audience whether this audience consists of academic peers, the lay public at large, or the policy-making community.

In an era of increasingly divided disciplines, scholars adopting a more pragmatic epistemological "middle ground," by virtue of their agnosticism, are likely to make the most critical contributions to whatever cumulation of knowledge is possible in the social sciences. These scholars are in a better position than those at the extreme ends for the purpose of generating and sustaining greater dialogue across different disciplines, theoretical approaches and intellectual movements precisely because their assumptions prevent them from hastily dismissing a study on grounds that are only meaningful to a subgroup within the wider community of scholars. In the absence of meaningful dialogue across different intellectual communities— whether delimited by disciplines, paradigms or methodological schools— the social sciences risk becoming permanently "balkanized," with scholars passing up opportunities to glean valuable insights from intellectual products developed on the basis of different foundational assumptions.

Notes

1. Stanley Fish, *Doing What Comes Naturally* (Durham: Duke University Press, 1989), p. 344; also cited in Pauline Rosenau, *Postmodernism and the Social Sciences* (Princeton: Princeton University Press, 1992), p. xi.

2. The "agent-structure problem" is not addressed here since, in practice, this has become more of a methodological issue rather than an onto-logical or epistemological one. The choice of whether agent-centered analysis or structural analysis is certainly nested in the larger questions addressed here concerning the objective/subjective nature of collective experiences and patterns in social reality and the primacy of induc-tive/deductive logics in theory-building. Nevertheless, the "debate" over agency and structure in IR has been carried out primarily as a methodological one, with limited references to ontological issues. A rare exception is Alexander Wendt, "The Agent-Structure Problem in International Relations Theory," *International Organization* 41, 3 (1987): 335–370.

3. Emanuelle Kant, *The Critique of Pure Reason*, trans. Max Muller, 2nd ed. (London: Macmillan, 1927).

4. David Hume, *An Enquiry Concerning Human Understanding* (La Salle: The Open Court Publishing Company, 1946).

5. John Stuart Mill, *A System of Logic* (New York: Harper and Row, 1888).

6. See Durkheim, *The Rules of Sociological Method* (Glencoe: Free Press, 1949). The ontological assumptions of Durkheim, Kant, and Hume are captured nicely in Steven Collins, "Categories, Concepts or Predica-ments," in Michael Carrithers, Steven Collins and Steven Lukes, eds. *The Category of the Person* (Cambridge: Cambridge University Press, 1985), pp. 49–51.

7. Husserl's phenomenology may have been influenced by a Hegelian view of an "intersubjective" social reality located in transcendent ideas embodied in a universal subject. Both Husserl and Hegel reject Kant-ian positivism, but both accept a general notion of a transcendent, unobservable reality that can be accessible to insightful philosophers despite the utter subjectivity of mundane experiences. See Edmund Husserl, *Ideas Pertainingto a Pure Phenomoenology and to a Phe-nomenological Philosophy* (London: Boyce-Gibson, 1931); and the discussions of Husserl and Hegel in Alfred Schutz, *Collected Papers: Volume I, The Problem of Social Reality* (The Hague: Nijnhoff, 1962).

8. Alfred Schutz, *The Phenomenology of the Social World* (Evanstown: Northwestern University Press, 1967); and Robert Nisbet, *Social Change and History* (London: Oxford University Press, 1967).

9. Although hermeneutics may be traced to the German idealism of Herder and Dilthey, Heidegger probably deserves the most credit for providing the foundation for contemporary hermeneutics by focusing on how language and communication provided subjects with a shared sense of "being-with-others" and rendered their actions meaningful in

society as a whole. From this existential philosophy of language, there have emerged a number of interpretive approaches based on the model of translation with Gadamer perhaps representing the most influential figure in postwar hermeneutics. See Martin Heidegger, *Existence and Being*, translated by D. Scott, R. F. C. Hull and A. Crick (London, 1949). Heidegger's existential ontology is summarized in Schutz, pp. 186–187, and his importance to hermeneutics is demonstrated by Dallmayr and McCarthy, "Hermeneutics and Critical Theory" in Fred Dallmayr and Thomas McCarthy, *Understanding and Social Inquiry* (Notre Dame: University of Notre Dame Press, 1977), pp. 285–287.

10. Paraphrased by Habermas in "A Review of Gadamer's *Truth and Method*," reprinted in Dallmayr and McCarthy, pp. 335–363, quote from p. 336.

11. See Paul Rabinow and William Sullivan, *Interpretive Social Science: A Second Look* (Berkeley: University of California Press, 1987), p. 2. Unlike postmodern deconstructionists, Gadamer sees social reality as decipherable because of the formation of habits ("habituodo") through repeated social practice, but at the same time, Gadamer is explicitly concerned with the primacy of context as well as the inseparability of culture from social practice. One cannot transcend the context of social practice and seek universal theoretical reason; one can only rely on the role of language and *practical* reason for contextual insights into the consciousness of human communities. See Gadamer, "The Problem of Historical Consciouness," reprinted in Rabinow and Sullivan, and his *Philosophical Hermeneutics* (Berkeley: University of California Press, 1976); see also Paul Ricoeur, "Ethics and Culture: Habermas and Gadamer in Dialogue," *Philosophy Today*, 17, 3 (summer 1972): 153–165.

12. Without going into the essential features of each scholar's approach here, it is possible to recognize that all of these authors share a subjectivist ontology but, in the place of the antirepresentationalism of more extreme relativists, offer some sort of meaningful interpretation of social practices though bound by the immediate *context* of the practices. See Peter Winch, *The Idea of a Social Science and Its Relation to Philosophy* (London: Routledge and Kegan Paul, 1958); Charles Taylor, "Interpretation and the Sciences of Man," *Review of Metaphysics* 25 (1971): 3–34, 45–51, reprinted in Rabinow and Sullivan; and Paul Ricoeur, "The Model of the Text: Meaningful Action Considered as Text," *Social Research* 38 (1971): 529–555.

13. Grand theorists such as Parsons have argued that Weber's own writings on the nature and task of social science were to be taken in the context of the intellectual currents of his time which included Marxism, utili-

tarianism and especially the German idealism of Troeltsch and Dilthey. In Parsons's view, Weber was essentially an objectivist, but employed the language of *verstehen* (interpretive understanding) in order to make his social analyses more palatable to his colleagues. I suspect, however, that this interpretation was developed on an ad hoc basis solely to make Weber's epistemology more consistent with Parsons's. See Talcott Parsons, "Value Freedom and Objectivity," in Otto Stammer, ed., *Max Weber and Sociology Today* (New York: Harper and Row, 1971), reprinted in Dallmayr and McCarthy, pp. 56–65.

14. Max Weber, "'Objectivity' in Social Science and Social Policy," in *The Methodology of the Social Sciences*, ed. E. A. Shils and H. A. Finch (Free Press, 1949), reprinted in Dallmayr and McCarthy; esp. pp. 25–34.

15. Weber, "Basic Sociological Terms," in Dallmayr and McCarthy, pp. 42–43.

16. See Durkheim, *Rules of Sociological Method;* as well as his *Suicide: A Study in Sociology* (Glencoe: Free Press, 1951), and *The Division of Labor in Society* (Glencoe: Free Press, 1933); and previously cited works by Kant, Hume, and Mill.

17. For formal deductive theory, see the definitive application of structural realism of Kenneth Waltz, *The Theory of International Politics* (Reading: Addison-Wesley, 1979); the classic discussion of the "rational actor model" in Graham Allison, *The Essence of Decision* (Boston: Little, Brown, 1971); the application of expected utility theory to conflict studies in Bruce Bueno de Mesquita, *The War Trap* (New Haven: Yale University Press, 1981) and T. David Mason and Patrick J. Fett, "How Civil Wars End: A Rational-Choice Approach," *Journal of Conflict Resolution*, 40, 4 (December 1996); the applications of iterated games in Robert Axelrod, *The Evolution of Cooperation* (New York: Basic Books, 1984), Kenneth Oye, ed. *Cooperation Under Anarchy* (Princeton University Press, 1986), and Vinod Aggarwal, *Debt Games* (New York: Cambridge University Press, 1995); and formal approaches to institutions seen in Elinor Ostrom, *Governing the Commons: The Evolution of Institutions for Collective Action* (New York: Cambridge University Press, 1990). Elsewhere in the social sciences, deductively driven analysis is evident in such well-known works as Talcott Parsons, *The Social System* (Glencoe: Free Press, 1951); Mancur Olson, *The Logic of Collective Action* (Cambridge: Harvard University Press, 1965); George Homans, *Social Behavior: Its Elementary Forms* (New York: Harcourt Brace, 1974); Peter Blau, *Approaches to the Study of Social Structure* (New York: Free Press, 1975); Michael Hechter, *The Principles of Group Solidarity* (Berkeley: University of California

Press, 1987); James Coleman, *Foundations of Social Theory* (Cambridge: Harvard/Belnap Press, 1990); and Richard Ellis, Michael Thompson and Aaron Wildavsky, *Cultural Theory* (Boulder: Westview, 1990).

18. Examples of quantitative approaches in IR include J. David Singer, ed. *Quantitative International Politics: Insights and Evidence* (New York: Free Press, 1968); Paul Diehl, "Arms Races to War: Testing Some Empirical Linkages," *Sociological Quarterly*, 27 (1985): 322–349; and Claudio Cioffi-Revilla, *The Scientific Measurement of International Conflict* (Boulder: Lynne Rienner, 1990). For a more general discussion of empiricism in IR theory, see Michael Nicholson, *The Scientific Analysis of Social Behaviour: A Defense of Empiricism in Social Science* (London: Pinter, 1983).

19. Many comparative-historical, neoliberal institutionalist, and constructivist studies of IR offer good examples of a more qualitatively oriented inductive approach to IR theory. See, for example, John Ruggie, "International Regimes, Transactions, and Change: Embedded Liberalism in the Postwar Economic Order," *International Organization* 36, 2 (1982): 379–415; Ernst Haas, *When Knowledge Is Power* (Berkeley: University of California Press, 1990); Steven Weber, *Cooperation and Discord in U.S-Soviet Arms Control* (Princeton: Princeton University Press, 1991); Peter Katzenstein, *Cultural Norms and National Security: Police and Military in Postwar Japan* (Ithaca: Cornell University Press, 1996); and Elizabeth Kier, *Imagining War: French and British Military Doctrine Between the Wars* (Princeton: Princeton University Press, 1997). Elsewhere in the social sciences, examples of different kinds of qualitative approaches range from Clifford Geertz, *The Interpretation of Cultures* (New York: Basic Books, 1973), to more comparative approaches of varying degrees of causal significance such as Barrington Moore, *The Social Origins of Dictatorship and Democracy* (Boston: Beacon, 1966); Theda Skocpol, *States and Social Revolutions* (Cambridge: Cambridge University Press, 1979); Charles Tilly, *Coercion, Capital and European States* (Oxford: Blackwell, 1990); and Liah Greenfeld, *Nationalism: Five Roads to Modernity* (Cambridge: Harvard University Press, 1992).

20. Thus, I do not include Immanuel Wallerstein's world-systems theory in the category of deductive theorizing where most structuralist arguments would normally located. Wallerstein makes it very clear that his world-system is an emergent, historically generated structure; although this structure is no less determining of contemporary outcomes than Waltz's international system, it is a result of historical processes rather than universally valid laws of human behavior, and the outcomes

explained by the world-system can ultimately be traced back to consequences of historical conjunctures. See Immanuell Wallerstein, *The
Modern World-System*. 3 volumes (New York: Academic Press,
1974–1988), and "World-Systems Analysis—The Second Phase,"
Review 13 (Spring 1990): 287–293. For an additional contrast that
emphasizes the ontological irreducibility of Wallerstein's world-system
(as opposed to Waltz's international system where the units remain
ontologically primitive), see Wendt.

21. It is not surprising that attempts to "bridge" the agent-structure divide
in the social sciences are typically constructed on the basis of either a
deductive or an inductive approach, with each of the "middle
grounds" between agency and structure only extending the number of
levels at which the deductive/inductive debate can be conducted.

22. Bueno de Mesquita, "Toward a Scientific Understanding of International Conflict," *International Studies Quarterly*, 29 (1985): 121–136,
quote from p. 128; emphasis original.

23. Thus, even if many deductivists reject Kant's critique of "pure reason,"
they are at least "neo-Kantian" in assigning primacy to pure, universal
categories of human understanding.

24. James Coleman, a rational choice theorist, suggests that even zealots
seeking martyrdom are utility-maximizing in that they seek rewards for
their self-sacrificing behavior in a future life. This is certainly more creative than simply describing zealots as "irrational," but how one views
death and whether one feels protected by divine intervention may have
a great deal to do with how costs, risks, and benefits are calculated by
a potential zealot. The values and beliefs that shape the individual's
definition of interests and the historical circumstances that shape the
choice situation confronting a potential martyr are absolutely integral
if we are to draw meaningful inferences about the choice itself. See
James Coleman, "Free-riders and Zealots," in Karen Cook, ed., *Social
Exchange Theory* (Newbury Park: Sage, 1987), pp. 59–82.

25. On this point, see Victoria Bonnell, "The Uses of Theory, Concepts and
Comparison in Historical Sociology," *Comparative Studies in Society
and History* 2, 2 (April 1980): 156–173.

26. Weber, "'Objectivity' in Social Science and Social Policy," pp. 34–35.

27. Charles Taylor, "Interpretation and the Sciences of Man," p. 125
(emphasis added).

28. Quoted in Dallmayr and McCarthy, "The Crisis of Understanding," in
Dallmayr and McCarthy, p. 4.

29. Rabinow and Sullivan, p. 6.

30. While Parsons might regard this ambiguity as an attempt by Weber to
mask his positive commitment to causal explanation in an academic

environment where positive science was increasingly becoming unfashionable (ff. 13), others see him using causal formulations solely as heuristic devices to advance his primary goal, to understand and interpret the meanings attached by actors to their actions in specific historical contexts. See, for example, the interpretation of Reinhard Bendix in *Max Weber: An Intellectual Portrait*, 2nd ed. (Berkeley: University of California Press, 1977).

31. Weber, "'Objectivity' in Social Science and Social Policy," pp. 34–35.
32. Weber, "'Objectivity' in Social Science and Social Policy," pp. 25–34.
33. In practice, Weber's search for a middle ground between explanation and understanding is evident in his comparative study of world religions, and also comes across in his famous argument in the *Protestant Ethic and the Spirit of Capitalism*. *The Protestant Ethic* does not posit a causal theory of the rise of capitalism as some have assumed. Rather, Weber offers a *partial* account of the role of cultural "rationalization" (as evident in Calvin's reformulation of Christian religious doctrines) in establishing and legitimizing capitalism and the middle-class way of life as a viable basis for a new, more "rationalized" political economy. This account is derived from Weber's own "analytic accentuation" of the relationship between changes in religious doctrine and the role of religion on the one hand, and the institutionalization of a new type of economic organization on the other. See Max Weber, *The Protestant Ethic and the Spirit of Capitalism* (New York: Scribner's, 1958).
34. Among classical social scientists, Durkheim is a perfect representative of this perspective: As long as empirical observation was the basis for the generation of concepts and theories, values could be identified and examined objectively by the theorist even if bias is involved in the choice of a question. The designation of "crucial facts" was a scientific exercise and uncompromised by whatever biases the investigator might harbor. Durkheim's epistemology is mostly outlined in *The Rules of Sociological Method* (ff. 7). See also the discussion of Durkheim's methodology in Neil J. Smelser, *Comparative Methods in the Social Sciences* (Englewood Cliffs: Prentice-Hall, 1976), chapters 3 and 4.
35. See Karl Popper, *The Open Society and Its Enemies* (London: Routledge and Sons, 1945), and *The Logic of Scientific Discovery* (New York: Science Editions, 1961). Note, however, that "intersubjective convention" can include the smuggling in of common shared values.
36. Martin Landau, *Political Theory and Political Science: Studies in the Methodology of Political Inquiry* (New Jersey: Humanities Press, 1972), p. 45.
37. Karl Mannheim, *Ideology and Utopia* (New York: Harcourt, Brace and World, Harvest edition, 1965), p. 28.

38. See, for example, the classic statement by Alvin Gouldner in "Anti-Minotaur: The Myth of a Value-Free Sociology," in Irving Louis Horowitz, ed., *The New Sociology: Essays in Social Science and Social Theory in Honor of C. Wright Mills* (London: Oxford University Press, 1964).

39. Weber, "Objectivity' in Social Science and Social Policy," in Dallmayr and McCarthy, p. 29.

40. Weber, "Science as a Vocation," in H. H. Gerth and C. W. Mills, *From Max Weber* (New York: Oxford University Press, 1949), p. 129–158.

41. Weber, "Science as a Vocation" and "Politics as a Vocation" in Gerth and Mills.

42. Horkheimer, "Traditional and Critical Theory," (1937), quoted in Phil Slater, *Origin and Significance of the Frankfurt School: A Marxist Perspective* (London: Routledge and Kegan Paul, 1977). This "critical theory" position was clearly influenced by Marx's own legacy of "praxis," consisting of an objective theory of dialectical change ("historical materialism"), a critique of bourgeois capitalism, and writings advocating programs and strategies of revolution. Marx attempted to outline his theoretical project of "historical materialism" (based on the superimposition of a Hegelian dialectic on the objective material conditions in history) in *The German Ideology*. The critique of capitalism includes *Grundrisse: Foundations of the Critique of Political Economy* and *Capital*, 3 volumes. The involvement in real political struggles for revolutionary change is represented in the *The Communist Manifesto* by Marx and Engles in 1848 shortly before the political upheavels in France. Representative excerpts for all of these works may be found in Robert C. Tucker, ed., *The Marx-Engels Reader*, 2nd ed. (New York: Norton, 1978).

43. See Habermas, "Modernity Versus Postmodernity," in Rabinow and Sullivan. Habermas, despite his obvious admiration for many aspects of Weber's epistemology, criticizes him on this point: "A reified everyday praxis can be cured only by creating unconstrained interaction of the cognitive with the moral-practical and the aesthetic-expressive elements. Reification cannot be overcome by forcing just one of those highly stylized cultural spheres to open up and become more accessible" (p. 152).

44. Thus, I am more sympathetic to Habermas's "communicative rationality" project than to the more programmatic search for "praxis" seen in Horkheimer's "ideology-critique" or Adorno's position in *Negative Dialectics* (London: Routledge and Kegan Paul, 1973).

45. A similar position is taken by Ernst Haas in his "Reason and Change in International Life: Justifying a Hypothesis," *Journal of International*

Affairs (Spring/Summer 1990), esp. pp. 230–231. Although Haas's language is not too different from the language of positivists (e.g., he draws a stark distinction between "scientific knowledge" and "ideology"), his emphasis on the role of self-reflection and self-correcting procedures in the quest for modest truth-claims distinguishes him as a "soft" positivist.

46. A somewhat more sophisticated formulation is described as "neojustificationism": although final confirmation through external validation is seen as impossible, it is nevertheless reasonable to accept a theory if the evidence overwhelmingly supported it. "Justificationism" and "Neojustificationism" are defined and critiqued in Imre Lakatos, *The Methodology of Scientific Research Programs*, volume 1 (London: Cambridge University Press, 1978).

47. Bueno de Mesquita, "Toward a Scientific Understanding . . . ," p. 122.

48. Popper, *Logic of Scientific Discovery*, pp. 40–41 (emphasis added).

49. See the excellent discussion of Popper's criteria for the refutation of theories in Imre Lakatos, "Falsification and theMethodology of Scientific Research Programmes," in Lakatos and Alan Musgrave, eds., *Criticism and the Growth of Knowledge* (Cambridge: Cambridge University Press, 1970), pp. 106–112.

50. Karl Popper, *Conjectures and Refutations* (London: Routledge and Kengan Paul, 1963), pp. 216–217, also quoted in Landau.

51. Bueno de Mesquita, "Toward a Scientific Understanding . . . ," p. 122.

52. Lakatos, *The Methodology of Scientific Research Programs*, p. 32.

53. "Intertextuality" in postmodernist approaches is discussed by Rosenau.

54. Kuhn, passim.

55. Paul Feyerabend, "Consolation for a Specialist," in Lakatos and Musgrave, and his *Against Method: Outline of an Anarchistic Theory of Knowledge* (London: New Left Books, 1975).

56. See Rabinow and Sullivan, p. 5.

57. See, for example, Richard Bernstein, *Beyond Objectivism and Relativism: Science, Hermeneutics and Praxis* (Philadelphia: University of Pennsylvania Press, 1983). For similarly flexible understandings of "rationality," see Stephen Toulmin, *Human Understanding* (Princeton: Princeton University Press, 1972).

58. Margaret Archer, "Resisting the Revival of Relativism," in Martin Albrow and Elizabeth King, eds., *Globalization, Knowledge and Society* (London: Sage, 1990), pp. 19–33

59. Even at this extreme, as evident in my distinction between categories 7 and 8, it is possible to distinguish the deconstructionists such as Derrida and Lyotard from writers like Foucault who at least attempt to

produce a historically rooted alternative narrative in order to challenge truth claims based texts reflecting the perspective of those in power. On this point, see Rosenau's distinction between "affirmative" and "skeptical" postmodernists as well as Callinicos's contrast between "textualist" and "contextualist" postmodern epistemology; the latter may be found in Alex Callenicos, "Postmodernism, Post-Structuralism and Post-Marxism?" in *Theory, Culture and Society,* 2: 3 (1985) 85–102.

60. From the positivist end, the convergence on a Weberian "center" may be evident in the Jurgen Habermas *The Theory of Communicative Action, Volume 2: Lifeworld and System*, trans. T. McCarthy (Boston: Beacon Press, 1983); Haas, "Reason and Change"; and Peter Katzenstein, contribution to "The Role of Theory in Comparative Politics: A Symposium," *World Politics* 48, 1 (October 1995): 10–15. Some of the earlier interpretive approaches that appear to converge on the center from the subjectivist or historicist end might include: Clifford Geertz, "Thick Description: Toward an Interpretive Theory of Culture," in *The Interpretation of Cultures* (New York: Basic Books, 1973); Peter Berger and Thomas Luckmann, *The Social Construction of Reality* (Garden City: Doubleday, 1967); Robert Bellah's essays in *Beyond Belief* (New York: Basic Books, 1973); and Pierre Bourdieu, *The Logic of Practice* (Cambridge, UK: Polity Press, 1990).

7

THRESHOLDS IN THE EVOLUTION OF SOCIAL SCIENCE

WADE L. HUNTLEY

> The fault, dear Brutus, is not in our stars,
> But in ourselves, that we are underlings.
> —William Shakespeare, *Julius Caesar*

> Good fences make good neighbors.
> —Robert Frost, "Mending Wall"

In the twentieth century, the exercise of social analysis—development of social facts through rigorous rational practices for the purpose of explaining and understanding human life—has become increasingly characterized by specialization, compartmentalization, and narrow focus. Such "boundaries" now abound in the social sciences, delimiting disciplines, epistemologies, paradigms, methodologies, and relevance to social practice.[1] Criticism of this condition has made the issue itself yet another point of differentiation, yielding yet another apparent boundary. As if there are not enough problems and conflicts in the "real" world, many social analysts today seem devoted to pursuing agendas defined as narrowly as possible and to competitively promoting their chosen agendas over all others, consequently inventing ever more problems and conflicts in our efforts to understand and assess that world.

This essay presents a collection of observations on this condition. My principle aim is to distinguish between the illusory and legitimate difficulties for social analysis that the proliferation of specializations and "boundaries" presents. My hope is that a clearer understanding of the nature of this proliferation will reveal the virtues as well as the vices of such boundaries, and point to paths of escape from their most vexing consequences.

My thesis has two points of departure. First, I shall argue that the notion of "boundaries" itself is a misnomer. Rather, the distinctions in the social sciences that the term characterizes are better thought of as "thresholds." Whereas the concept of "boundary" connotes forced separation and perhaps antipathy, the concept of "threshold" inheres suggestions of both separation and joining—one "crosses" a "threshold." This latter idea, as I shall seek to explain, better describes the nature of most delineations of human inquiry— between theories and research traditions, physical and social sciences, differing social science disciplines, or social science and public policy.

The second point of departure for my argument is recognition of the historical origins of, and hence explanations for, the ongoing proliferation of such thresholds. I shall argue that, when viewed in proper historical perspective, the proliferation of thresholds in social analysis was—and still is—a natural and inevitable stage in the development of social analysis. Rather than representing a breakdown in the vocation and a lost hope for theoretical integration and cumulation, the "crisis" of proliferation indicates the potential culmination of this stage. Indeed, this culmination represents perhaps the next threshold in the history of social analysis, crossing which will require not nostalgia for a long-past simplicity but rather development of new perspectives and modes of approach to solving problems.

In thinking about this problem, I have found it useful to consider, as a heuristic device, certain metaphors and analogies to developments in human understanding of the physical universe. In this essay, I employ this device liberally, in order to make several points about the nature, function, difficulty, and desirability of thresholds in the social sciences. First, I utilize contemporary understandings of the nature of the physical universe as a metaphor to describe what I take to be the inevitability of both thresholds themselves and their problematic nature. Second, I note how this understanding of the physical universe arose from physical sciences' confrontations with epistemological issues analogous to those presently at issue in the social sciences, in order to draw out several useful lessons for understanding the relationships between contesting approaches. Finally, I consider how these metaphorical and analogical descriptions omit certain problems unique to the social sciences, centered on the existence of human sentience, intentionality, and the relevance of knowledge claims to moral choices. I conclude that "thresholds" are "made," and that they are made to be crossed. This understanding of the present condition holds the most promise for translating the *accumulation* of human knowledge into *cumulative* understanding of, and practical improvement of, the human condition.

The Expanding Universe of Knowledge

Physicists tell us that the universe is expanding. According to current theories, the universe began some 10–20 billion years ago in a "Big Bang" previous to which there was . . . nothing—not space, not time, not any physical property of which knowledge survived the "Big Bang" itself.[2] On the momentum of this instant of creation the universe has grown. In its earliest moments the great miasma constituting existence began coalescing into identifiable entities, combining and reacting to produce unique structures, ever more distinct from their neighbors. With this coalescence came the eruption of spaces between these structures. The very gathering of galaxies necessitated the vast voids between them. Today, still riding the momentum of creation, the galaxies that populate the universe continue to race away from one another at inconceivable speeds, stretching the distances between them into equally inconceivable gaping voids of empty space.

To human comprehension, this understanding of the physical universe is very new (as is our appreciation of our own minuscule, peripheral, and perhaps wholly insignificant place in that universe). Hence, the understanding itself has an historical origin and context. Accordingly, while constituting a fascinating advance in human comprehension of the known world, this understanding also reflects the continuing limitations of that comprehension. These limitations are evident in the baffling and complex paradoxes inherent to this understanding that remain beyond the grasp of most human minds. They are also obvious in the persistent questions (and, indeed, contradictions) that this understanding has not solved or resolved.[3]

Importantly, both the cutting edge and the trailing wake of this understanding denote its stage of historical development. Most important ideas have similar life histories. The idea that our world is round was itself, not too long ago, an individual insight that took time to gain knowledgeable adherence, more time to overcome both knowledgeable and political resistance, and more time yet to gain widespread acceptance and *intuitive* appreciation. The subsequent idea that the world is a planet that orbits in a predictable fashion around one star among many billions of other stars also faced such a process. Indeed, Galileo Galilie's early seventeenth century contests with the Catholic church over this Copernican theory is one of the more famous examples of this process, as well as a formative period in the history of both physics and epistemology.[4] Today, most people experience little difficulty grasping these concepts. In similar fashion, there likely will come a day when high school students grasp with equivalent intuition the current "cutting edge" understanding that our world does not in fact travel in a circular orbit around a star, but rather in a straight line through a curved "space-time" whose geography is defined by the gravitational forces of the various stars and planets that populate it.

An additional feature of current understanding of the physical universe is its very dependence on the limitations of our perception—or, more accurately, our understanding of those limitations. The very idea that the universe is expanding, that celestial bodies grow ever more distant from us, arises only by virtue of a *distortion* in the images of these bodies that we receive. Many of us are already familiar with the way the sound of a train whistle or a car engine seems to change its tone as the train or car passes us by. Early in the twentieth century, astronomers discovered that this "Doppler effect" could also be employed to measure the relative velocities of other galaxies. For galaxies moving away from our own, the "Doppler effect" would shift the light we receive from them into lower (or "redder") frequencies than those at which the light was emitted. Because types of galaxies emit characteristic patterns of light frequencies, astronomers can discern the pattern of any given galaxy and then measure the extent of this lowering of frequencies—that is, the "red shift."[5] Because a galaxy's "red shift" represents the distortion produced by that galaxy's movement away from the earth's galaxy, the extent of this shift yields a measure of the velocity of that movement.

In the 1920s, Edwin Hubble, already famous for demonstrating the existence of other galaxies and measuring their distances from our own, used measurements of galaxies' red shifts to discover that *all* galaxies are moving *away* from our own. This discovery was startling enough, insofar as it contradicted the expectation that galaxies moved in more or less random fashion (and hence that some would be moving toward our own). Yet Hubble went on to establish that the velocity at which other galaxies are moving away from ours is exactly proportionate to their distance from ours. Discovery of this ratio—now known as "Hubble's constant"— became the basis for the determination that the universe is expanding, revolutionizing cosmology. Thus, contemporary understandings of the basic nature of the universe depend on appreciation of how perceptions can be systematically distorted.

These features of contemporary understandings of the physical universe—its historicity, its limitations as a function of its progress, and its dependence on appreciation of distortion—provide, *metaphorically*, a mode of understanding of the present state and dynamic evolution of the "universe of human knowledge." We can conceive of human knowledge as having a moment of origin—a "Big Bang"—occurring with the emergence of human sentience. From this moment on, human knowledge proceeded to (and continues to) expand, in the sense that the "quantity" of human "ideas" about the world, available (at least potentially) to any individuals seeking to answer their own questions about the nature of the worlds they perceive, is characterized by continuing growth.[6]

One way to conceive of this notion of the "expansion of knowledge" is by envisioning a *sphere*: its internal space represents knowledge, while its surface represents the "frontiers" of knowledge. These frontiers are the places where the newest ideas of what we "know" give way to the next immediate questions concerning what we do not know. Each new question answered brings that idea within the sphere, expanding the sphere and pushing out its surface, thereby extending the frontier to reach even newer questions. Just as it is literally impossible to envision what lies beyond the known limits of the physical universe, so with the universe of knowledge is it impossible to conceive of knowledge yet to be achieved. We do not know what we have yet to come to know—we cannot place ourselves outside the sphere's frontier. Thus, so long as we retain the consciousness to inquire, the expansion of knowledge can perhaps proceed indefinitely.[7] To complete the image, all that remains is to envision not a sphere but a more complex, amorphous shape, expanding in a myriad of directions and dimensions, including protrusions and pockets of ever greater complexity.[8]

At the dawn of sentience, the domain of knowledge was small. Just as at some primordial early moment the entire universe was within an arm's reach, so at some early moment was all knowledge, in a manner of speaking, within a single mind's reach. Relative to today, the domain of knowledge remained relatively small for much of human history. Thus, individuals contemplating the nature of "the world" would naturally—and necessarily—come to master a wide variety of topics in human knowledge. More accurately, Aristotles and Galileos, although seeking answers to consciously conceived questions through some manner of rational thought, were relatively oblivious to rigorous distinctions among differing disciplines and methods. With less preexisting knowledge available, questions of all types were more obviously related to one another, and mastery of many topics was realistically attainable.

However, as each "master" added to the stock of human knowledge, the inexorable expansion of this stock soon brought a close to the era in which any one person could be such a "master." Each new thinker brought a new perspective of inquiry; with growing perspectives of inquiry, new questions proliferated, beyond the capacity of any one individual to address more than a handful. Also, questions became more distant from one another, their mutual relevance more obscure. With the acquisition of such ideas as, for example, that changes in the weather could be traced to causes independent of the will of the gods, questions as to the most efficient ways to grow crops and the most just ways to distribute the harvest began to move away from one another—perhaps first in the minds of forefront thinkers, but eventually and inevitably in more common thought as well.

Moreover, the proliferation of questions necessarily brought with it a proliferation of answers, beyond the capacity of any one individual to learn more than a handful. Absent the time or capacity to familiarize themselves with so many bodies of knowledge, thinkers could hardly hope even to know what questions others were asking, let alone what answers they were generating. Not only the mutual relevance of differing topics of inquiry, but also the results of these inquiries, were becoming increasingly obscure. What awareness one could obtain for the agendas and results of other foci of study necessarily became increasingly partial and unrepresentative. Just as the increasing distances among galaxies dimmed and distorted the light they exchanged, so did increasing distances among foci of inquiry breed unfamiliarity and distortion of insights.

Inevitably, thresholds among differing "galaxies" of inquiry began naturally to emerge. This process was reinforced by concomitant expansion *within* each emerging galaxy. Thus, for example, the accumulation of knowledge about the nature and causes of the weather, and about the proper social organization of crop distribution, in turn yielded more detailed and sequestered analysis of weather and distribution, respectively. In this manner, a relentless expansion of the scope and complexity of human knowledge has come to characterize the modern (post-Enlightenment) era of human history. Individuals inquiring into the nature of "the world" now necessarily move through ever-growing galaxies of available knowledge before finally reaching an area of knowledge's frontiers. As these frontiers themselves continue growing, those reaching them discover within their range of comprehension only a small portion of that frontier.

Thus, today, individuals seeking sincerely to contribute to the advance of human knowledge face long sequences of choices among questions to address and preexisting answers to master. Once finally reaching that venerable opportunity to ask and answer questions truly unasked and unanswered before, individuals discover that the thresholds separating these questions from even closely related topics are now considerable, if not immense. Moreover, the now extensive thresholds between bodies of knowledge necessarily *distort* the communications among them. Foci of inquiry have become so distant and unfamiliar to one another that the very languages they utilize are often mutually incomprehensible. To the extent that patterns among divergent foci are also difficult to discern, there also is no "thought shift" (akin to the astronomical "red shift") to reveal even the character of this distortion.

The emergence of "international relations" exemplifies this process. In its own context, Thucydides' *History of the Pelopenesian War* is as much a work of literature as of history or political analysis. Similarly, although Thomas Hobbes is widely regarded as having provided one of the earliest modern evocations of international political theory, his *Leviathan* is a work of philosophy as much as of politics, and is only peripherally concerned with international relations per se.[9] The notion of expanding human knowledge helps explain why tracing roots of the discipline to Thucydides and Hobbes is nevertheless more than appropriate. In their day, the discipline of international relations had not yet emerged, and so few questions yet existed on the topic to which their analysis could be widely applicable. Rousseau, although less renowned in international relations theory than Hobbes, in fact devoted greater specific attention to problems of international politics. Yet he also still explicitly conceived of these issues as part of a more general set of problems of political organization.[10] But while these early thinkers' works might be viewed as crossing "boundaries" between disciplines and methodologies, in fact their thought depicts an era in which thresholds simply were less profligate.

Only in the nineteenth century did political analysis truly diverge from political philosophy, and "social science" in its modern sense truly come into being. As bestowed by Comte, Spencer, Durkheim, Weber, and others, this new threshold between philosophy and political analysis delimited epistemologies and methodologies as much as fields and disciplines. By the end of the nineteenth century, this threshold itself was giving rise to new thresholds within the broader discipline: sociology became but one form of social science, accompanied by economics, psychology, anthropology, "political science," and others.[11]

Finally, in the twentieth century, as a result of the continuing expansion of knowledge and proliferation of thresholds (as well as the dominant impact on human society of interstate wars early in the century), thresholds developed marking off "international relations" as a discipline in its own right. Previously seen as an aspect of philosophy, history, and law, the study of international relations began to emerge as a nomothetic social science only with the coming of the First World War.[12] In the aftermath of the Second World War, the work of such eminent theorists as Hans Morgenthau and E. H. Carr was aimed specifically at further carving out "international relations" as a separate subject matter.[13] The work of Kenneth Waltz, renowned rather statically as a foundation of modern "realism," when viewed dynamically also nicely conveys this development: of Waltz's two most notable works, the earlier evokes the synthesis of philosophy and analysis characteristic of the works of Hobbes, Rousseau, and the other philosophers the work assesses, whereas the latter strongly conveys the self-consciously and clearly defined disciplinary and methodological boundaries Waltz and other contemporaries then conceived and advocated for the vocation.[14]

Today, the field of international politics alone has expanded to the point of encompassing a growing selection of subdisciplinary specialties and contending methodologies. Following the initial divergence of security studies and international political economy, scholars have now come to focus their attentions on global patterns, regional circumstances, discrete events, effects of regime type, psychological and interpersonal dimensions of decisionmaking, and a host of other topics. Analysts employ a range of qualitative and quantitative methodological techniques, ascribe to epistemological dispositions ranging from positivist to postmodern, and offer analyses and conclusions evincing realist, liberal, and radical perspectives.

This emergence, coalescence, evolution, and subsequent fracturing of international politics as a discipline of study simply exemplifies a broader trend throughout intellectual inquiry toward the proliferation of what we now view as "boundaries" among disciplines, epistemologies, and methodologies of human inquiry. This proliferation is a simple function of the expansion of the "universe of human knowledge" over time.[15]

More important than this point itself are the issues the observation raises. Most debates over the nature and function of "boundaries" in social analysis revolve around issues of their propriety—that is, whether "boundaries" are in some sense or another "good" or "bad." However, understanding the issue instead as a proliferation of *thresholds* resulting from the inevitable expansion of human knowledge reveals the former formulation of the problem to be misconceived—we might as well ask if it is good or bad that the sun rises and sets. Delineation and specialization are neither good nor bad, but rather the ineluctable and inevitable result of the natural expansion of human knowledge. Indeed, the proliferation of the former is something of a measure of the latter. The emergence of thresholds and apparent boundaries in this universe of human inquiry is then an inevitable and irreversible byproduct of the progress.

Or, I should say, *apparently* irreversible. Here, the metaphorical use of the understanding of the expansion of the physical universe given by contemporary physics is particularly apt. Albert Einstein's "general theory of relativity" posits that the universe is a "space-time" medium in which time and space are simply differing dimensions, and that this medium is not constant or "flat," but distorted or "curved."[16] Contemporary theory now holds that the universe is expanding, and galaxies receding, not because they are "moving" away from one another per se, but rather because the space-time medium of the universe *itself* is expanding. Moreover, less than a century after Albert Einstein established the speed of light as the universal limit to velocity, thereby seemingly placing nearby stars—let alone other galaxies— forever beyond human reach, cosmologists now speculate on the possibilities of simply transcending, rather than traversing, these impossible distances. This prospect emerges from the understanding of the universe as a *curved* "space-time" medium, in which distant points in the universe might be linked as simply as folding a sheet of paper links its opposite edges.[17]

The useful point that this image suggests is that the universe of human knowledge is expanding, and differing disciplines *apparently* receding from one another, not because the topics of inquiry are becoming any more inherently distant or disassociated, but rather because ongoing inquiry expands the *medium* of knowledge, creating the *appearance* of pushing knowledge on various topics farther away.

Hence, the manner of thought most fruitful to overcoming the apparently expanding thresholds of knowledge might not be striving to bridge them by ever-longer and more tenuous linkages. Rather, what is needed is to *transcend* these thresholds, by formulating a new and more imaginative understanding of the nature of knowledge, and exploring new dimensions of inquiry within which the natural bonds across disparate thresholds might be rediscovered. Contemporary understandings of the nature of the physical universe invite us to conceive of linkages in the universe of human knowledge as intellectual "geodesics," which appear long and complex only because of the limitations of our understanding of this universe itself.

The field of international relations again offers a good representative example of this point. Many have judged that the proliferation of boundaries and thresholds marks a disintegration and hence diminution of the activity of intellectual inquiry in its broadest sense, producing more immediate and discernible costs as well. Many have hence sought explicitly to develop new specializations that are "cross-boundary" or "interdisciplinary"—such subfields as "political psychology" or "economic sociology" are examples. Conceived as efforts to link disparate disciplines or methodologies, the intention is to develop lateral connections that will stitch back together what is perceived to be a disintegrating domain.

These efforts are laudable, but potentially misguided, in two senses. First, cross-disciplinary linkages may provide immediate benefit for proximate topics of inquiry, but to the extent that these links themselves become quite specialized, they also create new thresholds (and perhaps new boundaries) of their own. Hence, the proliferation of such lateral linkages reinforces rather than countervails the process of increasing specialization, thus evincing rather than transcending the current trajectory of proliferation. Moreover, such efforts are in a sense destined to be futile, requiring ever-greater efforts and ever-more complex contrivances.

This leads to the second and more central point: the conviction that the universe of knowledge requires restitching in the first place is based on a misperception of the proliferation of thresholds as a problematic *disintegration* rather than as simply a stage of evolution, an era in a historical continuum. Placing the current era of proliferation into its proper historical context reveals that the objective cannot be to reclaim the primordial conditions of a prior era, but should be instead to prepare for and perhaps facilitate the arrival of a future era whose form is as yet unknowable. The objective ought to be to transcend rather than combat thresholds, and this requires first embracing the inevitability—and in many cases the merits—of those thresholds.

I have argued that the variety of thresholds of all types in social analysis arise from the nature and success of inquiry itself. Thresholds are in this sense inevitable. However, they are also useful in so far as they provide *location*. Thresholds among disciplines create a *geography* of knowledge, illuminating the form of the expanding substance. If questions that previously seemed intimately related now, at the frontiers of knowledge, seem apparently quite distant, the thresholds between constitute the data of that distance. Cosmologists, thinking long enough about the data of the distance separating disparate points of the physical universe, reconceived the very medium of that distance as a curved entity that transcends the distances. In the same manner, inquiring into and learning about the *nature* of the proliferating thresholds in the universe of knowledge offers the best promise, instead of painstakingly traversing the distances between profligate and disparate loci of the intellectual universe, of discovering new modes of inquiry that by their very nature *transcend* these distances.

Relativity and Relativism

Among the more extensive thresholds to emerge in the expanding universe of human knowledge are those that separate differing ontologies and epistemologies—definitions and judgments on what constitutes knowledge itself and how knowledge may be generated. Such questions have long bedeviled philosophers, dating at least to Plato's Cave Allegory, one interpretation of which is the idea that knowledge is essentially perceptual, or subjective—that what we see depends on where we stand.

Plato, however, was perhaps less concerned about the nature of knowledge itself than in establishing the privileged position of the philosopher, who would be king. Modern credit for this idea is more aptly traced to Immanuel Kant, whose landmark philosophical insight—his self-termed "Copernican revolution"—was to locate the foundation of human knowledge not in experiences themselves, but in constructions the mind produces for the purposes of understanding those experiences. Direct knowledge of the "noumenal" world of "things as they are" is not possible; experiencing only the "phenomenal" world of "things as they seem," the mind must impose its own order. Hence, "we can know *a priori* of things only what we ourselves put into them . . . knowledge has to do only with appearances, and must leave the thing in itself as indeed real per se, but as not known by us."[18]

The proliferation of contrasting answers to questions concerning the nature of knowledge is also a more modern phenomenon. In the field of international relations, as in many other fields in the social sciences, the fissures between advocates of "positivist" or "materialist" viewpoints on the one hand, and "postmodern" or "constructivist" viewpoints on the other, have perhaps never been greater. These differences constitute some of the most obstructive thresholds in the contemporary study of human society. Ontological and epistemological issues, however, have also confronted students of the physical universe for quite some time. Although, on first consideration, the discipline of physics might seem an odd place to look for insights and advice in consideration of the epistemological conflicts bedeviling contemporary social science, some of the ways in which physicists have met and resolved the problems these issues pose can be instructive to social analysts.

I do not make this latter claim to resurrect the hackneyed notions that the rigorous study of human society must always takes its cues from inquiries into the nature of the physical world, or—worse yet—that "hard science" can by its nature produce knowledge with a level of certitude impossible in the realm of human relations, imposing a permanent inferiority and yearning embodied in the appellation "social science" itself. I shall argue in the third section that this dichotomy is false in any event. Here I would like merely to begin with a somewhat more modest claim: that students of the physical world (at least in the discipline of cosmology) have met and to some degree overcome the epistemological quandries still bedeviling social analysts in ways that can be helpful—but only partially—to social analysts.

The primary revolutions in physics that introduced Kantian epistemological insights into understandings of the physical world were the introduction of Albert Einstein's concept of "relativity" and Werner Heisenberg's contemporaneous positing of his "uncertainty principle." The view of the physical world given by these theoretical insights, in contrast to the preceding view given by the theories of Isaac Newton, evoke and in some respects embrace the *perceptual* basis of all knowledge. Crucially, however, both Einstein's and Heisenberg's arguments rely precisely on the classical presumption of the objectivity (i.e., the replicability and commensurability) of sensory data from the point of view of human observers, *given the same conditions of perception (i.e., frames of reference).*[19] This paradoxical result obtains from the unique synthesis of vying ontological and epistemological positions inherent in modern theoretical physics. I argue below that the nature of this synthesis offers useful insights to social analysts grappling to reconcile similarly contrasting ontological and epistemological positions—though often through analogy, rather than replication.

Einstein stands as the progenitor of modern theoretical physics chiefly for his introduction of the notion of *relativity*. The most colloquially familiar application of the "special theory of relativity" built on this idea is the unity of matter and energy given in the famous equation $E = MC^2$. However, more relevant here is the central implication of the theory: even perceptions of the measures of time and space depend on the situation (in particular the velocity) of the observer. The theory establishes the velocity of light as the maximum velocity obtainable by anything anywhere in the universe, but also as a *constant* regardless of one's own particular velocity. In fact, it posits that all laws of physics, including the speed of light, are the same for all freely moving observers, regardless of the observers' own velocities. Thus, individuals traveling at half the speed of light would perceive nothing unusual about the passage of time on their own ships—and would perceive a light shown forward to be traveling still at the speed of light! Suggesting something of a reverse Doppler effect, the theory thus posits that moving observers, instead of perceiving a change in the speed of light, instead experience a change in the passage of time—more precisely, as velocity increases, time passes more slowly. Thus, in theory, space travelers could roam the universe at near-light speeds and return after a few years to discover that on earth centuries had passed. In sum, by embracing the universal constancy of the speed of light, the "special theory of relativity" discards the idea of "absolute time"—that is, that time passes at a uniform rate everywhere in the universe.[20]

Of perhaps even greater epistemological significance, to both the physical sciences and social analysis, is Heisenberg's demonstration of the existence of a fundamental limit to the precision with which any natural phenomenon can be measured. Heisenberg's "uncertainty principle," an inescapable property of the universe, fully undermines *naive* scientific determinism: because, even in principle, the exact status of the universe at any given instant can never be known, the future behavior of the universe can never be perfectly predicted. Heisenberg and others used the uncertainty principle to develop the theory of quantum mechanics, which holds that one can predict only the approximate proportions among a range of outcomes of multiple measurements, not the specific outcome of any single measurement.[21] As Stephen Hawking notes:

> The uncertainty principle had profound implications for the way in which we view the world. Even after more than fifty years they have not been appreciated by many philosophers, and are still the subject of much controversy. The uncertainty principle signaled an end to Laplace's dream of a theory of science, a model of the universe that would be completely deterministic. . . . Quantum mechanics therefore introduces an unavoidable element of unpredictability or randomness into science.[22]

Thus, the uncertainty principle, and the theory of quantum mechanics built on it, suggest something of a Kantian ontology for the physical universe: we can posit the existence of an objective universe, and even posit laws and equations concerning its operation, but perfect observation of it must always elude us.[23]

These ideas concerning the intrinsic unpredictability of the *natural* universe might at first appear, in the realm of social science, to hand victory in epistemological debates to positivism's staunchest critics, and in particular postmodern theorists who have long sought to storm the ramparts of positivist social science with assertions of the subjectivity of all human knowledge. Indeed, insofar as these developments in modern physics can be construed to underscore Kantian epistemological positions, it is not difficult to see why constructivist arguments as to the perceptual basis of all social organization are seen by so many contemporary analysts to border on self-evident (so to speak).

However, the lessons of relativity in physics for the relativism of knowledge are not so obvious. First, as noted above, Einstein's and Heisenberg's arguments as to the relativity of perception to frames of reference, and the intrinsic error of perception, were built on commitments to fundamentally positivist scientific methodologies. Moreover, despite having been transcended, Newtonian explanations of the world still suffice quite well for most day-to-day purposes. The Einsteinian worldview, while now deemed more "correct," in fact corrects only at the margins our understandings of the way most things work. For example, one early demonstration of the validity of Einstein's challenge to Newton was its ability to account for a slight deviation in the orbit of Mercury that Newton's theories could not explain.[24] Thus, the impact and relevance of Einstein's insights were at once monumental and marginal.

To extend these observations by analogy to the social sciences offers an intriguing if speculative way of conceiving of a synthesis of perceptual and materialist ontologies. Rather than concluding that the merit of "postpositivist" approaches necessitates wholesale reconstruction of all knowledge derived from positivist epistemologies, we might instead take the more constructive approach of asking how these newer paradigms help answer questions and solve problems for which prior frameworks fell short.[25] Such an approach would provide a basis for accepting, at the same time, that postmodern theorists might be "right" about the perceptual basis of all social organization, and that nevertheless this new paradigm might necessitate only marginal corrections to positivist descriptions of the social world.

One potential avenue exemplifying such an application of insights from physical sciences to achieve syntheses of vying ontological and epistemological positions in the social sciences is through the use of *chaos the-*

ory. In effect, chaos theory combines Heisenberg's uncertainty principle with the notion of "nonlinear causality"—that is, effects do not follow in a simple, proportional manner from causes. A chaotic system manifests "sensitive dependence on initial conditions"—a marginal deviation in the status of the independent variable can cause dramatic impacts on dependent variables. Because this property holds for any arbitrarily small alteration of the initial conditions, while at the same time the Heisenberg principle precludes precise measurement of initial conditions below a certain level of precision, chaos theory offers the paradoxical prospect that certain systems in the physical universe are simultaneously deterministic and indeterminable.[26]

The implications of chaos theory have been occasionally misinterpreted and widely ignored by international relations students. Physicists and other physical scientists now appreciate and embrace the necessity and utility of envisaging systems as operating under the dictates of complex and sometimes chaotic nonlinear causal properties. Yet, most international relations scholars remain guided by a Newtonian image of systemic dynamics described by strictly linear equations, and so never move beyond seeking to build ever-more complex models and to accumulate ever-more detailed data in the hope of achieving a modest predictability.[27] In contrast to this Sisyphian ambition, chaos theory offers one mode of thinking about how a system can be both simply predictable in theory and fully unpredictable in practice, thus also suggesting how perceptual and deterministic ontologies in the social sciences might be synthesized. A few scholars have sought to conceive of arms races, alliance formation, the outbreak of war and other specific forms of international phenomena in terms of mathematically modeled chaotic systems.[28] However, the implications of chaos theory for conceiving international relations—and, indeed, many dimensions of politics and human relations more generally—could be more profoundly applied at a heuristic level.[29]

Be this as it may, I should like to argue that contemporary social science faces ontological and epistemological divisions beyond those described above, including dimensions not faced in the physical sciences, and hence for which few analogies from the physical sciences can be drawn. Central to these is the problem of the relationship of knowledge to action—specifically, social knowledge to political action. I now turn to these more unique problems.

Social Knowledge and Political Action

In this section I shall argue that one of the most important—and least attended—thresholds to have opened up in the past century of social analysis is between studying the human condition to achieve knowledge and understanding the human condition in order to make it better. As with the other types of thresholds discussed above, I will assert that the objective ought to be not to build transient links across this threshold, but to transcend it.

I will also argue that perceptual and deterministic epistemologies in the social sciences, although diametrically opposed in so many respects, share important common presumptions on the crucial issues of how knowledge can and should be used to guide individual action and public policy. In particular, both manifest the trend, dominant in the social sciences in the nineteenth and twentieth centuries, to treat human action *behaviorally* rather than *morally*.

Central to the conception of science throughout the modern era has been the notion that the standards of scientific progress are distinct from those of other activities, intrinsic to scientific activity itself, and measured against the aim of contributing to "a system of ideas about Nature which has some legitimate claim to 'reality.'"[30] In the twentieth century, the capacity of the scientific endeavor to take place so independently from the "human world" has come under sustained critique.[31] As pertaining to social analysis specifically, positivist and deterministic approaches are commonly also deemed to be pervasively amoral. As Hannah Arendt comments:

> Under the concerted assault of the modern debunking "sciences," psychology and sociology, nothing indeed has seemed to be more safely buried than the concept of freedom.[32]

However, this charge also applies more commonly than realized to postmodern approaches. These latter approaches, focusing on the perceptual basis of reality, necessarily emphasize the capacity of the human mind to "shape" that reality. However, these approaches tend to sidestep the implication that this shaping is affected by conscious *judgments*, and so say virtually nothing about the basis—moral or otherwise—of such judgments.

A return to Kant here is instructive. A central premise of Kant's moral and political philosophy is that the relationship between "phenomenal" and "noumenal" worlds (described above) also conveys a symbiosis of epistemology and moral decision. Kant perceives a fundamental dualism in human life: people are both instinctive creatures, expressing a variety of desires that are the stuff of experience, and conscious agents with free wills, able to recognize and make moral choices. Although moral rules and principles must be founded on knowledge independent of experience itself, moral judgments can be made only by applying this knowledge to experience. Indeed, the human "fact of reason" is a constituent of experiences. Hence, there are "two kinds of causality for whatever happens, namely

either that of nature or that of freedom."[33] Through reasoning about perceived conditions in the realm of *nature*, individuals discover within themselves the realm of *freedom* and the purpose of moral autonomy. We
discover *in ourselves* Kant's supreme moral law, the categorical imperative.

Thus, a symbiosis of epistemological and moral purposes is fundamental to Kant's political theory: knowledge is the basis of moral choice,
which is in turn the inspiration for knowing. The viewpoint hearkens to the
Socratic identification of the "good person" with the "good citizen": one's
obligations to oneself, which Socratic philosophy defines in terms of pursuit of knowledge for the purpose of discovering "the good," are identical
to one's obligations to others, defined in terms of community responsibility and citizenship. In effect, the imperatives to *know* truth and to *act* on
its basis are intimately related.

The separation of epistemological and moral purposes is another
threshold of the modern era. Archetypically, Machiavelli provides one of
the earliest modern arguments as to the *necessity* to separate the obligations of the "good person" and the "good citizen." The Prince, in order to
meet his duty to lead, must turn his back on the moral conditions applying
to others, and explicitly learn "how not to be good."[34] In international relations today, this position finds expression in the concept of *raison d'état*,
which offers to diplomats, leaders and, in principle, to the responsible citizens of functioning democracies, a certain moral insulation as a result of
the duties of citizenship.[35]

This divergence of the obligations of personal and public conduct
extends beyond foreign affairs, permeating modern attitudes toward most
public action. Politics today is widely perceived as an arena into which one
brings predefined objectives for purposes of achievement. Such objectives
may be morally based, but the process of politics itself has little to do with
determining them. Thus, politics is an instrument, a technique, a mere
"vocation"—it is no longer a good in and of itself (except for those few
whose *interests* in participating happen to be "ideal"), but resolutely a
means to other ends.[36] This viewpoint founds the now common depiction
of ideal liberal-democratic government as akin to a free market, in which
interests determine actions and capabilities settle outcomes.[37]

The modern positivist turn in social analysis well suits this view of
political action. The view that to be a "scientist" requires adopting and
achieving a posture of "objectivity" cuts the intimate bonds between
knowledge and moral choice that the Greeks took for granted and Kant
viewed as central. However, disassociating knowledge creation from moral
action in this way has not necessitated cutting all bonds between knowledge and political action. This results because the Machiavellian separation
of obligations of "right" and "duty" liberates political action from moral

oversight beyond expediency. Thus, today, knowledge can be "objective" but still also "policy-relevant." Scientific analysts and political actors can intercourse freely, without compromise to the duties of their positions, precisely because they both share an interest in "just the facts."

Contemporary "postmodern" turns in epistemological theory reject the possibility of achieving the objectivity premised by positivist approaches. As discussed in the preceding section, modern physical sciences have already had to face this problem squarely, and have done so in ways that acknowledge elements of the postmodern emphasis on the perceptual basis of not only human knowledge but also decisions and institutions. However, postmodern turns in contemporary social science replicate rather than reverse the positivist bifurcation of analytical and moral knowledge. Put another way, postmodern epistemologies abandon objectivity without reclaiming morality.[38]

Consider, for example, contemporary "constructivist" international theory, such as that provided by Alexander Wendt.[39] The constructivist position challenges realist and neorealist presumptions that "self-help" is intrinsic to international anarchy, and hence that state sovereignty and *raison d'état* are definable—at least in principle—by objective laws of politics. Constructivism rejects the "materialism" it sees underlying these presumptions, emphasizing the insufficiency of building international relations theories on simplistic assumptions of a general depravity in human nature. On this point, the constructivist position converges with Kant (as well as Rousseau and a host of other challengers of Hobbes).

In place of such assumptions about human nature, however, constructivism offers the argument that states and their environments are "mutually constituting," and hence that sovereign authority is made legitimate "intersubjectively." This formulation offers no equivalent of a Kantian moral law by which differently constituted configurations of power and authority may be judged. Judgments are merely preferences, and preferences themselves merely functions of "identities" that are constituted (and reconstituted) through interaction, leaving them subject to the ebbs and flow of history.[40] Constructivism provides no basis on which even to know progress toward a better world when we see it, because seeing is only believing, not knowing. The approach thus lacks—or rather deliberately eschews—critical and prescriptive value.[41]

Much "critical" international relations theory goes considerably farther than Wendt in questioning the epistemological grounds on which Kantian and other Enlightenment moral philosophy and political theory are constructed.[42] Ever since Hegel took the final step that Kant would not, denying fully the existence of the autonomous realm of moral certitude beyond human experience that Kant asserted had at least to be assumed, critical theory has purported that no guide to the right can be found beyond the limits of our own minds. An important source of this twentieth-century skepticism has been the failure of liberal Enlightenment ideals, often traced to Kant, to prove to be as "universal" as they were purported to be. Instead, the triumphal proselytization of "pan-human" Enlightenment values often masked baser and more immediate Western interests, and so worked significantly to erode liberalism's appeal in much of the non-Western world.[43]

For this reason, the key figure to whom to look for guidance in sustaining a connection of a moral compass to social analysis is not Kant but Marx. In the context of the topics addressed here, Marx is a genuinely "threshold" figure: rooted in Enlightenment theory and yet a seminal critic of it; enamored with the promise of science, technology and progress rampant in his day and yet committed to an epistemology rooted in social conscience and liberation. In the nineteenth century, Marxist thought epitomized the convergence of philosophy and political action. In the twentieth century, this Marxist legacy became itself somewhat bifurcated: as its call to action became increasingly appropriated by Leninism and, in turn, Stalinist totalitarianism, Marxist thought in the West survived in nonradical circles through a focus on its analytical dimensions that neutralized or sterilized its politically programmatic intentions. In this form alone—the *Communist Manifesto* as *theory*—does Marx survive in many mainstream academic departments (at least in the U.S.).[44]

A recent reincarnation of purposeful Marxism (which also has its articulation in international relations theory) can be found in feminist theory—in particular, feminist standpoint theory. Feminist standpoint theory as applied to international relations (as well as other topics) seeks to uncover the epistemological bases of gender bias, challenging the presumption that "objective" knowledge is possible and emphasizing the need to design concepts and research practices from the *standpoint* of neglected groups and issues. However, the critique is not merely epistemological, but political: feminist standpoint theory judges that prevailing analytic practices, under cloak of objectivity, serve society's dominant groups, and disguise the subjectivity of knowledge claims in a manner that reinforces that dominance. This impetus of feminist standpoint theory is self-consciously Marxist in origin, intending to employ Marx's emphasis on the standpoint of the proletariat as a paradigm to validate the emphasis on the standpoint of women's life experiences.[45] Feminist standpoint theorists translate the Marxist origins into feminist terms by asserting that women's standpoints offer certain *superior* vantage points from which to observe, and learn about, gender relations.[46] Feminist theorists of international politics apply this idea to assert that the "lens of gender" offers a point of view on issues of conflict and cooperation sufficiently unique to constitute a paradigm shift that subsumes and displaces "idealist" as much as "realist" approaches.[47]

This privileging of the epistemological validity of women's lives has generated criticism precisely for "essentializing" women's experiences into a single standpoint and thereby undermining feminist standpoint theory's own core assumption that "all knowledge is located and situated."[48] However, many feminist standpoint theorists, sensitive to the issues of "essentializing," nevertheless resist embracing postmodern metaphysics out of concern that it precludes building the kind of systemic knowledge necessary for positive social action. Thus, feminist standpoint theorists, in international relations study and elsewhere, wrestle with a larger dilemma that the postmodern alternative to positivist epistemology has failed to address, much less resolve: how to formulate the inevitable relationship between knowledge and action.

The relationship of Kantian moral and epistemological theory to the Enlightenment's "positivist" legacy provides only a partial answer to this dilemma.[49] Although Kant establishes the *cognitive* foundation of all human knowledge, his metaphysics nevertheless assert that reestablishing a foundation for knowledge necessitates positing *a priori* truths, against which experiences can be assessed. However, Kant views such "truths" as discernible only in *form*; their *content* is wholly beyond the grasp of human reason, and so "truth" can never be "uniquely captured" by any particular representation. Thus, the Kantian formulation posits certainty as possible only for knowledge in its most formal, abstract sense, not in any real-world sense enabling a Marxian programmatic purposefulness.

Critical theorists since Hegel have assiduously rejected the Kantian formulation—but with opposite intent. Rather than seeking certainty in real-world knowledge, critical theorists have sought to establish that knowledge is necessarily wholly perceptual and contingent. Whereas the Kantian position offers at least a formal moral guidepost by which to orient oneself in experience, the post-Hegelian position denies even this abstract certitude, leaving moral compasses as subjective as all other perceptions.

Thus, the problem of meaningfully reassociating knowledge and action in the modern context is quite different—and far deeper—than commonplace hackneyed depictions. The issue is not simply whether it is possible to contain our moral "subjectivity" while we pursue "objective" scientific endeavors. Nor, conversely, do we face merely abandoning the hope of attaining meaningful knowledge of human affairs because, in a twisted Heisenbergian sense, the creation of such knowledge inevitably affects human action. What we learn about ourselves affects how we behave, and inevitably changes what we know, not just in the sense that

specific "policy relevant" knowledge can affect specific government policies, but in the sense that basic understandings of the world can ultimately
affect basic judgments about human values and purposes. Thus, at the
deepest level, this absence of a sure foundation for knowledge not only
truncates the political meaningfulness of knowledge claims, it also undermines the very motivation for genuine political action in its classical sense.

The creation of knowledge imposes on its creators a certain responsibility for the implications of that knowledge, pertaining to the uses and
potential abuses of that knowledge. Again, the realm of physics offers a
good example: Einstein and many other physicists, having enabled humanity to harness on earth the power of the sun, subsequently took very seriously their responsibility for the political consequences of this
achievement.[50] However, the creation of knowledge about the human world
imposes a second responsibility, not only for the effects of knowledge on
our purposeful actions, but even more deeply for its pertinence to our
understandings and moral judgments of purposes themselves. So long as
humanity has recognized its capacity to have knowledge, this has been the
case. Only in the modern era has the inevitable role of knowledge in guid-
ing action been viewed as a *problem,* rather than precisely the point.

Modern positivism has sought to flee from this responsibility by hid-
ing behind a facade of objectivity and scholastic self-righteousness. Postmodern relativism does not reclaim this responsibility; rather, it exchanges
the facade for abandonment of all foundation. To reconnect the imperatives requires rediscovering how, to paraphrase the Socratic formulation, to
be both a "good citizen" and a "good scholar."

However, there can be no return to the simplistic Socratic identification of the two imperatives, as though the threshold between them had
never been opened. Rather, this threshold must be transcended. To return
to a main point of the first section (and thereby bring this essay full circle),
transcending such thresholds now itself defines the threshold of the universe of human knowledge. Should the continuing expansion of that universe bring an end to the era of proliferating thresholds, there is hope that
it will bring with it a transcendence of this threshold as well, and renew the
human capacity for creating knowledge that serves progressive pan-human
purpose.

Conclusion

The emergence of thresholds in social analysis—among disciplines, epistemologies, paradigms, methodologies, and relevance to social practice—has
been an inevitable product of growth of knowledge. The apparently excessive and obstructive proliferation of thresholds marks a stage in the histor-

ical development of the growth of knowledge, one period among many in the unending development of the human capacity to learn. Hence, this proliferation is not to be lamented and resisted as a symptom of the deterioration of the Enlightenment project to widen the scope of human knowledge through the judicious application of the faculty of reason. Rather, this proliferation needs to be accepted, and indeed built on, in part through anticipation of the next stage in the process, which may entail transcendence of the Enlightenment project itself.

Accepting the inevitability of this proliferation of thresholds, in turn, suggests a more appropriate response than seeking to reverse the proliferation or to outrace it by constructing a maze of links among disparate positions. A wiser aim is certainly to begin seeking *transcendence* of present conditions through formulation of a new understanding of the complex geography of human knowledge. The emergence of thresholds is providing an ever more detailed map of this geography, viewing which requires only the development of our own capacity to rise above perceiving these thresholds as "boundaries." Our judgments as to topics of attention, epistemological viewpoints, and the like, thus can serve to *locate* us, rather than *limit* us, if only we can rise above the choices themselves.

To analogize to the depiction of the universe as curved "space-time," the objective then is to transcend rather than traverse the existing "paradigm" of the "universe of knowledge." To analogize to chaos theory, which finds predictability in unpredictability, this objective to transcend the ever-greater complexity of human knowledge can be achieved by developing an approach to the search for knowledge that itself reveals the *unity within the chaos of the proliferation.* Such an attitude and approach requires an as yet inconceivable new "paradigm" of the nature and function of human knowledge. Although we cannot now say how this new paradigm will emerge, or what it will look like when it does, certainly the first step must be to begin looking.

Notes

1. I use the terms "boundaries" and "thresholds" in this inclusive sense throughout this essay, unless specified otherwise.
2. For a good layperson's description of modern developments in physics and cosmology discussed in this essay, see Stephen Hawking, *A Brief History of Time* (Toronto: Bantam Books, 1988). On the theological implications of positing the "Big Bang" as the origin of space and time, see Hawking, pp. 8–9, 46–47, and the critical opinion piece by Robert L. Park, "A Cosmology of Your Very Own," The *New York Times*, October 9, 1992.

3. In particular, theorists have yet to reconcile the theory of relativity (which applies to very big scales) and the theory of quantum mechanics (which applies to very small scales). Hence, the challenge today is to derive a "quantum theory of gravity," or what Hawking calls a "theory of everything." See Hawking, pp. 155–169.

4. See Hawking; and Paul Feyerabend, *Against Method* (London: New Left Books, 1975), chapters 6–12.

5. One can visualize this process by imagining multiple printouts of this page of text, some with smaller than normal left margins. Holding a normal sheet and an aberrant sheet up the light, one can align the printed text and then compare the edges of the pages to discover the "left shift" of the aberrant sheet's text. This process will still work even if different pages of the text have different "normal" left margins, because each page has a distinct "pattern" of text with which aberrant copies of the same page can be matched.

6. By "quantity," I do not mean facilely that we could, even in theory, "count" the "number" of "things" that we know. Rather, I am suggesting that the "cumulation" of knowledge (e.g., in Lakatos's or others' senses) necessarily involves a certain degree of "accumulation" of knowledge. By "ideas" I mean mainly facts, but also expectations, presumptions, and judgments of a perhaps more "quasi-scientific" nature, which, while perhaps not established with sufficient rigor to deserve the mantle of "scientific truth," nevertheless function to inform our understandings of our life worlds with sufficient perspicacity so as yet not to have been replaced with other, "better" ideas. My intention here is simply to sidestep epistemological questions for the moment—I would assert that the tendency toward expansion holds at any arbitrarily narrowed definition of the acceptable domain of "knowledge."

7. Can knowledge contract? The human capacity for forgetfulness— sometimes willful—suggests certainly yes. In fact, humanity may very well be forgetting more than we learn; strictly speaking, then, human knowledge may not be expanding at all. An analogous problem in physics today addresses whether or not black holes, when they consume matter and energy, destroy the "information" that the matter and energy contained; see Leonard Susskind, "Black Holes and the Information Paradox," *Scientific American* (April 1997), pp. 52–57.

8. Fractal images given by chaos theory well evoke such imagery. Of particular note for this metaphor is this feature of fractals: their complexity obtains at any level of detail. One can zoom a tiny portion of a fractal image to full size an infinite number of times, and the fractal pattern will remain. Similarly, the shape of the frontier of the universe of knowledge is infinitely complex.

9. As Hedley Bull has remarked, "In the vast mansion of Thomas Hobbes' philosophy, what he has to say about relations among states does not occupy more than a small cupboard." See Hedley Bull, "Hobbes and the International Anarchy," *Social Research* 48 (1981), pp. 717–718.

10. Rousseau's views on international politics are scattered among his unfinished essay, "The State of War," his "Summary" and "Critique" of the Abbé de Saint-Pierre's *Project for Perpetual Peace*, and portions of several other larger works. The relative inattention to Rousseau's thought in modern IR theory may be due in part to the deep ambiguities in his treatments of the topic, which have over time given rise to widely varying interpretations of its import for modern world political theory. See Grace G. Roosevelt, *Reading Rousseau in the Nuclear Age*. (Philadelphia: Temple University Press, 1990), pp. 4–9. Rousseau's own frustrations with these questions led him ultimately to abandon an ambitious project on political institutions—a work that would have exemplified the "trans-disciplinary" nature of his thought and his era. Extracts from this work of material dealing only with the narrower question of citizenship in a single society eventually became *The Social Contract*.

11. For an insightful discussion of the emergence of social science disciplines, see Immanuel Wallerstein, et. al., *Open the Social Sciences* (Stanford University Press, 1996), pp. 1–32.

12. For differing renditions of this genealogy, see Steve Smith, "Paradigm Dominance in International Relations: The Development of International Relations as a Social Science," in H. C. Dyer and L. Mangasarian, eds., *The Study of International Relations: The State of the Art* (New York: St. Martin's, 1989); and Jeremy Larkins, "Representations, Symbols and Social Facts: Durkheim and IR Theory," *Millennium: Journal of International Studies* 23:2 (1994): 239–264.

13. E. H. Carr, *The Twenty Years Crisis* (London: Macmillan, 1946); and Hans Morgenthau, *Politics Among Nations* (New York: Alfred Knopf, 1985 [1948]).

14. Kenneth Waltz, *Man, the State, and War* (New York: Columbia University Press, 1959); and Waltz, *Theory of International Politic.* (Reading, MA: Addison-Wesley, 1979.)

15. This assertion takes for granted certain epistemological presumptions discussed in the next section, but is easily grasped at an intuitive or practical level.

16. The general theory of relativity posits that gravity is not a "force" like other forces, but rather a consequence of the "warping" of the space-time medium of the universe itself by the unevenly distributed masses

and energies within it. Thus, objects (like our earth) do not move in curved orbits around more massive objects (like the sun); instead, they move through curved "space-time" in approximate straight lines called "geodesics." For example, the surface of the earth is itself a two-dimensional curved space, and the routes of airliners along the shortest distances between airports follow geodesic lines. In Einstein's general theory of relativity, "space-time" is an analogously curved medium of four rather than two dimensions. See Hawking, pp. 28–34.

17. See Lawrence M. Krauss, *The Physics of Star Trek* (New York: Harper Collins, 1995), chapters 3 and 4. At the time of publication, Krauss was Ambrose Professor of Physics and Professor of Astronomy and Chair of the Department of Physics at Case Western Reserve University. See also the discussion in the book's "Forward" by Stephen Hawking.

18. Immanuel Kant, *Critique of Pure Reason,* trans. Norman Kemp Smith (New York: St. Martin's Press, 1965), pp. 23–24; see also Hannah Arendt, *Lectures on Kant's Political Philosophy,* ed. Ronald Beiner (Chicago: University of Chicago Press, 1982), pp. 9–10.

19. In other words, "relativity" is not the same as "relativism." In this section I am seeking to relate these concepts by analogy, not directly. On this issue. see Stephen Toulmin, *Human Understanding* (Princeton: Princeton University Press, 1972), pp. 89–91.

20. See Hawking, pp. 15–29. The idea of varying rates of time, while difficult to comprehend intuitively, follows from a simple logic based on the fact that velocity is simply the distance a thing travels in a given amount of time: $V = D/T$. Observers on earth and on the ship would both perceive the ship's light to travel at the same velocity. But because the movement of the ship itself affects the travelers' perceptions of distance, velocity can be constant only if it also affects their perception of the passage of time. Einstein's proposition explained for the first time the results of the famous 1887 Michelson-Morley experiment, which showed that the speed of light is unaffected by the velocity of the earth's own rotation, and has since been observed in many ways. For example, time passes approximately one ten-millionth of 1 percent slower on the space shuttle than on the earth's surface, and the precision of modern global positioning satellites would be impossible without taking this relativity into account. Einstein later extended this proposition into the "general theory of relativity," discussed earlier, in order to account for the contradiction that gravity appears to "travel" at infinite speed.

21. Hawking, pp. 53–55. Heisenberg's limit is known as Planck's constant, named after Max Planck, who first formulated the quantum theory of energy.

22. Hawking, pp. 55–56.
23. To be precise, however, the implications of the uncertainty principle are subtly but crucially different than Kant's position. Kant also brings into question positivist assumptions about the replicability and commensurability of measurements themselves. To this extent, the implications of the theory of relativity for social science ontology is, as noted earlier, through analogy rather than replication. Driving a wedge into this distinction is the added problem that in social analysis, unlike physical analysis, measurement of phenomena, in addition to being intrinsically inaccurate, produces knowledge that in turn alters the phenomena (i.e., social behavior). I elaborate on the nature and implications of this distinction in the following section.
24. General relativity predicts that the long axis of Mercury's elliptical orbit itself rotates around the sun once every 3.6 million years. Although this variation from Newtonian expectations is minute, it had already been observed when Einstein's theory appeared in 1915. See Hawking, p. 31.
25. In other words, whether and how they satisfy Lakatos's standards for "sophisticated falsification." See Imre Lakatos, *The Methodology of Scientific Research Programs* (London: Cambridge University Press, 1978), p. 32.
26. For a good layperson's introduction to chaos theory, see James Gleick, *Chaos: Making a New Science* (London: Macdonald & Co., 1988). The tie of chaos theory to Heisenberg's uncertainty principle is indirect, but crucial: again suggesting a Kantian ontology, chaotic systems are determinate *a priori* (as in the derivation of fractals) but indeterminate in practice (as in the predicting the weather). Gleick relates that "turbulence"—a principle problem that chaos theory addresses—was one of the two phenomena (the other was relativity) of which Heisenberg, on his deathbed, declared that he would seek an explanation from his maker—and the one about which he did not expect an answer. See Gleick, p. 121.
27. See Wallerstein, et. al., p. 61; and Gleick, p. 14. The indictment holds even for self-consciously "sparse" theories (such as neorealism) nevertheless rooted in linear logic. Neorealism leaves itself an "out"—factors that are not deemed "systemic" can still affect international outcomes. But the theory is still linear in two senses: first, such factors do not affect long-term patterns of outcomes; and second, such factors are exogenous to the theory.
28. For representative examples, see Alvin M. Saperstein, "Alliance Building Versus Independent Action: a Nonlinear Modeling Approach to Comparative International Stability," *Journal of Conflict Resolution*

36, 3 (Sept, 1992); Siegfried Grossman, and Gottfried Mayer-Kress, "Chaos in the international arms race," *Nature* 337, 6209 (Feb. 23, 1989); and Alvin M. Saperstein, "Chaos—a model for the outbreak of war," *Nature* 309 (1984). Much of this work builds on the original ideas of L. F. Richardson; see *Arms and Insecurity* (Pittsburgh: Boxwood Press, 1960) and *Statistics of Deadly Quarrels* (Pittsburgh: Boxwood Press, 1960).

29. To my knowledge, no attempt has ever been made to utilize chaos theory in this way to derive a theory of global politics pitched, as is neorealism, at a sparse and conceptual level. An approach to such use can be found in some relatively recent work of James N. Rosenau, *Turbulence in World Politics: A Theory of Change and Continuity* (Princeton: Princeton University Press, 1990), and "Security in a Turbulent World," *Current History* 94, 592 (May, 1995). Although Rosenau employs some of the language of chaos theory (references to the "nonlinearity" of global politics), the argument does not adopt chaos theory itself as a conceptual model to depict world political systems, and the use of the language of chaos theory does not appear to carry with it the conceptual innovations underlying that language.

30. See, for example, Stephen Toulmin, *Foresight and Understanding: An Enquiry into the Aims of Science* (New York: Harper and Row, 1963), pp. 13–17, 114–115.

31. The seminal work in this regard is Thomas Kuhn, *The Structure of Scientific Revolutions* (Chicago: University of Chicago Press, 1962).

32. Hannah Arendt, *On Revolution* (London: Penguin Press, 1962), p. 11.

33. Kant, *Critique of Pure Reason*, pp. 24–28.

34. Niccolo Machiavelli, *The Prince*, trans. A. Robert Caponigri (Chicago: Henry Regnery Co., 1963), p. 85.

35. Strictly speaking, Machiavelli, and later Carr and Morgenthau, in positing IR as an independent realm, do not depict it as amoral, but rather as inhering a separate morality. This understanding does not negate my subsequent points.

36. The classic discussion of the problems posed by the fact/value distinction for policy-relevant social analysis is Max Weber's essay "Politics as a Vocation" in H. H. Gerth and C. W. Mills, eds., *From Max Weber* (New York: Oxford University Press, 1949).

37. For the classic statements, see Joseph Schumpeter, *Capitalism, Socialism, and Democracy* (New York: Harper and Row, 1942), esp. pp. 232–302; and Robert Dahl, *A Preface to Democratic Theory* (Chicago: University of Chicago Press, 1956). For an articulation of this position at its logical extreme, see Anthony Down, *An Economic Theory of Democracy* (New York: Harper and Brothers, 1957). For critical reac-

tions, see Carole Pateman, *Participation and Democratic Theory* (Cambridge: Cambridge University Press, 1970); and C. B. Macpherson, *Democratic Theory: Essays in Retrieval* (Oxford: Clarendon Press, 1973).

38. For a good recent discussion of the place relation of social action to both positivist and postpositivist international relations theory, see Justin Rosenberg, "The International Imagination: IR Theory and 'Classic Social Analysis,'" *Millennium: Journal of International Studies* 23:1 (1994), pp. 85–108; and the rejoinder, Mervyn Frost, "The Role of Normative Theory in IR," *Millennium: Journal of International Studies* 23:1 (1994), pp. 109–118.

39. Alexander Wendt, "Collective Identity Formation and the International State," *American Political Science Review* 88 (1994), esp. pp. 394, 399–401.

40. And since, consistently, constructivism also dismisses anarchy's "putative causal powers," and definitely refutes "that the logic of history is progressive," we have no hope that progress will occur despite the absence of human moral intentionality.

41. The constructivist approach also says little about how and when we might expect intersubjective judgments to gravitate toward or away from one configuration or another, hence sacrificing predictive value as well. For an elaboration of this critique, see Wade L. Huntley, 'Kant's Third Image: Systemic Sources of the Liberal Peace,' *International Studies Quarterly* 40, 1 (March 1996), pp. 45–76, p. 61.

42. For a good recent survey, see Chris Brown, "Turtles All the Way Down: Anti-foundationalism, Critical Theory and International Relations," *Millennium: Journal of International Studies* 23 (1994), pp. 213–236. Brown adopts a "generic" definition of "critical theory" that includes all approaches which share the belief that Enlightenment political and social theory is now in "crisis" (p. 214). By this definition, Kant, a key Enlightenment figure, is not considered a "critical" thinker in terms of "critical" international theory. This position is somewhat ironic in that Kant's own "Copernican revolution" in metaphysics—rejecting that *a priori* knowledge of "things in themselves" is possible—opened the door to contemporary "antifoundational" epistemologies which now reject Kant's claim that truths can still be found within the human mind. See Kant, pp. 23–24.

43. Ironically, realist theory also warns against the same tendency for particular interests to operate under the guise of moral truths. For an emblematic and notorious example of the kind of liberal triumphalism that leads realists and critical theorists alike to question liberal ideals, see Francis Fukuyama, "The End of History?" *The National Interest*

16:3–18, and *The End of History and the Last Man* (New York: Avon Books, 1992). Fukuyama grounds his arguments in the thought of Georg Hegel and portrays Hegel as fulfilling the promise only outlined in Kant's proposal for a "Universal History." (See Immanuel Kant, "Idea for a Universal History with Cosmopolitan Intent," in *The Philosophy of Kant*, edited and translated by Carl Friedrich (New York: Random House, 1949), pp. 116–131.) However, Fukuyama fails to convey how Hegel fundamentally and self-consciously rejected Kant's philosophy in crucial ways. For critiques of Fukuyama, see Joseph M. Knippenberg, "Kant, *thymos*, and the End of History," in Timothy Burns, ed. *After History? Francis Fukuyama and His Critics* (Lanham, MD: Rowman & Littlefield, 1994), pp. 47–54; and Susan Shell, "Fukuyama and the End of History," in Burns, ed., pp. 39–46. On how Kant's conception of history offers a healthy corrective to liberal proselytization, see Huntley, "Kant's Third Image."

44. Marxism is probably about one or two decades away from making a serious comeback, not only for its inspiration to translate analysis into action (discussed below), but also for its incisive insights into the inner workings of capitalist economies. In particular, the fading of the Soviet experience into history will allow Marx's original analyses to emerge from this shadow, enabling a rediscovery of the applicability of Marxist categories to contemporary "globalization." For one look at this prospect, see John Cassidy, "The Return of Karl Marx," *The New Yorker*, October 20 and 27, 1997.

45. Nancy Hartsock, one of feminist standpoint theory's founders, notes that it was defined in terms evoking a Marxist sense of the interrelation of epistemology and politics: "Standpoint theories are technical theoretical devices that can allow for the creation of accounts of society that can be used to work for more satisfactory social relations." See Nancy Hartsock, "Comment on Hekman's 'Truth and Method: Feminist Standpoint Theory Revisited': Truth or Justice?" *Signs: Journal of Women in Culture and Society* 22, 2 (Winter 1997), esp. 368–370.

46. For early formulations of this position, see Alison Jaggar, *Feminist Politics and Human Nature* (Totowa, N.J.: Rowman & Allanheld, 1983), and Dorothy Smith, *The Everyday World as Problematic: A Feminist Sociology* (Boston: Northeastern University Press, 1987).

47. See Grant, Rebecca, and Kathleen Newland, "Introduction," in Rebecca Grant and Kathleen Newland (eds.), *Gender and International Relations* (Milton Keynes: Open University Press, 1991); and Anne Sisson Runyan and V. Spike Peterson, "The Radical Future of Realism: Feminist Subversions of IR Theory," *Alternatives* 16, 1 (Winter 1991).

48. Susan Hekman, "Truth and Method: Feminist Standpoint Theory Revisited," *Signs: Journal of Women in Culture and Society* 22, 2 (Winter 1997), pp. 341–365, at p. 349.
49. For discussions of the relationship of Kantian moral and epistemological theory to feminist standpoint theory as it applies to IR, see Wade L. Huntley, "An Unlikely Match? Kant and Feminism in IR Theory," *Millennium: Journal of International Studies* 26:2 (1997).
50. Einstein's involvement in politics began with his opposition to World War I, which included advocacy of refusing conscription and participation in antiwar demonstrations. There is also Einstein's famous advocacy of U.S. construction of a bomb during World War II (out of fear that Nazi scientists would provide the bomb to Hitler first) and his subsequent and enduring involvement in efforts to prevent nuclear war. Einstein himself described his life as "divided between politics and equations." See Hawking, pp. 177–178.

8

THE DISCIPLINE AS
DISCIPLINARY NORMALIZATION

Networks of Research

TIMOTHY W. LUKE

This chapter explores the normalizing effects of disciplinary practices and values in contemporary American political science. It attempts to account for the behaviors and beliefs of thousands of professional-technical workers whose individual careers are unfolding in hundreds of colleges, government offices, and universities within the obvious, but also vague, confines of acceptable professional performance set by the discipline of political science. This critical reinterpretation is essential, because the uncritical voices many hear speaking through "the literature," "the discipline," or "the association" of American political scientists all too often ignore the origins and outcomes of disciplinary normalization.

In this fashion, it begins to apply the "strong program" in the sociology of science to political science.[1] This approach suggests there is no transcendent context of rational justification that renders some scientific hypotheses more credible than others; hence, an explanation of why some forms of science are found to dominate in any given context depends on cultural/economic/political/social qualities of the context rather than some intrinsic merits in the system of science.[2] Consequently, it critically re-reads political science, conducting a literary, political, or social analysis of its disciplinary culture as the best means of elucidating the context of production/consumption/circulation/accumulation in political science.[3] Political science still is a flexible form of narrative social knowledge as much as or more than it is rigorous technical knowledge about society.

The orderly conduct of any single political scientist's professional career in a shared disciplinary context typically expresses an implicit system of rules, which exerts, in turn, a normalizing effect on both thought and action. One perhaps expects these outcomes as part of the discipline's intellectual integrity or overall authority; unfortunately, their effects also can prove to be remarkably pernicious, destructive, and undemocratic. Therefore, this analysis purposely provides a more disorderly or malconducted reconsideration of this discipline's disciplinarity, which might, in turn, refocus or reshape our understanding of the more destructive sides of the discipline's punishing discipline. "In the long run," as Easton maintains, "political science has become what the political scientist does."[4] Despite their professed behavioralism, few political scientists openly discuss what political scientists actually do, choosing instead to hide in shopworn abstractions about the maturation of their subfield's paradigm, the integration of their methodological techniques, or the sophistication of their professional society. This critique takes Easton at his word, suggesting that the discipline of political science does become what its disciplining does to political scientists as they "do" political science. It can be illustrated by reconsidering some of what happens when political scientists "just do it" by playing against the multiple meanings of discipline for the discipline.

While there are many ways to approach these problems, this study focuses on three aspects of discipline in the discipline. First, on the most general level, it examines how the discipline provides some ontological stability for a larger social order with its own disciplinary systems of power/knowledge by recasting the state, government, and society so they can be read in a fairly secure fashion. Second, it traces out the symbolic economies of professional-technical life that enforce the normalizing expectations of professional correctness as part and parcel of attaining success in the discipline. And, third, it investigates the disciplinary demands of reputation in the nomenclatures of prominence, effectiveness, and significance looming over any individual scholar's or department's disciplinary presence.

The Discipline as an Ontological Stabilizer

One phase of discipline, as it seems to be exerted by the discipline of political science, is its persistent implication within the reproduction of existing systems of social control. Vocational analyses of political science might presume that political science instruction should train citizens, politicians, or government operatives to become better citizens, politicians or operatives. Such Aristotlean visions of political science as the master science, however, have not held true in modern America as most forms of citizenship have devolved into passive routines of consumeristic clientage. Many politicians are really trained in law, business, or media/journalism schools, and most government operatives are tutored in neoliberal microeconomics. Nonetheless, scores of thousands continue to enroll in political science courses in college, thousands start graduate work in political science, and hundreds take Ph.D.s every semester in political science, even though the narrow research practices of the discipline increasingly do not prepare them for anything other than doing such narrow research.

Instead of bickering about why so many political scientists are sitting at separate methodological tables, most political scientists simply promote the ongoing tabular separation of citizens, communities, and cultures into zones of instrumentally rational calculation for capital, the state, and technoscience as the necessary outcome of liberal democratic capitalism.[5] The professional-technical compromise of Charles Merriam, who coped with not becoming "the Woodrow Wilson of the Midwest" in Chicago politics by turning to the tasks of "making citizens" in his scientific rhetoric and activity, reflects one important facet of the discipline in political science's power/knowledge rising out of its disciplinarity in the academy and society.

The drill of discourse in political science reveals its "knowledge" shaping and shifting with "power" in many remarkably useful ways. Almost all of them, however, undercut the liberalism, democracy, and markets of liberal democratic capitalism. Rational choice theorists routinely illustrate the economic irrationality of voting, the coalitional strangulation of public goods provision, and the inefficiency of democratic decision-making. Voting behavior specialists reshape the public into psychodemographic niche markets whose buttons can be pushed with sufficient air time and money to produce specific voting outcomes. Public opinion analysts reveal how truths and untruths can be vended effectively in the news cycle to paralyze individual initiative or mobilize collective outrage. Pomo normative theorists tear up foundationalist ethics, rationalizing an agonistic free-play of hectoring moralizers that leave almost everyone unclear and uncertain about how to behave. The reduction of politics to psychosocial behavioral events, rational choice acts, or ungrounded discursive textuality permits the discipline of other structures, markets, or rhetorics to circulate as productive power behind/below/beyond the liberal humanist anthropology unconsciously accepted as normal by most political scientists.

Here, political science promotes the smooth operation of larger disciplinary systems among the general population through its first principles: epistemological, psychological, social. The inherent conservatism of most political scientists and much of political science becomes an ontological stabilizer that, particularly now at the end of history and liberal capitalist democracy's triumph over illiberal state socialism, assuringly assumes this is the best of all possible worlds certain to bring all of the best into the world.[6] Simplistic modernist assumptions about human agency, structural stability, natural predictability, defensible values, or useful knowledge all underpin most political scientists' normalizing studies of who normally gets what, how, where, when, and why. Political science, particularly the normal science of empirical analysis, is integrally involved, to be Latourian about it, in "the pasteurization of America" by operating as "science (in)action." What is known as "science" basically "does not exist" in political science; rather, "it is the name that has been pasted onto certain sections of certain networks," in which political scientists "write" over, about, on, through, in, or with in "trials of strength" against other more heterogenous intellectual networks.[7]

What political science "is" works best as an ontological generator, tying together normalizing associations of people and things through its networked inscriptions of industrial democracy. The very definition of politics, the state, or society, following Latour, . . .

> is the final outcome, in Sociology Departments [or *Political Science Departments*] in Statistical Institutions, in journals, of other scientists busily gathering surveys, questionnaires, archives, records of all sorts, arguing together, publishing papers, organizing other meetings. . . . The results of what society is made do not spread more or faster than those of economics, topology, or particle physics. These results would die if they went outside of the tiny networks necessary for their survival. A sociologist's interpretation of society [or *a political scientist's interpretation of politics*] will not be substituted for what every one of us thinks of society without *additional* struggle, without textbooks, chairs in universities, positions in the government, integration in the military, and so on, exactly as for geology, meteorology or statistics.[8]

As normalizing forces, then, political scientists are essential links in the reproduction of the power/knowledge networks animating contemporary forms of the economy, government, and society.[9] The operational assumptions of the scholarly discipline as a discipline help to produce, and then reproduce, the empty forms of liberal democratic citizenship—passivity, clientage, cluelessness, quietism, tax-evasiveness, and disinformation—that permits such "pluralistic polyarchies" to function.

The Discipline of Professional Correctness

Comparable effects of the disciplinary regime in the political science discipline also can be read directly in the sign-value economies of professionally correct research. Here we can look at something else that political scientists do. In a society obsessed by measures of performativity, rank and rankings are a register of valorization and a mechanism of social control for the individual, the department, and the university. The covering myth of academic research claims that it is integrally involved in performative applications: teaching undergraduates, promoting economic growth, or furthering scientific development. Yet, all too often very little of what normal science is within any discipline really carries this payoff. Some of it might be useful in the classroom, but much of it is far too specialized to work there. A bit might be leveraged in economic growth campaigns; but, once again, most of it is useless for pragmatic pursuits. Odds and ends could be sellable in open markets, but only a few corporations or labs will make an occasional purchase. Still, many things that do not find use-value in teaching or exchange-value in external markets continue to be produced because of special symbolic economies of sign-value circulation within academic disciplines that compel academicians to sustain their own disciplined command economies of disciplinary repute, professional prestige, and administrative allocation.

These sign-value products may not be produced for use as such, but for use as signs; not for exchange as such, but for exchange as signs; and, not for signage as such, but for useful appearance as use-value and/or exchange value for the exchanges of sign-value economies in professional correctness. The research game, then, truly is a game of researchers, by researchers, and for researchers. The disconnect between the political science discipline's "leading" cadres of research science and "top twenty-five" departments, which are both embedded in numerical measurements of performative quality tied to publication of traditional research, and the quality of undergraduate and graduate instruction are widely acknowledged in political science.[10] Nonetheless, this acknowledgment also is cynically suppressed in the exaltation of a reward system that is grounded in research rankings.

This academic economy of invidious distinction represents the fusion of two disparate and allegedly antithetical material logics—the academic/scholarly and the capitalist/professionalistic—into an elaborate disciplinary system of knowledge production and producer valorization. As the university has become implicated increasingly in the reproduction of the larger national and transnational economy, its workers are expected to make it into an informational engine of economic growth and/or a reserve currency bank of accumulated conceptual capital. Criteria borrowed from the real worlds of exchange-value are now imposed on both the use-value producing regions of teaching and the sign-value generating realms of research. The results are both destructive and frightening in their implications for all concerned: society, students, and scholars.

Research outputs in this symbolic economy begin to operate as commodities in a complex accounting system of private, departmental, and institutional accumulation strategies tied to boosting their various values in rank and ranking systems. Having manufactured their products in accord with disciplinary standards of "good research" or "normal science," academics circulate them through local, regional, national, and international networks in multiple exchanges of compensation, reputation, and status. Political scientists rightly can say that these practices are true of all or most academic disciplines, and they might be correct. Yet, few other disciplines profess to have the same fundamental commitments to developing individual moral agency or promoting collective democratic life as political science. Hence, the collaboration of the political science discipline with such authoritarian disciplinary practices only worsens the cooperation of political scientists with this invidious disciplinary regimen.

On an individual level, for example, the placement of articles and books become the blue book on one's career or the means for assaying the placement of one's labor in departments, between different universities, or within the discipline itself. Without any other stable measure of value, the systems of continuous normalizing judgment typically use obvious indicators of status, like institutional location or professional position, to measure worth. Scarce timed positional goods, or those spaces appearing quarterly in the pages of high-prestige journals or intermittently between the covers of books from big-name presses, mark the range of high or low value as functions of the relative difficulty of gaining access to them. "Where" one publishes, and how often, then, clearly are accepted as a definition of "worth" for ranking in these networks of production. This is essential, because the ranking system of professional correctness that assays "where" one's work is done also defines "how" rewards are or are not allocated, "when" promotions do or do not occur, "why" status rises or falls, "who" wins or loses. Of course, "how much" also can determine "worth" within economies that accept "high volume" in lieu of "high visibility" output, but often only up to some point of saturation. At that juncture, "too much" often backfires in the ranking equations as badly as plain old "poor placement."

These arithmetical economies of professional correctness drive or stall careers. In these codes, each individual scholar is expected to become a professionally correct producer, mixing "good placement" with "steady volume," by marketing his or her research products to outlets with the highest potential yield of material payoff, measured as a mix of symbolic scarcity, disciplinary recognition, or professional interest. The act of publication itself marks new sign value production beyond what might be occupying meritously in the research, valorizing its significance via occupying scarce locations (limited journal pages), claiming rare options (limited book publishing contracts), or convincing tough review boards (limited grant funds). Likewise, in this ranking regime, each department becomes an open mutual fund of such symbolic values, pooling together personal rankings as the summation of the local faculty's university productivity and national disciplinary sign value. The department can tout its mutual fund's one-year, five-year, ten-year record of yield in the quest for more raises, new faculty, additional promotions, fresh students, and greater material support. Universities and disciplines, in turn, track their various cases of success and failure, growth and decline, winners and losers in this complex symbolic economy of pooled assets, joint stock companies, or mutual funds at the individual, departmental, college, and discipline level of aggregation.

Such circuitous conduits of professional sign-value production/consumption/circulation/accumulation are nicely illustrated by Miller, Tien, and Peebler in a recent *PS* (*Political Science & Politics*) article, which proposes criteria for establishing an *APSR* (*American Political Science Review*) "Hall of Fame." Arthur H. Miller and two students at the University of Iowa—one a graduate and one an undergraduate—assert without any trace of irony in *PS*—an official American Political Science Association (APSA) journal—that the *APSR*—another official APSA journal—is "the leading political science journal in the United States."[11] This fact is affirmed with self-evident legitimacy by yet another *PS* article by Garand.[12] The leading place of the *APSR* in actually existing American political science, in turn, is supposedly a function of several interrelated facts:

> *APSR* is substantively broad based, peer reviewed, high quality, widely circulated (16,000 subscriptions), and has an acceptance rate of about 10 percent. An article published in *APSR* indicates research of considerable merit and significance for the entire field of political science. Given the prestige and difficulty associated with publishing in *APSR*, we argue that accomplishing this task a number of times is a feat that should be recognized.[13]

Again without any sense of irony, Miller's two students, who apparently helped build "The University of Iowa *APSR* Data Set," uncover an odd fact: none other than their lead author and senior faculty colleague, Arthur H. Miller, is one of a tiny handful of most published and most cited *APSR* authors with ten total articles from 1974–1994, giving him admission to his own distinguished top dozen of *APSR* "Hall of Famers: 1954–1994."[14]

One former *APSR* editor claimed his executive command over the journal's editorial procedures was like conducting "a seminar by mail."[15] Before the bar of the *APSR*, then, all disciples of political science become, once again and forever more, student acolytes of the discipline's latest breaking editorial tastes. Most of those who enroll in this seminar by submitting manuscripts through the post are not worthy, and most of the editor's comments in return mail to them are about rejection for their unworthiness. Nonetheless, Patterson piously asserts such review, rejection, and rewriting only brings rigorously "constructive and useful critiques" to those eager to please the postal seminar's powerful conductor by strengthening their work for reassessment and reconsideration by "a quarterly journal of exceptional merit."[16] To be heard in the discipline, a clear discipline is leveled on all; in turn, only a very disciplinary few are worthy enough to be culled from the unruly remaining masses. Strangely enough, then, the *APSR* Hall of Famers oddly are willing multiple repeaters in this same little postal seminar, writing well enough inside of all the right lines to pass once again, over and over again.

Miller, Tien, and Peebler claim the *APSR* is substantively broadly based, but Patterson and Smithey indicate things actually are otherwise at the *APSR*. They suggest that over 40 percent of the journal's submissions are in American politics, the comparative and IR communities are very dissatisfied with the *APSR's* breadth, and "unconventional" approaches (nonquantitative, Marxist, critical, etc.) basically were not as welcome.[17] Of the distinguished dozen in the Hall of Fame four honorees (W. Miller, R. Niemi, K. Shepsle, R. Wolfinger) claim American government and politics is their game, and another five (W. Riker, P. Ordeshook, S. Brams, R. Erikson, M. K. Jennings) easily fit into the same box. Four (W. Riker, S. Brams, P. Ordeshook, K. Shepsle) are rational choice devotees, and the other eight (E. Muller, P. Abramson, M. K. Jennings, W. Miller, A. Miller, R. Niemi, R. Erikson, R. Wolfinger) are mostly big data-set empiricists. There are no public law, public policy, international relations, or comparative government Hall of Famers, although three (E. Muller, P. Abramson, A. Miller) are allegedly comparativists and three (W. Riker, P. Ordeshook, S. Brams) are supposedly political philosophers and theorists.[18] The *APSR* is widely circulated, but it is a compulsory piece of belonging to the APSA. That is, almost everyone gets it as part of their APSA member's "benefit package." Wide circulation has not meant broad readership, and the *APSR's* prestige, at least in part, is a self-fulfilling function of circulating as an official organ of the APSA. Likewise, a 90 percent rejection rate says much about the exclusivity of its timed scarcities of sign-value affirmation, making the 10 percent who make it into these pages quite special.

At the end of the day, Miller, Tien, and Peebler maintain the *APSR's* prestige is a function of innate propensities for making invidious distinctions that is a universal human trait:

one's curiosity regarding who published in *APSR* and how frequently is a reflection of our basic human desire for drawing
comparisons . . . there is a basic human drive to evaluate one's
own opinions and abilities, and that inevitably involved comparisons with others. In short, we all are curious to know who
has published most frequently in *APSR*.[19]

We are not curious about truth, what is strongly confirmed technoscience,
or how we might learn; on the contrary, we all are allegedly curious only
about who has the greatest sign-value, or who has published in *APSR* and
how often.

As Crewe and Norris argue, "a journal's overall impact is the product of its perceived quality and its familiarity among members of the academic community."[20] Quality perception and member familization, however,
may well be a function of repeated bureaucratic provision rather than real
utility, actual readership, or material quality. In Crewe's and Norris's analyses, the top 3 U.S. political science journals are the official organs of the top
3 political science associations, another 10 of the top 20 journals are also
official outlets of other scholarly societies. Wider circulation does mean
broader readership, but it does translate into higher familiarity. To succeed
one must accept these constraints: the discipline disciplines through such
unbalanced games of sign-value as its disciples seek to attain "visibility."

Transmitting knowledge to the next generation of students pales
beside generating the next generation of statistical applications certain to
win fresh citations in major journals, and thereby enhancing one's rankings. Challenging the classics of human knowledge falls to the wayside
against the need for publishing the classic challenge to disciplinary outlaws
who might be intent on destroying the integrity of the profession's scientific
enterprise. Writing the great book about enduring moral dilemmas slips in
favor of building a good book on one's career in the reputational trading
pits at national meetings where scholars swap puts and calls on individual
scholars' career futures in the examinations of perpetual surveillance. As
U.S. News and World Report annually identifies "up and coming universities," as gossips gauge the relative merits of the "emerging star," the "has
been," or the "never was" at national association confabs, or as college
deans target departments for "new hires" or "more cutbacks," these symbolic markets in sign-value work their magic. And such codes of professional correctness operate as a disciplinary regime, sustaining a level of
conformity, self-service, and corruption that cultural conservatives' night-
mare of political correctness on campus never begins to approach. More
important, as normal science produces normalized scientists and normalizing disciplines in the research game, it also produces suboptimal college

educations in substandard classroom performance by subverted researchers struggling to hit the big-time in the casino capitalism of collegiate careerism.

The Discipline of Reputational Development

The organization of a national political science association in the APSA during 1903, as well as the subsequent founding since then of various regional, state, and even city-based professional associations, still ground the multiple, automatic, and autonomous disciplinary powers of the discipline.[21] With the more focused thematic (Presidential Studies, Security Studies, History of Political Thought), race/gender/class-grounded (black, latino/a, asian, women's, gay and lesbian caucuses), ideologically grounded (New Political Science, Ecological Transformational Politics), and area studies (Conference Groups on China, French Politics, German Politics, Italian Politics, or the Middle East) associations now operating alongside the national and regional professional organizations, political science constitutes its knowledge in a vast network of scholarly disciplined relations, working both hierarchically and laterally, which sustains itself by the mechanisms of a calculated gaze from "out there in the discipline." With both scholarly performances and performance scores logged in from journals, books, newsletters, conferences, listserves, faxes, or phone calls, it is apparent that the layers of normalizing judgment exerted in/by/from "the discipline" continuously define and distribute individuals, programs, and universities in permanent and continuous fields of reputational development.[22] The apparently innocuous working of any network, as Foucault suggests, "enables the disciplinary power to be absolutely indiscreet, since it is everywhere and always alert, since by its very principle it leaves no zone of shape and constantly supervises the very individuals who are entrusted with the task of supervising; and absolutely 'discreet,' for its functions permanently and largely in silence."[23] In following the discipline's basic drill of surveillance, analysis, and judgment, everyone gets to become the judge who, in turn, is judged, freely accepting orderly forms of conduct from a disciplinarity that ironically forces one to be unfree.

Academic life is an existence pegged to perpetual examinations: seminar discussions, research papers, dissertation defenses, conference papers, journal submissions, book contracts, teaching evaluations, committee assignments, tenure hearings, academic promotions, annual reports. Somit corroborates these facts about the routines of continual judgment in the disciplinary operations of the discipline as those necessities that "constitute a recurrent aspect of academic life."[24] The means of correct training usually disclose some practicable mean of professionally correct behavior at every step in one's academic training. For one's superiors, peers, and inferiors, "all behavior falls in the field between good and bad marks, good and bad points . . . it is possible to quantify this field and work out an arithmetical economy based on it."[25] Reward and punishment almost always appear in these forms of ranking and rank—symbolically and materially. Such scaling maneuvers play a double role as an ordinal system of disciplinary valorization as well as an interval system for the discipline's rewards and punishments. The discipline of the discipline mostly rewards through "the play of awards, thus making it possible to attain higher ranks and places; it punishes by reversing this process. Rank itself serves as a reward or punishment."[26]

The discipline of ranking in/by/for the discipline is normalizing, and this normalization brings a loose administrative order through conventional modes of scholarly training that correct, mold, strengthen, or perfect through the symbolic economies of reputation. The training in the discipline of political science simultaneously is a discipline that develops by instruction, exercise, or standards into a powerful regime of normalizing thoughts and behaviors in most of its professional technical practices. The discipline of the discipline represents "a type of power, a modality for its exercise, compromising a whole set of instruments, techniques, procedures, levels of application, targets; it is a 'physics' or an 'anatomy' of power, a technology" for producing the "political scientist" as "a professionally correct" expert.[27] Political science also thereby becomes a "scientific politics" intent on creating the correctly disciplined disciple of its knowledge via personal surveillance and methodological instruction. In political science/scientific politics, one finds "the meticulous, concrete training of useful forces; the circuits of communication are the supports of an accumulation and a centralization of knowledge; the play of signs defines the anchorages of power; it is not that the beautiful totality of the individual is amputated, repressed, altered by our social order, it is rather the individual is carefully fabricated in it, according to a whole technique of forces and bodies."[28]

The professionally correct gauge the value and position of individual persons and departments, willingly and openly, as "names." One is "a big name," "a name," or "a no name." This reading can be taken immediately from almost any group of professionally minded political scientists. Reputation and its development in rankings, therefore, boil down, first, to building one's meganymic profile, and second, avoiding anymic obscurity or micronymic ineffectuality. While some cling to naive beliefs about better explanation, scientific progress, or accurate prediction to ground their careers, most political scientists are fully engaged in developing themselves as a meganym. Because power and prestige in American political science are organized around being "professionally correct," the small-scale campaigns for enforcing "politically correct" behavior on many campuses are at best a minor diversion. When all is said and done, Latino/a studies stars, pomo heavy-hitters, and stand-out feminist scholars often vary little from the rational choice artists or data grubbing experts. They all play the same professionally correct games, even within smaller politically correct discourses, at raise time and in the bars during their professional meetings. They too want to be meganymic presences. The substantive focus of the discipline is immaterial; the formal functioning of disciplinarity is the key material force.

Whether it is rational choice theory or queer theory, professional correctness uses the language of disciplinary examination to discipline individual behavior within academic disciplines by locating scholarly work in vague regions of "approval" (the mainstream, at the core, on the cutting edge) and/or "disapproval" (the backwaters, along the periphery, on the dull side). One's methodological stance in research practices is fitted into similar categories of "valorization" (sophisticated, leading edge, standard-setting) and/or "devalorization" (unsophisticated, old hat, completely lacking). In the same way, one's publication record can be graded in terms of "significance" (major journals, big-name presses, high citation counts) and/or "insignificance" (minor journals, no-name presses, no citation counts). At the end of the day, most academic political scientists cope with this system of professional correctness as a real material expression of disciplinary political correctness. Who gets what, where, when, and why in university departments, professional associations, and grant competitions depends on these ranking systems of invidiously ranked distinction. While the intrinsic worth of any widely sought after rewards—pay raises, tenure, promotion, corner offices, or administrative powers—are declining, the battle for them continues at full tilt. And, the strategies for winning success or evading failure totally are denominated in these codes of professional correctness as the normalizing judgment of superiors, peers, and inferiors iterate their evaluations in matrices of performative success and failure.

Living lives of perpetual anxiety about the dubious meaning of their work, when the purposelessness of anyone's career can be underscored by the vacant stares of 50 20-year-olds all wearing their baseball caps backwards in class, political scientists, like all academics or new class professionals, compulsively rank themselves, their departments, or universities in lists of prestige and repute. Many dismiss such rankings as philistine, but they do generate real and important meaning. In them, dark tales of scholarly self-affirmation create and then (re)valorize professional notions of significance out of signs of apparent status. Everyone hears these stories. Listen in the bars and hallways at any conference. First, "Sure, nobody gives a damn about my latest book, but I am at Johns Hopkins, and not out in the boondocks." Second, "Alright, everyone slept through my Wednesday lecture, but I am a member of one of the highest nationally ranked departments of political science, and not some second-rate shop at a third-rate school." Third, "Fine, the number of majors in public policy is dropping, but I have three articles in *The American Political Science Review*, and none in the *Political Science Quarterly*." Fourth, "Big deal, you just connected a manuscript with Iowa State University Press; I have three books with Yale University Press, and not a bad review anywhere on all of them." Outside of the fishbowls of academe, such psychosocial abilibis of self-affirmation might seem trivial. In the discipline, however, such mantras of invidious distinction give psychic meaning, professional purpose, and personal drive to often miserable lives otherwise racked with deep alienation and perpetual ambiguity.

At the bottom line, no one really can judge definitively if one's work is good or bad, important or unimportant, revolutionary or ordinary. Maybe History will be able to make those judgments. Almost everyone, however, can judge, albeit perhaps only provisionally, that Oxford University Press is better than University of Nebraska Press, the *American Political Science Review* is far more meaningful than *Political Research Quarterly*, or California-Berkeley outstrips East Carolina State in prestige. Like Calvinist entrepreneurs clinging to monetary wealth as signs of salvation, academic political scientists clutch their journal placements, publishing houses, citation counts, and department affiliations as *the* tangible markers of predestined significance and well-deserved success. Publishing a classic article with elegant arguments for all citizens in the Sunday paper is meaningless, but publishing a robotic research report in the *American Political Science Review* is truly exciting. Writing a great book with a big commercial press is very difficult, but publishing a small-selling Harvard University Press book easily proves that it is great as such. The signs on the spine or the code on the cover is the *sine qua non* of valued meaningful achievement. As any real estate agent can tell you, always go for "location, location, location" to measure worth.

Asking whether or not those Oxford University Press books are really good, if *APSR* articles really add more to human understanding than *PRQ*, or are Cal-Berkeley students truly are better educated than East Carolina students is very rarely done. Independent assessments simply would burst too many bubbles. Challenges from without almost always question the symbolic economies of meaning as they operate now. Those who benefit from them fear any intimations of *perestroika* that might disturb their benefits, and those who do not benefit them now often hope to do so in the future, so they too rarely question the prevailing regime of valorization. In point of fact, like indecipherable party tracts from old CPSU academics in the former Soviet Union, most high-prestige academic writing is printed and circulated in professional journals that exist because some bureaucratic body (say the American Political Science Association, the Southern Political Science Association, or the Midwest Political Science Association) makes a subscription a mandatory component of paying annual professional dues. Individuals frequently read the book reviews (to check the reputation markets) or skim the table of contents (to monitor the prestige placement exchange), but most articles go unread, uncited, and unremembered, like the collected works of Joseph Stalin or Enver Hoxha, as volume after volume of these dismal tracts are entombed in forgotten library stacks or dusty bottom shelves in faculty offices.

Because these symbolic economies are what both gives value to the academic process of production and drives faculty behavior in the workplace, the practice of liberal education is left pinched and gasping. The production of *American Journal of Political Science* or *American Political Science Review* articles not only may not add to humanity's stock of knowledge, it actually detracts from the processes of knowing by imposing high net opportunity costs elsewhere. The time and energy expended on writing articles virtually no one wants to read or journals no average lay reader will buy cannot be spent writing more useful materials, teaching more important things, or tending to more real intellectual challenges. In the final analysis, this excess of academic sign-value production becomes a perverse system of (ab)use value that prevents change as it ruins individual lives and educational institutions. Not surprisingly, surveys of *APSR* authors reveal that 61 percent publish there for its "prestige," or more plainly, here its sign-value, which is double the response of those seeking a wide audience in the discipline (31 percent), triple those convinced of the theoretical importance of their work (21 percent), and ten times those seeking serious peer review (6 percent) for their research.[29] Most *APSR* articles, then, do seem sought after, and published, in pursuit of meganymic development rather than some ideal quest for social enlightenment or rigorous review.

Meganymic development—and hence personal success—is based on playing in these elaborate symbolic economies of reward and punishment that disconnect individual scholarship from obligations of teaching, national academic disciplines from individual universities, and professional success from the rewards of professing. The work of academics becomes locked into insidious economies of invidious distinction that disciplinary associations, university administrations, and professional entrepreneurs all manipulate to advance their careerist interests without necessarily, or even occasionally, serving the more nebulous, but far more important, interests of society, students, or scholarship. Yet, it is for precisely these latter constituencies that academics say they allegedly serve by accumulating, storing, and transmitting knowledge across the generations. Of course, nothing could be farther from the truth.

The professionalization of most academic disciplines has introduced a cross-cutting influence in the life of many individual faculty, college departments, and entire universities. Bizarre intradisciplinary practices in each department, and not the profession of teaching or the life of scholarship, define what is valued, worthy, and practicable. The latest fads of disciplinary debate constitute what is and should be taught, the major journals of disciplinary associations become the prime target of academic research and writing, and national recognition in the discipline (meaning other faculty at other schools in the same area of research) often outweigh honest work at the craft of teaching (meaning working with students at one's own school in department courses). Most serious systems of ranking are done by research reputation in disciplines, not by academic strength of graduates or overall satisfaction of students; hence, everyone knows that focusing on the teaching tasks at hand will materially diminish, and not visibly enhance, one's real professional status and success.

Drawing comparisons between oneself and others, in turn, leads to regimes of classification to appraise relative visibility, professional reputation, or academic impact. In the argot of the profession, these appraisals are folded into a series of nominative judgments about the power, size, recognition, or circulation of authorial presence, or, more colloquially, "name." Is one "a name" to be reckoned with? Who are "the names" one needs to know in this or that subfield? What are "the big names" in this particular methological specialty? Why does one remain a "no-name" journeyman? How can one become a "big name?"

Professional success mostly revolves around developing from "an unknown name" to "a big name," and this meganymic process rests on the footnote fetishism of "citational analysis." A clear articulation of the disciplinary assumptions behind the citational currencies of these sign-value economies is found in Miller, Tien, and Peebler:

> One of our basic hypotheses . . . is that there would be a substantial correlation between the frequency of publishing in the APSR and the number of citations received in the *Social Science Citations Index*. Assuming that the profession is essentially a reflection of the intellectual interest of those who do the very best work in the field, then both of these approaches convey the same basic portrait of where the profession has been, where it is currently, and where it may be going in the future. If this is

true, then an even more accurate ranking of scholarly impact on the profession would be obtained by combining the number of *APSR* publications with the number of citations.[30]

Here, footnote fetishists contrive an intriguing new index, or PVI (Professional Visibility Index), to weight and rank the repute of true macromeganyms among the fame of mere meganyms. By multiplying the total number of *APSR* publications (for those top 4 percent of *APSR* authors with 5 or more articles) times the total number of SSCI citations and dividing by 1,000, Miller, Tien, and Peebler affirm the meganymic value of 72 big names, positioning Professor Miller, strangely enough once more, among the elite top 10 of the mighty 72.[31]

At the same time, the disciplinary thrust of such disciplinary comparisons is stated quite succinctly by the PVI's functionality as a ranking mechanism. That is, the PVI is cast as "a valid and reasonably accurate measure of visibility and performance, as it considers both publishing in the discipline's top peer review journal and the number of citations from one's peers."[32] Footnote fetishism, then, becomes the marker of visibility and performance: big names have high citation counts, medium names have smaller counts, little names have small counts, no names have no citations. One cannot publish anywhere; one must publish in SSCI-surveyed journals, because the SSCI only surveys allegedly "the top journals." Visibility equals performance, and performance must become visible. The sighting of meganyms derives from citings of them by others; sign-value accrues from and to those who value such signs.

Miller, Tien, and Peebler push their footnote fetishist measuring system from the individual level out on to the collective level by asserting their objective assessments of PVI also can be used to assess departmental quality in terms of aggregate faculty research visibility and teaching performance.[33] Instead of judging how broadly a research faculty's work effects public life positively or how well its students learn their ethical, political, or social obligations, meganymic developmentalism brings the discipline of the political science discipline to full force. That is, how often does a department's faculty publish in the *APSR* or get citations from the *APSR*? More important, how well does it train—as *APSR* publishing masters—its students—as wannabe *APSR* publishing apprentices—to get published in the *APSR* and gain citations from their *APSR* publications? Instead of relying on purely reputational analyses, like those of the National Research Council,[34] with their low evaluator numbers, small response rate, and high sampling error, these more "objective" meganymic assessments stay directly centered on the sign-value economies of real academic life.[35]

Conclusions

For most academics living and working on the margins beyond the more disciplined centers of American political science, the surrealistic debate of the past decade about why most political scientists have split apart to sit at one of four "separate tables" (the soft left, hard left, soft right, and hard right), leaving behind some unifying methodological core is essentially incomprehensible.[36] They could be dismissed, following Professor Almond's diagnosis, as either just more of those sorry political theorists "traumatized by the diffusion of scientific aspirations and methods into political science, and seduced by the simplistic temptations of 1960s and 1970s thinking,"[37] or even worse, as more sad cases of "the Marxist, neo-Marxist and 'critical theory' approaches" that follow "unfalsifiable truths discovered and stated in the works of Marx and elaborated by his associates and followers."[38]

Something else materially links together the separate tables that Almond describes, namely, the discipline in/of/from the power/knowledge practices of the discipline itself. Again, the "professionalism" he connects to the search of general scientific objectivity, in many ways, is a destructive obligation to enforce very specific forms of scientific subjectivity as "professional correctness." That is, "professionalism in the sense of affiliation to professional associations, peer accreditation, and reviewing of recruitment and scholarship and the like" or "professionalization (in the sense of the establishment of multi-membered, meritocratically-recruited, relatively non-hierarchic, departments; the establishment of associations and specialist societies, refereed journals; and so on)."[39] This professional correctness is where the unifying disciplinary core of the discipline emerges; and, this also is where the disciplinary downside of political science becomes what it "is" because of what, as Easton observes, political scientists "do."[40]

Outside the confines of political science, many observers now accept the social construction of scientific knowledge. As Pinch and Bijker assert,

> There is widespread agreement that scientific knowledge can be, and indeed has been, shown to be thoroughly socially constructed. . . . The treatment of scientific knowledge as a social construction implies that there is nothing epistemologically special about the nature of scientific knowledge: It is merely one in a whole series of knowledge cultures (including, for instance, the knowledge systems pertaining to "primitive" tribes). Of course, the successes and failures of certain knowledge cultures still need to be explained, but this is to be seen as a sociological task, not an epistemological one.[41]

This analysis has explored a few ins-and-outs in the knowledge regime of American political science, which still holds, by and large, to stories of individual discovery/confirmation via methodological rigor as its premium model of scientific knowledge despite its professed intellectual pluralism, to examine some of sociological sources of its continuing successes, at least within the ambits of its own little disciplinary networks.

Seeing how disciplines discipline their producers and consumers helps us understand the social construction of political scientific knowledge by disclosing the conventional understandings manifest in many of the acts and artifacts generated within the knowledge cultures of political science. The disciplinary lore of this academic formation does not acknowledge its own social construction; instead, it still purports to show political science as a very special project of data-driven, positivist explanation intent on discovering generalizable tendencies, testing deductive nomological propositions, and confirming naturalistic laws of human behavior. Seeing these practices as pure epistemological necessity, most political scientists ignore the more impure sociological contingencies, like the discipline of disciplinarity, that power such knowledges.

In this somewhat confused state, one recent retrospective compendium, *A New Handbook of Political Science*, touts essentially vague sociological goods, like methodological maturation, conceptual integration, or organizational professionalization, as being the signs of truly scientific advances.[42] While it is never clear how such "advances" work, "the general pattern is clear enough" for Goodin and Klingemann, namely, "There are highly differentiated subdisciplinary communities making great advances . . . the old aspiration of a Unified Science might still remain a chimera. But at the turn of the century, ours looks like a potentially unifiable science."[43] On the one hand, Goodin and Klingemann graciously admit their survey is "incomplete" and "somewhat idiosyncratic," because such survey projects are by their very nature "inherently selective."[44] Yet, on the other hand, this inherent selectivity is how and why, once again, disciplinary discipline can be exercised in affirming or ignoring certain practices, methods, and ideas as worthy of attention in unifying scientific potential. If Goodin and Klingemann ignore you, they suggest, then it is probably a function of random selectivity; but, if they include you, then your meganymic energies probably are pulling you inexorably toward the right disciplinary direction in the reputation exchanges.

If politics is "the *constrained use of social power*," and the study of politics examines "the *nature and source of those constraints* and the *techniques for the use of social power* within those constraints,"[45] then Goodin's and Klingemann's "authoritative survey," or social construction, of political science becomes an interesting example of the disciplinary constraints at play in scientific politics. Their belief in a positive social science

as being somehow epistemologically special constrains Goodin, Klingemann, and another "42 of the most famous political scientists worldwide"[46] included in this edited volume from admitting much Marxism,
critical theory, feminism, or postmodern deconstruction into their potentially unified science, although even they admit these are somewhat unset-
tling silences. Presenting the "most important" political science literature
as that of the past twenty years, which coincidently is the time when most
of these 44 professionals' academic lives and networks were being formed,
the experts here suggest that the only important work is the work that they
cite: less than 10 percent comes before 1960, 50 percent comes since 1985,
and over 60 percent comes since 1975.[47]

This work might be epistemologically special and highly scientific,
but these closely networked political scientists also seem to be socially constructing an intriguing scientific politics in which the most famous political
scientists worldwide get to write about and then cite the most famous political science in this common exercise of joint network defense, namely, what
they, or their friends and neighbors, have produced in a professionally correct fashion since 1975. And, the best measure of their veracity is, of
course, a "bibiliometric analysis" of their own footnotes. It is the best measure "for all sorts of purposes," not because it might reveal truth, utility, or
accuracy, but rather the goals of "gauging the reputation and standing of
individuals and departments within the profession, for assessing the intensity of use of any particular piece or type of work or of works by a particular individual, and so on" in their professional networks.[48] All of these
analytical outcomes are attributed to epistemologically special, method-
ologically rigorous, and technoscientifically driven causes. Social connections, cohort networks, ideological hegemonies, methodological prejudices,
school ties, and political agendas are not considered as probable causal
forces behind the findings of such bibiliometric analyses, which simply
mobilize statistical techniques as a source of social power for those who
wish to write and cite this sort of advances-making "science."

The self-referential certainty of Goodin's and Klingemann's retrospective survey of the field underscores again how thoroughly the discipline
of the discipline engenders trained incapacities or promotes a decline in disciplinary discourses.[49] The same decades that have brought thousands of
newly normalized political scientists to the academic tasks of methodological maturation, conceptual integration, and organizational professionalization in political science also have seen this sort of scientific politics do
very little to arrest the abnormal coarsening of public life, the corruption
of many civic institutions, and the erosion of once vibrant democratic practices. The celebratory certainty of such political science surveys cannot
negate the discipline's neglect of real politics. For all of its advances, the

normal science produced by adherents of political science's disciplined normalization has failed to anticipate or adapt many major changes, ranging from the end of the welfare state or the implosion of state socialism to the maldevelopment of the Second, Third, and Fourth Worlds or the spread of wild social chaos in many regimes. At this juncture, too much is in doubt and at stake in civic life for the hermetic discourses of most mainstream political science to remain entirely self-absorbed in a discipline that interprets its traditional epistemic realism, technocratic operationalism, and apolitical professionalism as real "advances" for human scientific awareness.[50] Other subjugated knowledges outside of the existing disciplinary ambit of political science instead must be reconsidered, if political science is to deal effectively with the very real crises that now challenge the state formations and university systems that historically have sustained it.

To conclude, this study has sought to understand the discipline enforced by the political science discipline by looking at what political scientists "do." Even so, it only explored a handful of concerns by playing one version of "the strong program" against mainstream political science, which values professional correctness as a system of "dogmatic wisdom."[51] First, it indicated how political science aids in the reproduction of social controls for industrial democracy, suburban consumerism, or liberal capitalism by ontologically stabilizing a system of disciplinary assumptions about our collective life. Second, it examined how participation in the discipline soon compels its members to trade actively in the sign-value economies of professional correctness, forcing would-be professionals to adhere correctly to very clear disciplinary expectations in order to succeed in the discipline. And, third, it discussed how reputational development functions as a system of discipline, forcing professionals to accept certain research practices to gain professional visibility, while broader and bigger public groups, who need what they should be teaching, often are left to fend for themselves.

Acknowledgments

This paper is extracted from a larger book-in-progress, entitled *Beyond the Boundaries: Discourse, Discipline and Dissent in Contemporary Political Science,* and some parts of it previously appeared in *Telos* 97 (Fall 1993). It was also presented at the Annual Meeting of the American Political Science Association, Washington D.C., August 28–31, 1997.

Notes

1. See Barry Barnes and David Bloor, "Realism, Rationalism and the Sociology of Knowledge," in M. Hollis and S. Lukes, eds. *Rationality and*

Relativism (Cambridge: MIT Press, 1982); and Michael Lynch, *Scientific Practice and Ordinary Action: Ethnomethodology and Social Studies of Science* (Cambridge: Cambridge University Press, 1997).

2. Helen Longino, *Science as Social Knowledge: Values and Objectivity in Scientific Inquiry* (Princeton: Princeton University Press, 1990), 10.

3. See Ben Agger, *Reading Science: A Literary, Political, and Sociological Analysis* (Dix Hills, NY: General Hall, 1989).

4. David Easton, *The Political System: An Enquiry into the State of Political Science* (Chicago: University of Chicago Press, 1971), 94.

5. Gabriel Almond, "Separate Tables: Schools and Sects in Political Science," *Political Science & Politics*, 20, 4 (December, 1988), 828–892.

6. Bruno Latour, *We Have Never Been Modern* (Cambridge: Harvard University Press, 1993).

7. Bruno Latour, *The Pasteurization of France* (Cambridge: Harvard University Press, 1988), 216–226.

8. Bruno Latour, *Science in Action* (Cambridge: Harvard University Press, 1987), 257 [Italics added].

9. For additional discussion of these points, see Timothy W. Luke, "The Discourse of Development: A Genealogy of 'Developing Nations' and the Discipline of Modernity," *Current Perspectives in Social Theory* 11 (1991), 271–293; "Political Science and the Discourses of Power: Developing a Genealogy of the Political Culture Concept," *History of Political Thought* 10, 1 (Spring 1989), 125–149; "Methodological Individualism: The Essential Ellipsis of Rational Choice Theory," *Philosophy of the Social Sciences* 17, 2 (September 1987), 341–355; and, "Reason and Rationality in Rational Choice Theory," *Social Research* 52, 1 (Spring 1985), 65–98.

10. Peter Zwick, "Mainstreaming Political Science Instruction: An Additive Approach," *Political Science & Politics* 25, 4 (December 1992), 714–717.

11. Arthur H. Miller, Charles Tien, and Andrew A. Peebler, "The *American Political Science Review* Hall of Fame: Assessments and Implications for an Evolving Discipline," *Political Science & Politics* 29, 1 (March 1996), 73.

12. See James C. Garard, "An Alternative Interpretation of Recent Political Science Journal Evaluations," *Political Science & Politics*, vol. 23: 444–451.

13. Miller et al., "Hall of Fame," 73.

14. Miller et al., "Hall of Fame," 78.

15. Samuel Patterson and Shannon K. Smithey, "Monitoring Scholarly Journal Publication in Political Science: The Role of the *APSR*," *Political Science & Politics*, 23, 4 (December 1990), 656.

16. Patterson and Smithey.
17. Patterson and Smithey, 647–656.
18. Miller et al., "Hall of Fame," 78.
19. Miller et al., "Hall of Fame," 73.
20. Ivor Crewe and Pippa Norris, "British and American Journal Evaluation: Divergence or Convergence," *Political Science & Politics* 24, 3 (September 1991), 526.
21. For more discussion, see David Ricci, *The Tragedy of Political Science*, 209–248.
22. For another classic reading of this process, see C. Wright Mills, *The Sociological Imagination* (New York: Oxford University Press, 1959), 76–118.
23. Michel Foucault, *Discipline and Punish* (New York: Vintage, 1979), 177.
24. Albert Somit, "From Professor of Political Science to Professor Emeritus," *Political Science & Politics*, 25, 6 (December 1992), 719.
25. Foucault, 180.
26. Foucault, 181.
27. Foucault, 215.
28. Foucault, 217.
29. Patterson and Smithey, 652.
30. Miller et al., "Hall of Fame," 74.
31. Miller et al., "Hall of Fame," 80–81.
32. Miller et al., "Hall of Fame."
33. Arthur H. Miller, Charles Tien, and Andrew A. Peebler, "Department Rankings: An Alternative Approach, *Political Science & Politics*, 29, 4 (December 1996), 709–710.
34. "Ranking Research Doctoral Programs in Political Science," *Political Science & Politics* 28, 4 (December 1995), 734–737.
35. Miller et al., "Department Rankings," 714–716.
36. Almond, "Separate Tables," 34–36.
37. Gabriel Almond, "The Nature of Contemporary Political Science: A Roundtable Discussion," *Political Science & Politics* 23, 1 (March 1990), 35.
38. Gabriel Almond, "Political Science: The History of the Discipline," in Robert Goodin and Hans-Dieter Klingemann, eds. *A New Handbook of Political Science* (Oxford: Oxford University Press, 1996), 51.
39. Almond, "Political Science: The History," 84, 50.
40. Easton, *Political System*, 94. These professionally correct standards for scholarly success circulate freely and openly through intradisciplinary communication channels. A recruitment letter from Pennsylvania State University, for example, touts the frequency of "success" that the

Department of Political Science there recently has experienced. With a new dean, department chair, and new senior faculty at Penn State, "all indicators of excellence (everything from faculty publications in the *APSR* and *AJPS* and university press books, to Fulbright and NSF grants) are up dramatically," Stuart A. Bremer, "Dear Colleague," Department of Political Science recruitment letter (October 6, 1997). Thus, departmental prestige and scientific success are not measured by creating workable solutions to pressing dilemmas in American political affairs, advancing sage answers to enduring moral questions, or training more effective citizens. Instead it is marked by the frequency and extent of any given faculty's publication of nameless, and mostly likely forgettable, papers in those journals that such correctly disciplined authorities regard as "the best." Excellence such as this thereby boosts those authors' and that department's PVI scores. To just make sure, the constituent components of PVI calculations constantly are revalorized in such self-referential intradisciplinary communiques to colleagues, possible students, and other departments.

41. Trevor J. Pinch and Wiebe E. Bijker, "The Social Construction of Facts and Artifacts: Or How the Sociology of Science and the Sociology of Technology Might Benefit Each Other," *The Social Construction of Technological Systems*, ed. W. Bijker, T. Hughes, and T. Pinch (Cambridge: MIT Press, 1987), 17, 50.
42. Goodin and Klingemann, 3–22.
43. Goodin and Klingemann, 26.
44. Goodin and Klingemann, 3.
45. Goodin and Klingemann, 7.
46. Goodin and Klingemann, jacket.
47. Goodin and Klingemann, 27.
48. Goodin and Klingemann, 23.
49. Ben Agger, *The Decline of Discourse: Reading, Writing, and Resistance in Postmodern Capitalism* (New York: Falmer Press, 1990).
50. See Theodore J. Lowi, "The State of Political Science: How We Become What We Study," *American Political Science Review*, 86 (March 1992), 1–7.
51. See Russell Jacoby, *Dogmatic Wisdom* (New York: Free Press, 1994).

9

BEYOND BOUNDARIES?

A Tentative Appraisal

EILEEN M. DOHERTY

> Elegance remains, I suppose, a general scientific ideal; but in the
> social sciences, it is very often in departures from that ideal that
> truly creative developments occur.
>
> —Clifford Geertz[1]

The Questionable Status of Boundaries
in the Evolution of International Relations

Knowledge about social and international phenomena is essentially inter-disciplinary in nature. This book is motivated by the suspicion that the fragmentation and disciplinary specialization that allow us to achieve empirical focus and theoretical parsimony may be accompanied by serious negative consequences. This concluding chapter has three purposes. First, it reconsiders the issues raised in the introduction regarding the problem of disciplinary fragmentation and the fruitlessness of interparadigm debates. Whereas the introduction focused on the broad evolution of the study of international life in the social sciences, this chapter examines more specifically the evolution of the international relations subfield of political science. Second, this chapter discusses the value of interdisciplinary dialogue by considering the specific ways in which the contributions in this volume speak to each other—and by extension, the ways in which various disciplines can inform each other. The articulation of areas of convergence and divergence among the contributors constitutes the beginning of an interdisciplinary dialogue among them. This kind of dialogue can refocus existing debates and highlight useful directions for future research for scholars across a range of disciplines. Finally, the chapter returns to the recommendation that was proposed in the introduction: the acceptance of an alternative, problem-driven approach to research. Disciplinary specialization should not be abandoned, but must be accompanied even more by the conscious integration of the knowledge accumulated via various research endeavors. Without that integration, we risk something more dangerous than simply missing the forest for the trees. We risk misperceiving the forest itself.

As Sil notes in the introduction, beginning in the nineteenth century a "division of labor" emerged within the social sciences. This was manifested in the proliferation of disciplinary structures and research traditions. For the most part, these divisions have been regarded as not only inevitable, but useful, in that they allowed for the emergence of distinct areas of expertise to increase the stock of knowledge from which academicians and policy makers could draw. This belief—that an academic division of labor is both natural and efficient—has been reinforced by institutional incentives that push researchers to carve out original research. In the attempt to carve out unique niches of specialization, there is even less incentive to pursue activities that involve replication or integration of prior research. The result has been a proliferation of boundaries, not only among academic disciplines, but also among subdisciplines and research traditions. The themes of this volume are twofold: First, a stringent disciplinary division of labor is neither natural nor necessarily beneficial in increasing our understanding of social phenomena generally, and international relations in particular. Second, traditional discipline-specific research is valuable—and therefore should by no means be abandoned—but it is necessary to supplement such research by comparing and synthesizing the insights that emerge within various disciplines and research traditions.

Disciplinary distinctions do not come easily to social science problems, either in conceptual or in practical terms. First, at a conceptual level, it is simply not possible to separate the political, economic, sociological, psychological, and anthropological aspects of international phenomena (whether international cooperation, conflict, or collective identity) into distinct empirically observable categories. At best, we can outline only rough guides to where these boundaries lie. Second, we face the problem of operationalization. That is, even if it were possible to identify conceptually the "political" variables of interest, it would not be possible to isolate those variables in a way that would come anywhere close to a laboratory experiment. The economic, sociological, cultural, and psychological dimensions not only affect, but are intertwined with, the political. This makes social science fundamentally different from physical sciences,[2] in which it is possible to isolate particular aspects of a problem and to manipulate variables with much greater precision.[3]

The starting point of this volume was that "international relations" is an intrinsically multidisciplinary rather than a conceptually distinct subfield. This did not use to be a controversial proposition. International relations theory qua theory is a young field. Prior to World War II, the international relations literature tended to involve broad understandings that emerged from philosophical speculation, legal discourse, and historical interpretation. Not only was international relations theory inextricable from law and philosophy, it was by definition normative. Realists viewed conflict as an inherent part of the international system, but focused on the ways that statesmanship and foreign policy could mitigate the tendency toward war in international relations. Idealists sought to understand international relations in order to change the international political order, to create institutions and rules that would lead to peace rather than war. Neither group concerned itself with hypothesis-testing and model-building.

This started to change in the postwar period. Much of the change stemmed from a widespread conviction among scholars and policy makers that the naiveté of some prewar idealists had been a destabilizing factor in the era leading to World War II:

> In dealing with international morality, which they were inclined to confuse with international law, [prewar idealists] contributed only a narrow and uncritical rectitude which exalted the international interest over national interests (but without asking how the former was to be determined), constitutional reform over revolution as the means of transcending the society of sovereign states (but without considering whether states could become the agents of their own extinction), and respect for legality over the need for change (but without facing up to the fact that the international legal system, as they construed it, could not accommodate change).[4]

International relations as a rigorous social science had its birth, then, partly as a reaction to the failure of normative prewar works—works that, according to Stanley Hoffman, engaged in "the kind of 'as if' thinking that mistook the savage world of the 1930s for a community, the League for a modern Church, and collective security for a common duty."[5]

The first "scientific" treatment of international relations was E. H. Carr's *Twenty Years Crisis*, which laid the foundations for postwar realism.[6] As postwar international relations theory evolved, the focus shifted largely (but not completely) from "ought" to "is"—a shift that transformed the nature of international political inquiry. Or, as Raymond Aron put it, "in crossing the Atlantic, in becoming power politics, Treitschke's *Machtpolitik* underwent a chiefly spiritual mutation. It became fact, not value."[7] In the form of postwar realism, international relations theory had taken the first step from away from philosophy and toward analysis.[8]

Since then, the field of international relations theory has been riddled with sharp debates about the nature of the inquiry itself. In particular, there have been contentious debates about the nature of international relations, with neorealism and neoliberalism emerging as competing research traditions (or "paradigms").[9] The debate between neorealist and neoliberal research traditions defined the study of international relations for much of the 1970s and 1980s, and indeed, it lingers today.[10] Neorealism emerged as distinct from traditional realism with the publication of *Theory of International Politics.*[11] Kenneth Waltz argued that if scholars were going to build a successful theory of international politics, it was important to highlight what was in fact was distinctive about interstate relations as opposed to domestic politics. Waltz argued that it was the existence of anarchy in the international system that created a distinctive structure to international relations. The resultant self-help system pushes states to be concerned about changes in the international distribution of power, and hence, engage in balancing behavior. Focusing solely on the systemic level of analysis, he argued that neorealist theory produces useful, albeit limited insights: "Elegance in social-science theories means that explanations and predictions will be general. A theory of international politics will, for example, explain why war recurs, and it will indicate some of the conditions that make war more or less likely; but it will not predict the outbreak of particular wars."[12]

Even if we accept Waltz's theory of international politics as a parsimonious explanation of some elements of international behavior,[13] others have argued that it is not enough—especially since neorealism tells us little about successful international cooperation.[14] Whereas the focus of neorealism has tended to be on state behavior, international conflict, concerns with relative gains, and (generally) security issues, neoliberalism has focused on nongovernmental and transnational actors, international cooperation, concerns with absolute gains, and (generally) political economy issues. The seminal work in the neoliberal research tradition was Keohane and Nye's *Power and Interdependence,*[15] which emphasized the importance of domestic or other trans-national actors in constructing explanatory theories of international relations. From the focus on issue-specific research emerged a broad literature on international cooperation and regimes.[16] The interparadigm debate of the 1970s and 1980s focused on the strengths and weaknesses of each of these competing approaches, as well as on the question of whether bridges can be built across the paradigms.

What is most interesting for our purposes is that the "neo" part of both neorealism and neoliberalism was the emphasis on theory-building and parsimonious explanation. As these research traditions evolved, each became more focused in its claims and research focus. Neorealist theorists sought to investigate the effect of anarchy on international balancing behavior; neoliberals examined the role of institutions in shaping international cooperation. In this process of redefining themselves as positivist research traditions, both neorealism and neoliberalism became "leaner and meaner."[17] They also became increasingly compatible in their emphasis on specifying relationships between variables, hypothesis testing, and theoretical parsimony. Not surprisingly, then, discussions of the "interparadigm debate" evolved from a debate about two seemingly incompatible approaches to discussions about the ways a unifying "rationalist" approach could by forged by building bridges or constructing a division of labor between neorealism and neoliberalism.

What has been called the "fourth debate" emerged in the late 1980s, partly as a reaction to the emphasis on rigorous theory-building by neorealists and neoliberals. This debate between "rationalists" and "reflectivists" has centered as much on the epistemological and ontological foundations of the field as on substantive theoretical claims and methodologies.[18] Reflectivist scholars—including critical theorists, poststructuralists, and constructivists—have objected to "scientism" in international relations, excessive emphasis on theoretical parsimony, overoptimism about the ability to achieve objective inquiry, overemphasis on explanation rather than interpretation, and a misguided focus on unidirectional causality rather than mutually constitutive relationships.[19]

In sum, international relations theory has emerged during the postwar period as a separate field of inquiry, distinct from law, philosophy, and other nomothetic social science disciplines. At the same time, the field has been marked by shifting, but consistently contentious, debates between research traditions defined by competing methodologies, analytic frameworks, theoretical claims, and sometimes, epistemologies. The emphasis of this volume has been on prospects for the cumulation of knowledge through systematic and deliberate (if eclectic) construction of integrative theoretical frameworks organized around empirically grounded emergent questions. In our view, such integrative approaches need to play a more crucial role in the social sciences, complementing the protracted debates about neorealist versus neoliberal research traditions, or about rationalist versus reflectivist epistemologies. It is more fruitful to move beyond discussions of these divisions—and to reestablish empirical questions as the center of the discipline. By starting inquiry from substantive problems (rather than by identifying new questions from within an established research tradition), a broader range of concepts, theories, interpretations, and research can be brought to bear on the inquiry itself. As Alexander Wendt has argued:

> The state of the social sciences and, in particular, of international relations, is such that epistemological prescriptions and

conclusions are at best premature. Different questions involve different standards of inference; to reject certain questions because their answers cannot conform to the standards of classical physics is to fall into the trap of method-driven rather than question-driven social science. By the same token, however, giving up the artificial restrictions of logical positivist conceptions of inquiry does not force us to give up on 'Science.' Beyond this, there is little reason to attach so much importance to epistemology. Neither positivism, nor scientific realism, nor postructuralism tells us about the structure and dynamics of international life. Philosophies of science are not theories of international relations.[20]

This is not terribly different from Hedley Bull's warning 25 years ago:

It . . . appears to me that what Morton Kaplan has called "the new great debate" between the classical and the scientific approaches has gone on long enough: it is a bad sign in a subject that it should be preoccupied with questions of methodology rather than substance.[21]

Beyond Disciplinary Boundaries?

The authors in Part I of this volume all attempt to look beyond traditional discipline-bound research programs in international studies. All consciously attempt to move beyond the constraints of disciplinary boundaries and traditional research traditions by stressing integrative theoretical approaches to substantive problems. The focus on interdisciplinary research does not necessarily mean the rejection of existing research traditions, but rather, expanding the explanatory capability of existing approaches through the conscious integration of new bodies of research into existing research traditions.

The works by Doherty and Clunan illustrate the ways in which different integrative approaches can inform each other, even across epistemological divides. Working from a "soft" positivist perspective, Doherty examines the process by which individuals understand and tackle problems. As she argues, experimental research in judgment and decision making suggests that individual cognitive processes play an important role in international negotiations—and one that is not well accounted for in traditional international relations bargaining theory. Specifically, the assumption that individuals approach negotiations with a well-specified set of preferences and the ability to order those preferences obscures some important insights about the way that issues are actually evaluated and redefined during international negotiations. Multidimensional tasks that spur intuitive rather than analytical cognition may create obstacles to successful negotiations; moreover, the inconsistent signaling that is part of the process of experimentation may create potential for negotiation collapse even when learning is occurring. This suggests that theories of international negotiations should not ignore individual cognition. Rather, they should integrate the generalizable insights about the way that task (negotiating) environments affect individual actions and interpersonal communication.

This argument complements Clunan's emphasis on social "learning" as an integral part of identity construction. Drawing on theories of sociology, Clunan argues that there is an artificial boundary between international and national processes of identity formation.[22] Her work, which is premised on the social construction of reality, challenges strict rationalist views of world politics and seeks to build a conceptual bridge between domestic and international processes in the development of a constructivist research program in international relations. In response to Sil's call for question-driven research, Clunan also emphasizes the importance of breaking down large, fixed categories into more manageable concepts designed to address specific issues.[23] With her focus on learning, Clunan is focusing explicitly on the centrality of shared ideas as a mechanism for the transformation of the international political system.

An obvious question, then, is how ideas emerge and are transmitted. Consider again Emanuel Adler's concepetion of cognitive evolution (as discussed by Clunan):

> Cognitive evolution is a theory of international learning, if by learning we understand the adoption by policymakers of new interpretations of reality, as they are created and introduced into the political system by individuals and social actors. The capacity of institutions in different countries to learn and to generate similar interests will depend not only on the acquisition of new information, but also on the political selection of similar epistemic and normative premises. The political importance of these premises likes not in their being 'true,' but in their being intersubjectively shared across institutions and nation states."[24]

And, as Clunan notes, "the nature of learning, whether it is simple or complex, may be the key to developing a constructivist theory of change."

Doherty's chapter is entirely compatible with this premise, but brings some light to bear on the problems associated with intersubjective sharing. For example, to the extent that issues or problems are addressed through intuitive thought processes, it is difficult—often impossible—to explicitly share the thought processes behind the "learning" that is occurring. Moreover, research in experimental psychology suggests that as individuals interact, they may not recognize the fact that their ideas about cause/effect relationships and policy priorities may be converging. This suggests that Clunan's social learning may not occur naturally, because actors may fail to recognize cognitive convergence when it occurs. In this case, the social constructivists and the experimental psychologists meet each other over the issue of creating shared ideas, and the concept of "learning" creates the basis by which to have a cross-disciplinary dialogue through which to build insights about social change. The social constructivists remind us that knowledge is socially created, that it evolves over time. The positivists (at least from the experimental psychology camp) provide insights about the ways that the dynamics of interpersonal interactions affect the emergence and transmittal of these ideas.[25]

If Doherty and Clunan are interested in psychological and sociological dimensions of the way in which problems are conceptualized and interests are defined, Ripsman and Blanchard emphasize the complexity and variety of the material contexts shaping interstate economic relations and national decisions on security issues. Challenging the conventional wisdom about the inverse relationship between the levels of interdependence and international conflict, they argue that the very concept of "interdependence" must be viewed in a much broader context if we are to understand its real effect on international conflict. Theories of international relations have tended to measure interdependence by primarily utilizing quantitative measures of "political" and "economic" aspects of cross-national relationships. Ripsman and Blanchard call for a more nuanced measure that can account for the geopolitical context of those relationships. Consequently, the Strategic Goods Test and Contextual Sensitivity Estimator both are designed to provide a more comprehensive framework for the qualitative analysis of economic interdependence. In short, context matters.

The strategic, material, geographical, and technological context of trade affects decision makers' judgments about national vulnerability, while perceptions about alliances and financial stability affect judgments regarding national sensitivity. By using contextual, interdisciplinary, qualitative measures of interdependence, Ripsman and Blanchard's findings call into question the conventional wisdom about (1) the nature of interdependence before each of the World Wars; and (2) perceptions of decision makers about the constraints of dependence. Here is a case where an overemphasis on parsimony may, in fact, prompt misleading conclusions. By relying on simple quantitative measures of trade relationships, analysts may miss important elements of the decision making context that affect particular policy actions. We are reminded that emphasizing elegance in the social sciences may be a misguided endeavor—that the more useful goal may not be to seek simplicity, but rather, to seek complexity and then to order it.[26]

Thus, for Clunan, the findings of Ripsman and Blanchard can provide an important corrective to the overemphasis on ideational factors in much of the constructivist literature in international relations. Ideas take hold for various reasons, not least because some ideas yield more efficient policy means of achieving particular goals within particular material contexts. Conversely, work from the constructivist camp is broadly applicable to the more empricist approach taken by Ripsman and Blanchard. For them, Clunan's insights regarding constructivism and identity formation can help to identify further contextual variables in the shaping of security interests, and it is obviously only after specifying these interests that we can understand the most efficient means of achieving cooperation and preventing conflict. This kind of dialogue is possible partly because neither Clunan nor Ripsman and Blanchard adopt an epistemologically extreme position. Ripsman and Blanchard do not claim that geographic factors or primary-source historical analysis are sufficient in the analysis of interdependence, interest-formation, and decision-making. Nor does Clunan deny that the existence of "real world" conditions constrains state behavior. Opportunities for cumulation and learning would be lost by simply slotting into isolated niches of expertise either the empiricist research into trade and conflict, or the constructivist concerns regarding the origins and consequences of identities. Rather, these two chapters suggest that scholars who may embrace different epistemologies, but the same broad empirical questions can inform, supplement, and challenge each other in ways that create productive dialogues and deeper understandings of particular political phenomena.

Like Clunan, Anno is interested in questions of identity, but his approach brings a novel perspective to a slightly different substantive question concerning the formation of national identities in particular international contexts. Anno argues that the notion of identity itself defies disciplinary boundaries, and therefore, that there is an artificial division between economistic approaches (that emphasize the centrality of individual interests) and sociological approaches (that emphasize collective norms and understandings). By examining the psychological aspects of identity formation, and in particular, the benefits that individuals derive from their identity, Anno argues for a theoretical middle ground that allows for some convergence between rational, interest-based theories and sociological approaches to identity. Anno uses insights from microeconomics to highlight elements of identity in a fresh way, as well as to illustrate the limits of a positivist, rational choice approach to identity. The focus on microeconomics is an implicit challenge to the distinction that is often made between affect-oriented identity politics and interest-oriented material politics. To the extent that Anno's metaphor highlights the emotional "returns" to identity, he is able to provide insights about individuals' motivations for embracing and maintaining certain identity characteristics.

Central to the argument is the use of metaphor as a heuristic for social science inquiry. In the tradition of Rousseau's stag hunt, or realism's billiard ball model of the international system, Anno uses the investment portfolio metaphor to make a nebulous concept like "identity" resonate for the student of international relations.[27] The use of metaphor in academic research is a time-honored tradition, but it is generally relegated to the role of supplementing more "scientific" research. Yet, as Anno demonstrates, the careful use of metaphor adds a dimension to our understanding that can be centrally important. As Lakoff and Johnson note:

> [M]etaphor is pervasive, not merely in our language but in our conceptual system. It seems inconceivable to us that any phenomenon so fundamental to our conceptual system could not be central to an account of truth and meaning. . . . Metaphor is one of the most basic mechanisms we have for understanding our experience.[28]

By developing an argument via metaphor, Anno can highlight aspects of identity that might be more difficult with a more descriptive or analytical approach. The use of metaphor gives the reader a kind of "double vision" because the technique holds the object of inquiry in two points of view simultaneously.[29] Moreover, because the "emotional investment portfolio" underscores both rational and affect-oriented reasons for the emergence of particular identities, the metaphor effectively breaks down the artificial divide between economistic and ideational theories of development. The metaphor itself provides the argument for an integrative approach to complex issues of national identity.

Beyond Epistemological and Ontological Boundaries?

The central question in Part 2 of this book is the following: To what extent do epistemological and ontological differences splinter international relations research and prevent the cumulation of "knowledge" however defined? The three essays in this section approach this question from dramatically different perspectives. Sil cautions that absolutist epistemological positions have produced unnecessarily sharp divisions between seemingly irreconcilable research traditions, and argues that the possibilities for theoretical integration and communication among different kinds of social science endeavors may be greatest if we embrace a more pragmatic middle ground between positivism and relativism. Huntley's essay challenges the argument in this volume that disciplinary specialization has led to an unfortunate fragmentation; he argues that boundaries (or, his preferred term, "thresholds") are an inevitable part of the expansion of knowledge. For him, the unnatural divide is that between fact and value, and in particular, between theory and praxis. Luke questions the possibility of objective knowledge given the professional interests of political scientists—and examines the way that the political science discipline itself creates incentives for fragmentation, and potentially, the marginalization of political science from policy-relevant endeavors.

Sil argues that there is indeed a wide and varied "middle ground" between epistemological extremes. Offering a spectrum of epistemologies, he notes that the boundaries separating various epistemologies are often blurry, and that "positivists" and "relativists" often cannot even find agreement on epistemological issues within camps, much less between them. Rather than continuing to focus on "postivism versus relativism," Sil suggests that it is more useful to embrace an epistemological "middle ground" that emphasizes the indeterminacy of epistemological questions and instead encourages communication and learning among scholars who are studying similar kinds of substantive questions or empirical objects. While there may be little room for dialogue on the extreme ends of the spectrum (logical positivism on one end, postmodern deconstructionism on the other end), there is ample room for dialogue between the varied and nuanced epistemological "camps" between those two ends, camps that happen to include many of the most distinguished figures in a variety of social science disciplines. Moreover, in terms of theory-building, Sil suggests that in between context-bound interpretation and more sweeping causal explanations lies the goal of partial explanation, which focuses on comparing deep interpretations of similar phenomena in different contexts. For Sil, this middle ground is not a unifying center for all social science, but simply a pragmatic solution in an era where the level of fragmentation has far exceeded the possibilities for interfaces and exchanges between scholars working in different subfields and research traditions. Such a pragmatic epistemological position aims at keeping debates alive, encourages a wide variety of social analysis—and critically, enables all but the most extreme objectivists and subjectivists to communicate with each other and borrow relevant insights from each other.

Huntley takes issue with the argument that disciplinary or epistemological divisions are threatening to balkanize social science research. Rather, he argues that the divisions found in international relations theory are simply part of the broader trend in intellectual inquiry. As the universe of knowledge expands, so too, must the organization of fields of inquiry according to various disciplines, epistemologies, and methodologies. Whether this is "good" or "bad" is not the point, he says, but rather an inevitable outcome of the cumulative nature of knowledge over time. The fundamental disagreement between Huntley and the editors is not whether divisions exist between disciplines, subfields and research traditions, but what the significance of those divisions are for the long-term cumulation of knowledge in the social sciences. It is important to remember here that in invoking an evolutionist framework, Huntley is thinking about the origins and nature of boundaries on a quite different scale. In fact, Huntley may very well concur with the aims of this volume to the extent that he interprets new, integrative frameworks as products of a particular new stage in the cumulation of knowledge, products that are functional at present for dealing with the level of complexity in an ever-expanding universe of knowledge.

Huntley's concern is with another division, one he finds more problematic than disciplinary or epistemological boundaries: the artificial divide between knowledge and morality. Limiting discussions to the possibility of attaining objectivity in social science research, and not considering the role of moral purpose in scholarship, misses the point of social inquiry. Most scholars recognize that values or normative concerns influence scientific inquiry. They affect the selection of problems, as well as our notion of what constitutes "important evidence."[30]

But acknowledging that fact begs a much broader issue: To what extent should international relations research be explicitly normatively driven? On this issue, Huntley argues, neither positivists nor constructivists have anything to contribute. For positivist researchers, he argues, morality disappears in the quest for objective research: "To the extent that to be a 'scientist' requires adopting and achieving a posture of 'objectivity,' the posture cuts the intimate bonds between knowledge and moral choice that the Greeks took for granted and Kant viewed as central." And since constructivism offers no basis by which to identify "progress," there is little room for prescriptive research. In this respect, purposeful social theory-such as Marxist theory and feminist standpoint theory—stand as a challenge not just to the epistemology of more "mainstream" international relations, but also to its amoral nature. For Huntley, then, the line between knowledge and morality is the division about which to worry: "Basic understandings of the world can ultimately affect basic judgments about human values and purposes. Only in the modern era has this been conceived to be a problem, rather than precisely the point."

Luke echoes the concerns both about disciplinary fragmentation and the lack of a policy-relevant normative focus in international relations. The chapter, which is essentially a sociological study of the academic profession, examines some of the institutional structures that perpetuate the existing disciplinary fragmentation. Political science is what political scientists do, as Easton has observed. And political scientists, according to Luke, are engaging in research and activities that have a marginalizing effect on the discipline. If a case can be made that departments of political science should train citizens, politicians and government employees, then—compatible with Huntley's focus on the moral purpose of social inquiry—it is important to note the inadequacy of our institutional structures (especially at the graduate level), which are structured to train highly specialized researchers rather than practitioners. With regard to research, Luke argues that institutions of "professional correctness"—the journals and other measures that are associated with academic advancement—are structured in ways that actually minimize the possibility of doing policy-relevant work.[31] Further, there are considerable opportunity costs associated with the time and energy spent publishing in journal that are prestigious within the international relations scholarly community, but that are not widely read elsewhere. Thus, Luke argues that the discipline itself has certain 'normalizing' influences that do not tend to reward the very kinds of threshold-crossings that both Sil and Huntley view as essential to social inquiry.

A Tentative Appraisal

Although there is no clear consensus among the contributors in this volume, some tentative conclusions do emerge. With regard to disciplinary divisions, the editors of this volume are not persuaded by the claim that an increasingly complex division of labor in the social sciences can in and of itself contribute to the efficient expansion of the total reservoir of knowledge in society. What seems to have happened—in the social sciences, at least—is that the volume of research has indeed expanded. But given the extent to which various disciplines replicate (rather than draw from) each other's methodological debates within separate realms, or simply speak past each other, we are not sure that increasingly specialized realms of "knowledge" reflect an efficient or fruitful division of academic labor.

Unfortunately, to the extent that we see incentives for change, these seem to be in the direction of increased specialization and fragmentation. Even large research foundations are seeking to create new boundaries in their management of research activities. The National Science Foundation, for example, announced that as of January 31, 1999, its Division of Social, Behavioral and Economic Sciences (SBER) would be reconstituted as two distinct units, each designed to focus strategic planning for two sets of communities with different research priorities and methodologies. One of these divisions, the Division of Behavioral and Cognitive Sciences (BCS), would focus on such issues as human cognition, language, social behavior, and culture, while the other, the Division of Social and Economic Sciences (SES), would focus on economic, legal, political, and social systems. Within this framework, research on the influence of cultural or cognitive factors on economic policies or the design of international organizations might well fall right through the cracks!

It is likely that technological changes, especially recent advances in information technology, may actually be decreasing rather than increasing the incentives to reach into other disciplines. Access to the internet and other databases gives scholars the luxury of more data to work with, but that luxury now means that it is hard to keep up with the gold mine of empirical data that is now available at the stroke of a computer key. Therefore, while the information revolution has improved our capacity for empirical research, it is now often difficult to stay current even within a particular subdiscipline or niche. The need for cross-fertilization is even greater, we believe, as the expansion of data and research within particular fields or traditions becomes more complicated. Otherwise, we risk becoming victims of our own tunnel vision.

Moreover, we are concerned that the preoccupation with epistemological debates in international relations theory creates an exaggerated sense of incommensurability among various traditions.[32] At root, we are wary of the fragmentation resulting from unnecessarily sharp methodological divisions and from what Sil has labeled "epistemological absolutism." Too much enthusiasm for scientific methods in the social sciences approaches scientism—an excessive confidence in the ability of empirical observation to derive generalizable laws and principles to explain the variance in human behavior. Similarly, excessive emphasis on postmodern approaches renders impossible any meaningful dialogue among researchers, much less replication or generalization across issues. Except at the extreme ends of the spectrum, there is ample room for dialogue among various epistemological traditions.

What is needed, then, are conscious efforts to encourage the integration of various bodies of research across disciplinary, methodological, and epistemological lines. One possible strategy is to focus on question-driven social science, whereby various research efforts can illuminate and inform the activities of each other. Consistent with the recommendations of Immanuel Wallerstein and the Gulbenkian Commission on the Restructuring of Social Sciences, we believe that these efforts should emphasize temporary, integrated research programs that are formed to address particular questions, rather than the establishment of permanent interdisciplinary programs (since the latter threaten to become institutionalized in ways that only add to the number of entrenched, bounded units within university structures).[33] Mechanisms already exist to facilitate the integration process. Valuable interdisciplinary research centers create institutionalized opportunities for groups of scholars to meet and request funding for research programs that focus on particular empirical questions.[34] On a smaller scale, formal and informal interdisciplinary working groups allow opportunities for researchers to find intersections between work being done in different disciplines.[35] The alternative to these kinds of conscious integration efforts, we fear, is the tendency for international relations research to become an increasingly ghettoized field. In that ghettoized world, various disciplines, methodologies epistemologies, and research traditions may coexist, but they are not likely not to strive for meaningful communication.

E. M. Forster wrote, "Only connect!" In promoting integrative efforts, we do not mean to suggest that the social sciences need to "only connect." We do believe, however, that without more attention to the possibilities for connecting, we risk ignoring Ernst Haas's warning about the danger of "extreme differentiation without unification" when we attempt to solve the problems facing an increasingly complex and interdependent world.[36] In short, the existence of differentiated research endeavors joined with conscious attempts to unify and connect those endeavors will expand our ability to achieve deeper understandings of the social phenomena that stand at the center of contemporary international politics.

Notes

1. Clifford Geertz, "The Impact of the Concept of Culture on the Concept of Man," in Geertz, *The Interpretation of Cultures* (New York: Basic Books, 1973), p. 33.

2. Of course, this is not to deny the importance of interdisciplinary work in the physical sciences. Many of the most profound advancements in science have occurred at the interface of traditional disciplines. A powerful example of this involves scientific investigations into the properties of hemoglobin. Early research relied on traditional biochemical methods to describe the important functional details of the molecule. It was only with the advent of more sophisticated physics tools (x-ray crystallography and laser spectroscopy) that investigators were able to gain a fuller understanding of the properties governing the binding and release of oxygen from hemoglobin. In other words, research and methods from chemistry, biology and physics were combined in order to permit the achievement of what is now a full understanding of the major functional attributes of hemoglobin. The importance of this discovery for medical science is obvious. I owe this insight to Cather Simpson of Case Western Reserve University's Department of Chemistry.

3. This may also be one of the reasons for the somewhat different publishing practices in the physical sciences as compared to the social sciences. In the field of chemistry, for example, research is often reported in "communications" in addition to "full papers." The communication is a preliminary account of new discoveries that are not fully understood and for which there exist preliminary data. The precision of the research insight is highlighted by the fact that these communications are generally only two to three pages of published text. By contrast, a full paper—which is often no longer than ten pages long—is a complete and presumably final account of some aspect of the science. I owe this insight to John Protasiewicz of Case Western Reserve University's Department of Chemistry.

4. Hedley Bull, "The Theory of International Politics, 1919–1969" in James Der Derian, ed., *International Theory: Critical Investigations* (New York: New York University Press, 1995), p. 187. The essay originally appeared in Brian Porter ed., *The Aberysthyth Papers: International Politics 1919–1969* (London: Oxford University Press, 1972), pp. 30–50.

5. Stanley Hoffman, "An American Social Science: International Relations" in Der Derian, p. 215. The essay originally appeared in *Daedalus,* Vol. 106, No. 3 (Summer), 1977, pp. 41–60.

6. E. H. Carr, *The Twenty Years' Crisis, 1919–1939: An Introduction to the Study of International Relations* (London: MacMillan and Co., 1940).

7. Raymond Aron, *Peace and War; A Theory of International Relations* (London, 1966), p. 592. Of course, as many have noted, realists have often integrated morality into their arguments by emphasizing the moral duty of government actors to pursue the national interest of their state.

8. Even so, the result was a hybrid between historical interpretation and theory building. As Bull has noted, postwar realism was compelling—"brilliant and provocative in the case of Carr, systematic and comprehensive in the case of Morgenthau, learned and profound in the case of Wight—but the theory they employed was 'soft,' not 'hard.'" Bull, p. 191.

9. Marxism or world systems theory could be included as a third research tradition, although that has never been as influential in "mainstream" international relations research in the United States as realism and liberalism.

10. Just a few examples of these include David A. Baldwin ed., *Neorealism and Neoliberalism: The Contemporary Debate* (New York: Columbia University Press, 1993); Charles W. Kegley, Jr., ed., *Controversies in International Relations Theory: Realism and the Neoliberal Challenge*

(New York: St. Martin's Press, 1995); Andrew Moravcsik, "Taking Preferences Seriously: A Liberal Theory of International Politics," *International Organization*, Vol. 51, No. 4, Autumn 1997; Robert Powell, "Anarchy in International Relations Theory: The Neorealist-Neoliberal Debate," *International Organization*, Vol. 46, No. 2, Spring 1994; and Emerson M. S. Niou and Peter C. Ordeshook, "'Less Filling, Tastes Great': The Realist-Neoliberal Debate," *World Politics*, Vol. 46, No. 1, 1994.

11. Kenneth Waltz, Theory of International Politics (Reading, MA: Addison-Wesley, 1979).

12. Waltz, p. 69.

13. Waltz has been criticized for that position, by some who argue either that "anarchy" is a problematic concept or that the condition of anarchy is not unique to the international system. See, for example, Helen V. Milner, "The Assumption of Anarchy in International Relations Theory: A Critique, *The Review of International Studies*, Vol. 17, No. 1, 1991; and Alexander Wendt, "Anarchy Is What States Make of It: The Social Construction of Power Politics, *International Organization*, Volume 46, No. 2, Spring 1992.

14. See, for example, Robert O. Keohane ed., *Neorealism and Its Critics* (New York: Columbia University Press, 1986).

15. Robert O. Keohane and Joseph S. Nye, *Power and Interdependence: World Politics in Transition,* 2nd ed. (Boston: Little, Brown, 1989).

16. Central works in this literature include Stephen Krasner ed., *International Regimes* (Ithaca: Cornell University Press, 1983) and Robert O. Keohane, *After Hegemony: Cooperation and Discord in the World Political Economy* (Princeton: Princeton University Press, 1984).

17. See Ole Waever, "The Rise and Fall of the Inter-Paradigm Debate," in Steve Smith, Ken Booth and Marysia Zalewski, eds. *International Theory: Positivism and Beyond* (Cambridge: Cambridge University Press, 1996).

18. Waever, 1996.

19. Some of these debates echo the controversy about behavioralism in the 1960s. Those who were sympathetic to behavioral approaches stressed the need for rigor in social science theory-building; skeptics argued that it was not possible to achieve the kind of parsimonious or predictive theory in IR that is possible in the physical sciences. However, these debates tended to focus on the utility of particular methodological tools, such as multivariate regression and other statistical techniques, rather than on deep questions of ontology.

20. Alexander Wendt, "Anarchy Is What States Make of It: The Social Construction of Power Politics," *International Organization* 46, 2 (Spring 1992) pp. 391–425, quote as reprinted in Der Derian, pp. 164–165.

21. Bull, as quoted in Der Derian, p. 205. It should be noted that in the same passage, Bull recognizes that the focus on scientific rigor resulted in a useful heightened awareness of the "intellectually shoddy character" of much of the previous international relations work.

22. In this regard, Clunan's critique of Wendt and Haas is reminiscent of the levels of analysis debates that were largely inspired by the emergence of neorealism: Can we understand "systemic" or international influences on individual states without understanding something about those states? Waltz was criticized for his decision to blackbox the state in viewing the effect of anarchy on international relations (an approach that misses important insights such as the democratic peace phenomenon). In her contribution to this volume, Clunan argues something similar with regard to our understanding of national identity: "[I]t is crucial to look at the internal elements of identity and the domestic actors who create it. . . . Wendt's reification of the state turns our attention toward the interaction of states, and away from the domestic sphere and the historical experiences that the leadership of the state collectively remember and reinterpret in shaping the state's current identity."

23. Clunan says, for example: "The formation of a state's collective identity is not a seamless process that encompasses all aspects of a state's international affairs. Rather a state's collective identity is issue specific, with general elements of identity becoming salient with the particular exigencies of a given issue."

24. Emanuel Adler, "Seizing the Middle Ground: Constructivism in World Politics," *European Journal of International Relations*, Vol. 3, No. 3, September 1997. Quote as cited in Clunan's chapter in this volume.

25. On a more normative note, insights from judgment and decision making research can also inform investigations on how tasks might be framed in order to make it easier to communicate actors' changing interpretations of reality. Task characteristics matter; therefore, changing the way that issues are linked in terms of international discussions might affect the ability of actors to articulate their own cognitive processes and to share those subjective processes with others.

26. This phrase comes from Geertz, p. 34

27. Other important foreign policy metaphors include "ladder of escalation" and the "slippery slope." See Philip Tetlock, "Psychological Perspectives on International Conflict and Cooperation in Diane F. Halpern and Alexander E. Voiskounsky eds. *States of Mind: American and Post-Soviet Perspectives on Contemporary Issues in Psychology* (New York: Oxford University Press, 1997).

28. George Lakoff and Mark Johnson, *Metaphors We Live By* (Chicago: University of Chicago Press, 1980), p. 211. See also Andrew Ortony ed., *Metaphor and Thought* (Cambridge: Cambridge University Press, 1979).

29. See Peter Manning, "Metaphors of the Field: Varieties of Organizational Discourse," in John Van Maanen ed., *Qualitative Methodology* (Newbury Park, CA: Sage Publications, 1983) and Richard Harvey Brown, "Social Theory as Metaphor," *Theory and Society,* Vol. 3, 1976, pp. 169–197.

30. Viewed from this perspective, the positivist/postpositivist debate is the latest incarnation of the very old fact-value debate in the social sciences. For example, see Max Weber's attempt to steer between German idealism and nineteenth-century positivism in "'Objectivity' in Social Science and Social Policy," in *The Methodology of the Social Sciences,* E. A. Shils and H. A. Finch, eds. (Free Press, 1949), reprinted in Fred Dallmayr and Thomas McCarthy, *Understanding and Social Inquiry* (Notre Dame: University of Notre Dame Press, 1977). See also Sil's discussion of the fact-value distinction in his contribution to Part 2 of this volume.

31. Consider the emphasis placed in academic culture on the importance of advancing international relations theory. In contrast, those scholars who engage in policy-relevant endeavors risk earning the dubious title of "policy wonk." For a good discussion of the different cultures of the policy world and the academic world, as well as of the possibility of building bridges between government and academe, see Alexander George, *Bridging the Gap: Theory and Practice in Foreign Policy* (Washington, D.C.: United States Institute of Peace Press, 1993).

32. The preoccupation with methodological and epistemological divisions in political science is reflected in decisions of department names and categorizations. Do we choose to call ourselves a department of "government" or one of "political science"? The resistance to the term "political science" in the Departments of Government at Harvard, Princeton, and the University of Virginia was at least partly a statement of skepticism about the value of the behavioral revolution. More recently, it has become common to hear debates in university corridors about whether the study of politics should be embedded in the humanities or in the social sciences.

33. Immanuel Wallerstein et al., *Open the Social Sciences* (Stanford: Stanford University Press, 1996).

34. This kind of interdisciplinary work is being done, for example at the University of California-Berkeley's Institute of International Studies, which coordinates projects designed to bring together scholars from

various disciplines to explore questions of particular importance. As of early 1999, the Institute sponsored a variety of integrative efforts, including projects on multilateral governance; environmental politics in an increasingly globalized world; and the impact of "new geographies" on area studies. Similarly, the University of Pennsylvania's newly established Christopher H. Browne Center for International Politics (PennCIP) explicitly defines its intellectual domain as "wide ranging and not simply defined by preexisting disciplinary boundaries and geographical categories."

35. At Case Western Reserve University, for example, there is an institutionalized, weekly Public Affairs Discussion Group brown bag lunch. Inspired by a similar practice at the Brookings Institution, the CWRU group consists of focused discussions of local, national, and international policy problems by political scientists, historians, physicists, astronomers, lawyers, physicians, economists, and other scholars and practitioners.

36. Ernst B. Haas, "Reason and Change in International Life: Justifying a Hypothesis," *Journal of International Affairs* (Spring/Summer 1990), p. 214.

ABOUT THE CONTRIBUTORS

TADASHI ANNO is Assistant Professor at Sophia University in Tokyo, Japan, specializing in international and comparative studies. His doctoral degree is from the Department of Political Science at the University of California at Berkeley, and his dissertation is titled "The Liberal World Order and Its Challengers: Nationalism and the Rise of Anti-Systemic Movements in Russia and Japan, 1860–1950." His most recent publication, "*Nihonjinron* and *Russkaia Ideia*: Transformation of Japanese and Russian Nationalism in the Postwar Era and Beyond," will be appearing in Gilbert Rozman, ed., *Japan and Russia: The Torturous Path to Normalization, 1949–1999* (forthcoming, St. Martin's Press).

JEAN-MARC F. BLANCHARD received his doctorate from the University of Pennsylvania and is presently Visiting Scholar at the Department of Political Science at Villanova University. He is coeditor (with Edward Mansfield and Norrin M. Ripsman) of a special issue of *Security Studies* entitled "Purchasing Power and Peace: The Political Economy of National Security" (Autumn 1999). He is the coauthor with Norrin M. Ripsman of "Commercial Liberalism Under Fire: Evidence from 1914 and 1936," *Security Studies;* "Measuring Economic Interdependence: A Geopolitical Perspective," *Geopolitics and International Boundaries;* and "Asking the Right Question: When Do Economic Sanctions Work Best?" *Security Studies* (Autumn 1999). He is also author of "The U.S. Role in the Sino-Japanese Dispute over the Diaoyu (Senkoku) Islands, 1945–1971," *China Quarterly* (March 2000).

ANNE L. CLUNAN is a Ph.D. candidate in the Department of Political Science at the University of California, Berkeley. She is presently finishing her doctoral dissertation which explores the relationship between the formation of national identity and national interests in the context of Russia's postcommunist relations with the West, East, South, and the other post-Soviet states. Portions of her research have been presented at the Annual Meeting of the International Studies Association, the Institute of International Studies (Berkeley), and the Berkeley Program in Soviet and Post-Soviet Studies. Her other research interests include the development of international law, rules, norms, and governance, as well as the study of nationalism and integration in Europe and the post-Soviet space.

EILEEN M. DOHERTY is Assistant Professor in the Department of Political Science at Case Western Reserve University, with a secondary appointment at the CWRU Weatherhead School of Management. She is editor of *Japan's Investment in Asia* (Berkeley, CA: Berkeley Roundtable on the International Economy and The Asia Foundation, 1995), and coauthor of "Tales from the Global Economy: Cross-National Production Networks and the Reorganization of the European Economy," *Structural Change and Economic Dynamics* (March 1997). She is presently completing a book on the management of international financial crises. She has previously held appointments as Research Fellow at the Berkeley Roundtable on the International Economy (BRIE) and as Government Relations Analyst at the Japan Economic Institute of America.

WADE HUNTLEY is Program Director for Asia-Pacific Security at the Nautilus Institute for Security and Sustainable Development. He received his Ph.D. from the University of California at Berkeley in 1993, and has been visiting professor at the University of Hawaii at Hilo and at Whitman College in Walla Walla, Washington. His areas of expertise include international security, nuclear nonproliferation and arms control, political relations in the Asia-Pacific region, and political theory. Among his numerous publications are: "Nonproliferation Prospects after the South Asian Nuclear Tests," *The Nonproliferation Review* 6:1 (Fall, 1998); "An Unlikely Match? Kant and Feminism in IR Theory," *Millennium: Journal of International Studies* 26:2 (Fall, 1997); and "Kant's Third Image: Systemic Sources of the Liberal Peace," *International Studies Quarterly* 40:1 (March, 1996).

TIMOTHY W. LUKE is Professor of Political Science at Virginia Polytechnic Institute and State University in Blacksburg, Virginia. He teaches courses in the areas of international politics, comparative political economy, and political theory. His most recent book is *Capitalism, Democracy, and Ecology: Departing from Marx* (Urbana-Champagne: University of Illinois Press, 1999). He is presently completing another book titled *Beyond the Boundaries: Discourse, Discipline and Dissent in Contemporary Political Science*.

NORRIN M. RIPSMAN is Assistant Professor of Political Science at Concordia University, Canada. He received his Ph.D. in Political Science at the University of Pennsylvania in 1997 and was a Lady Davis postdoctoral research fellow at the International Relations Department at the Hebrew University of Jerusalem in 1997–1998. He is presently completing a book entitled *Democracies and Peacemaking: Domestic Structure, Executive Autonomy and Peacemaking after Two World Wars*. He has published articles (coauthored with Jean-Marc Blanchard) in *Security Studies* and *Geopolitics and International Boundaries*. He is also coeditor (with Jean-Marc Blanchard and Edward Mansfield) of a special issue of *Security Studies* entitled "Purchasing Power and Peace: The Political Economy of National Security" (Autumn 1999).

RUDRA SIL is Assistant Professor of Political Science at the University of Pennsylvania. His research interests span the history and philosophy of the social sciences, the political economy of development and transition, comparative industrial relations, and the politics of the Former Soviet Union and Asia. He is author of *Managing 'Modernity': Work, Community, and Authority in Late-Industrializing Japan and Russia* (Ann Arbor: University of Michigan Press, forthcoming). He is also author of "The Foundations of Eclecticism: The Epistemological Status of Agency, Culture, and Structure in Social Theory," *Journal of Theoretical Politics* (July 2000), and "The Division of Labor in the Social Sciences: Trade-offs and Interdependence Among Methods and Research Products," *Polity* (forthcoming 2000).

INDEX

Action: behavioral, 191; causal beliefs on, 33; choice and, 17; collective, 2, 14, 94; commitment to, 35; communicative, 148, 162; consequences of, 35; decisionmaking and, 34; expressive, 124; group, 120; human, 93; identity formation and, 102; international, 94; knowledge and, 19; meaningful, 148; moral, 191, 192; political, 19, 158, 190–196, 192; public, 192; purposive, 124; social, 42, 88, 117, 118, 131. *See also* Actors, Behavior

Actors: behavior of, 96; conceptions of rules and, 90; converging preferences of, 15; goals of, 93; identity and, 15–16, 90, 96, 97; individual welfare of, 119; interests of, 15, 89; judgment processes of, 50; loyalty of, 94; maximization of utility by, 33; rational, 36 (*see also* rationality); social, 108; states as, 98; strategies, 93

Adaptation, 99, 102, 106, 108; as mechanism of structuration, 106–108

Adler, Emanuel, 93, 106, 107, 108, 237

American Political Science Association, 213, 220

American Political Science Review, 213, 214, 215, 220

Analysis: "citational," 221; cultural objects of, 164; interdisciplinary, 13; political, 182, 183; purpose of, 18, 146; social, 16; specialization in, 177–197; stages of, 178; subjectivity in, 157; values and, 157

Anarchy: culture of, 90, 94, 98; formation of, 90; international, 193, 234; nature of, 90; order in, 92; social, 92

Anno, Tadashi, 14, 16–17, 117–133, 239, 240

Anthropology, 3

Arendt, Hannah, 191

Aron, Raymond, 233

Bargaining: breakdowns, 39; international, 14, 15, 39; strategies, 50; theory, 39. *See also* Negotiation

Barnett, Michael, 97

Behavior: of actors, 96; adaptive, 42; decisionmaking, 32–36, 40; determinants of, 107; egoistic, 94; expressive, 123; group, 118, 119, 121; human, 32, 37, 42; identity-oriented, 123, 123*fig*; inconsistent, 49; individual, 119; political, 92; purposive, 123; rational, 35; regulation of, 96; satisficing, 34, 50; social rules and, 90; state, 94; transmission of, 107; utility maximizing, 34, 50

SUNY series in Global Politics
James N. Rosenau, Editor

List of Titles